A SAVAGE BUSINESS

The Comeback and Comedown of Mike Tyson

RICHARD HOFFER

Simon & Schuster

SIMON & SCHUSTER
Rockefeller Center
1230 Avenue of the Americas
New York, NY 10020

Designed by Deirdre C. Amthor

Manufactured in the United States of America

1   3   5   7   9   10   8   6   4   2

Library of Congress Cataloging-in-Publication Data
Hoffer, Richard.
A savage business : the comeback and comedown of Mike Tyson /
Richard Hoffer.
p.   cm.
1. Tyson, Mike, 1966–   .   2. Boxers (Sports)—United States—
Biography.   I. Title.
GV1132.T97H64   1998
796.83'092—dc21
[B]   97-36582
CIP
ISBN 0-684-80908-7

All photos courtesy of AP/Wide World.

Acknowledgments

I couldn't have done this book—and certainly wouldn't have tried—without the resources *Sports Illustrated* allowed me. It was the magazine, after all, that first set me upon this story and permitted me to think of it as more than just a series of fights, although they may have grown uncomfortable once I decided it was opera. Special thanks to Evan Kanew of CNN/SI who, over the course of this book, rose from collaborator to co-conspirator.

Nor would I have gotten very far without the day-to-day coverage of certain fight writers, as cranky and suspicious a group of people ever assembled. They are also absurdly generous; no good story goes untold. Thanks to Michael Katz and Vic Ziegel of the New York *Daily News*, Wally Matthews of the *New York Post*, Greg Logan of *Newsday*, Jon Saraceno of *USA Today*, Ron Borges of the *Boston Globe*, Tom Friend of the *New York Times*, Bernard Fernandez of the *Philadelphia Daily News*, Ed Schuyler of the Associated Press, Royce Feour of the *Las Vegas Review-Journal*, and Tim Kawakami of the *Los Angeles Times*. I owe them all for their vigorous reporting. More than that: Their devotion to the sport, which is demonstrated in their continued aggrava-

Acknowledgments

tion of it, is what encourages me to think boxing might survive.

And finally I have the sport itself to thank. It is sometimes horrible, sometimes wonderful, and always impossible to justify. But it's pretty damn fun to write about.

To Carol

Contents

Chapter One

"Make way for Brother Mike!"

At this time of year, at this time of morning, it was still dark. A small crescent moon hung in the Indiana sky and, beneath it, four helicopters balanced, as if some fantastic throbbing mobile had been constructed for the occasion. The citizens stood in a field of corn stubble across the road, and, closer to the prison itself, reporters and photographers crunched back and forth across gravel. A garden of satellite dishes bloomed in the parking lot. And inside the yellow police tape, much closer to the prison, mysterious-looking men in black fedoras and big overcoats clustered, their garb and secrecy setting them apart from any other crowd. Black limousines slid back and forth across the entrance.

Mike Tyson was still in the Indiana Youth Center, a medium-security prison outside Indianapolis. He'd been there for three years, doing famous time for raping Desiree Washington, an eighteen-year-old contestant in the 1991 Miss Black America pageant. Many predictions of his self-destruction had been fulfilled with that act—George Foreman had long ago warned, "He needs to be sheltered like you would shelter a lion or a tiger. You lock him up, except when you want him to come out and jump through a few hoops" —and for three years a nation had been smug in its revulsion.

But now, the only athlete ever to have been imprisoned in the heat of his career was about to step from behind those walls to reclaim lost time, and that same nation—the world, even—had come to see how he'd do it. Fascination replaced disgust, many times over.

Even before his crime, he'd been a strange melding of melodrama and malevolence, more a presence than an athlete. His appetite for subjugation, which had been illegally satisfied behind closed hotel doors, was also the basis of his $70 million career. In his last full year of boxing, people paid $16 million to watch him consume the weak. What he'd done to Desiree Washington was horrible, of course, but it could also be seen as a failure to discriminate, a momentary inability to distinguish between teenage girls and heavyweight contenders. On his release, whether or not he'd been forgiven, he had perhaps become more interesting than ever.

Three years in prison, while he stewed in bitterness, might even have made him dangerous in ways beyond his previous flamboyance. Three years ripped right out of him, when it is time that is always the principal factor of wealth and achievement in an athlete's young life. That lost time denied him earning power, and maybe his place in boxing history. He had been stubbornly unrepentant in prison, so it didn't seem likely he'd forgive the debt. All the powers of the media were trained upon him this cold morning: What was he like? What would he do? How did he plan to make us pay?

One open question was, what was he worth? It was a tough calculation. He was already 28 years old on the day he was freed, and nobody knew if he could still fight. By most reviews, he had already been fading by the time he went to jail. His aura of invincibility, so impressive and effortless in his youth, had become a clunking and largely artificial apparatus. He'd been beaten by James "Buster" Douglas in Tokyo in 1990, and had fought two difficult fights with the otherwise unimpressive Razor Ruddock in 1991, leaving all those one-round knockouts of his early career, all those titles to be reconsidered. Still, even behind bars, he was the most exciting heavyweight in the world. And all this attention at his release demonstrated some kind of demand for his services, or maybe just for his personality.

There were, naturally, some people under that Indiana moon who wondered if he had any value as an athlete at all, whether time had changed or diminished him to the point where he no longer had a promotional utility. The sporadic reports that had come out of the prison in the three years past had Tyson reading cartons of Communist literature and taking instruction in the Muslim religion, which was probably not good news for the game. One interview he did put him at such odds with his former boxing persona that you might well have guessed he was planning to enter a far less secular line of work. He said he had been "wrong and disrespectful" to dehumanize his opponents, and he was sorry he had ever said he would make Tyrell Biggs cry like a girl or that he would make Razor Ruddock his girlfriend. "I will appreciate their forgiveness," he said. Also, he wanted "to see the great libraries" once he got out.

It was an interesting idea, that Tyson had devoted himself to some kind of intellectual and moral development, though it was clear he would only do so on his own terms. He surprised Maya Angelou on a visit when he recited her poetry back at her. Yet he could not pass the GED exam that might have shortened his sentence. He told interviewers he was reading Malcolm X, but he got into a jail-yard beef with a corrections officer. He had another con put broad likenesses of Arthur Ashe and Mao Zedong on his arms, but he refused to apologize for the rape, an act of contrition that also would have sprung him early.

If he remained a little enigmatic, or at least contradictory, in this exile, there wasn't that much concern about his future, not really. His self-styled rehabilitation was not going to lead him to a life of good works. As a property who could generate millions of dollars for each appearance, the quality of the appearances notwithstanding, he was not going to be allowed to do anything beyond boxing. The economic imperative that such earning power represents overrides personal considerations (if, indeed, he had any) every time. There can be no resisting such opportunity.

Still, opportunities take many shapes; Tyson's was in the form of that most American of ideas, the second act. Such rebirths are consistently doomed, but nevertheless popular. Who isn't intrigued by a fresh start? Themes of redemption and recovery are very popular in a 12-step society such as ours, and though we like our heroes fallen, we also enjoy their comebacks. Even if it had been more or less predetermined that Tyson would reenter the fray, it was still going to be interesting to watch him do it.

Outside the prison on March 25, 1995, dawn began to break. There was a glint of sunshine on the coiled razor wire. You imagined some bustle inside as the most prominent member of the prison population gathered his belongings (all those books!) and made his farewells. But you couldn't really know what was happening behind those walls. More black limousines slid back and forth across the prison entrance, disgorging more mysterious people. Everybody crunched back and forth on the gravel. It seemed you could actually watch time pass, the water towers beginning to leave their marks on the flat farmland. Standing at a window, Tyson may have enjoyed that same tracery of shadow, 1,095 times.

How would he make us pay for this, this interruption of life? This subtraction of it? Or, more cynically: Who would collect the tolls? The greatest intrigue on this cold morning was not whether he would fight or not, but whom he'd end up back in the ring with. His old promoter, Don King? The kid comanagers, John Horne and Rory Holloway? Would he return to his roots, reach back to the Catskills days and hire his former trainer Kevin Rooney to train him? Or would some wild-card promoter—and they all came to Plainfield, Indiana, to make their pitch, from convicted embezzler Harold Smith to former car salesman Butch Lewis—romance him away from all of that?

The media had gathered to watch, as if for white smoke from the Vatican, for clues as to the direction of Tyson's future, investing this pseudodrama with significance of their own creation. The rumors in the weeks before his release were of such a conflicting variety that you almost had to lay them to some mischief on Tyson's part. Butch Lewis said, "At least half a dozen people, maybe more, think they have a chance to manage or promote Mike once he gets out." Bill Cayton, who had once managed him along with the late Jimmy Jacobs—Cayton was the remaining link to Tyson's greatness—thought Tyson might want to go back to the Cus D'Amato era and retain Rooney, the Cus disciple who had trained him until 1988, when King got ahold of him and ousted the entire Catskills crew. Cayton believed that Tyson, from his jail cell, had made overtures to that effect, even though Rooney was then suing the fighter for $10 million for breach of contract.

Opinions elsewhere stressed the importance of Tyson's getting a fresh start, the kind America likes, with fresh management. These opinions had been especially popular among alternate managers. If King hadn't been the architect of Tyson's ruin, the thinking went, he had at least been its landlord. What Tyson really needed was . . . Harold Smith, or Rock Newman, or Butch Lewis, or Bill Cayton. You could just ask them.

Tyson had entertained most all of them at prison, inspiring

rumors of all manner of scenarios for his release. The King crowd had been similarly relentless in its courting of Tyson and would be presumed to have the inside track; still, there was a sense that Tyson was playing all sides from within those walls. It gave rise to much intrigue and not a little harrumphing from the King bunch.

Horne, a Tyson buddy who'd been installed as a sort of translator for the much older King, addressed the issue: "Every time somebody goes to Indiana to see Mike in prison, they come out swearing to God and to everybody else that they got him. When you're behind bars, you'll come out of your cell to see a jackrabbit if it came to see you."

An insider who'd noted the strange stream of visitors to this prison more or less confirmed that. "Mike likes company," he said. "It helps pass the time." Anyway, he said, it wasn't like King didn't understand his man. "No one is better in the world at getting into a fighter's psyche." It probably didn't hurt that King was covering all bases, dropping by a Los Angeles auto dealer to pick up a $300,000 turbocharged Bentley as a gift for Tyson.

Religion was a wild card, though; King had overseen Tyson's conversion from Catholicism to his own Baptist religion in a Cleveland church, and news that Tyson had converted again, to Islam, was not exactly a confirmation of the status quo. This spreading of religious wings was a small show of independence that, grown any larger, endangered their relationship. What was Tyson doing with a religious advisor, Muhammad Sideeq? Hadn't there been a great heavyweight champion before whose religious awakening had heralded his passing into the control of Muslim management?

King, all the time insisting that Tyson would return to the fold and it would be business as usual, seemed more nervous about Tyson's religious conversion than the possibility of a managerial change. His office debunked reports that the first thing Tyson intended to do out of prison was visit a mosque. For some reason, this became a persistent issue, as if any evidence of worship established a chink in their relationship. All these guys in their fedoras and bowties, they were worrisome to King. "Muslims," he told everybody who asked, "make good visitors, too."

At 6 A.M., among the odd comings and goings in the dimness of a Saturday morning, King himself produced a small excitement by climbing out of one of the black limousines and, with his minions Horne and Holloway, disappearing into the prison's visitors' center. It couldn't have been unexpected, but there nevertheless was a thrill among the crowd as it hit home: The battle for Tyson's life, maybe even his soul, had been no contest, a laydown.

Then, at 6:20 A.M., in the loneliness of a Hoosier countryside on a day that was turning gorgeous, a tall man holding his black leather overcoat open like a drape exploded from the door, and the same entourage that had entered before, but grown by one, rumbled through and into the waiting limousine. And that was that. Tyson, whose white skullcap reflected all the available light, was in the middle of the moving huddle, and it was impossible not to realize—a quickly arriving idea—that he was leaving jail with the same men who had delivered him there.

And yet . . . there was that white skullcap. A photographer registered Tyson's show of faith by that kufi cap and, shouting "To the mosque!" triggered a Mack Sennett kind of chase through the landscape. The helicopters tilted in the sky and raced ahead of the motorcade. Cars scrambled in pursuit, some of them cutting across the corn stubble, *Dukes of Hazzard* style. All of them hoped to convene at one of the few countryside mosques in America, which happened to be just two miles away from the prison, before Tyson did.

Indeed, Tyson meant to bow to Mecca before he'd return

to his estate in Ohio. This was a crushing blow to King's presumption, but nothing he couldn't ride out. Tyson was joined in the mosque by Muhammad Ali himself, and in a special prayer of thanksgiving from the Koran that was offered by Sideeq, they all bowed—even King, shoeless, right behind Tyson.

"It was a very big statement for Mike to make," said Sideeq later. "Instead of making two right turns to the airport. . . . It gives hope."

After prayer Tyson met with Ali and showed a determined deference to him. "Mike got up and helped Ali to a chair next to him," Sideeq said. "He showed great respect and concern for his brother Ali." A little later, with helicopters still thrumming over the mosque, Tyson posed for a picture with Ali and Sideeq, Tyson's girlfriend, Monica Turner, and a group of children. The picture, taken by Ali's longtime photographer and friend Howard Bingham, shows a smiling Tyson with a small boy kneeling in front of him. Tyson is pinching the boy's cheeks with his fingers so that the boy appears to be making a silly face for the camera.

Neither King nor his minions were in the photo, and the presence of Ali might have suggested that King was really, really out of the picture. And yet, after prayers ("Make way for Brother Mike! Please! Will security make a path for Brother Mike!"), it was King who directed the motorcade to Indianapolis International Airport, traveling at a great speed, for the trip back to Tyson's Ohio estate.

If a statement had been made, it was hard to find it in the day's hullabaloo. Among the last times Tyson had been seen in public, at a news conference on the eve of his trial, he was pretending to nap. Or he was joking with Horne. Or springing to attention at the sight of a female television reporter. Or running the media gauntlet on his way to jail, twisting his handcuffs, as if to mock the system that trifled with his arrogance. A visit to the mosque was an improvement over that, anyway, but as the limousine rolled out of Plainfield (A COMMUNITY OF VALUES), it was important to remember that, in most respects, he was returning to where he came from, with the same people who'd brought him here.

Indeed, all the deals for his comeback had already been made. He was to pick up just about where he'd left off. The whole scene had been poor theater, really. Anybody who stood in the Indiana cold that morning and attached any suspense to Tyson's release had to reckon himself a fool. The visit for prayers had been a nice and unexpected touch— hey, good to see Ali!—but the idea that there would be any deviance from a plan of bold commercial opportunism turned out to be plain ridiculous. Remember: Not only had Tyson left money on the table those three years—65 cents a day for prison work was the bitter comparison—but King had been reduced to an unseemly scrambling, his livelihood dependent upon Julio Cesar Chavez, a Spanish-speaking has-been of questionable loyalty and longevity.

They'd get it back, in a King-sized caper that would leave whole industries reeling. They'd get it back, and more.

It was funny, actually. All this time, as rival promoters pumped themselves up before Tyson, King had been making deals with broadcasters and casinos and sponsors, finalizing contracts, getting the dough up-front. Nearly the day Tyson had gone into prison, King had been visiting the MGM Grand Hotel, a fairly new property at the far end of the Las Vegas strip that was hoping to compete with Caesars Palace and the Mirage. One Las Vegas insider remembered that the industry was nearly wheezing with laughter over the idea that Tyson would end up with anyone but King, doing anything but what he had done before. "What a joke," he said.

By the time Tyson had emerged in his kufi cap, King had agreed to and broken three different deals with the MGM

Grand before finally taking a fourth deal that called for six
fights (and this only after MGM officials nearly booted him
for his escalating demands). The pact with Showtime had
been agreed upon with much less pain and gave the fighter
to Showtime's pay-per-view arm, Showtime Event Television
(SET), for three years. It was later estimated that King had
wrangled a total of $35 million in up-front money from the
two concerns, although those familiar with the contracts
have said they signed secrecy agreements and could not discuss the terms. With long-term guarantees, the take was
much higher: $100 million the day Tyson hit the street, King
bragged.

Oh, Tyson would fight again, all right. The great libraries
would wait. As Tyson had mocked us before, wriggling his
cuffs as he entered prison, he mocked us now, his serenity
masking a sense of entitlement that prison time had not reha-
bilitated, but inflamed. Was it possible that King and Tyson,
all the old gang, were setting out on a comeback that would
settle scores, make them rich and famous, place them in history, and reclaim the three years? Was that the second act?

It was a gloomy thought. But the intrigue that underpinned
Tyson's release unleashed a cynicism that just would not tol-
erate the notion of fresh starts. If this was just going to be
business as usual, it could end—it certainly would—in some
sort of chaos or disgrace, with bystanders in jeopardy again.
If all King imagined for Tyson, if all the fighter wanted, was
a quick strike for the money, it could finish ugly. The particulars would be impossible to predict. From that distance did
one see an undisputed champion, with his wife and daughters
gathered around him, happy in his accomplishment? Or
could one imagine savagery unleashed, opponents frozen in
the ring, chips scattered on a casino floor, men gunned down
in city streets?

Wherever this was going, it was going to go easy for its

central figure. There was an economic appetite for Tyson. He had become an imagined form of entertainment, one that had grown more important in his absence than it had been even in his prime, creating incredible bargaining power for the former inmate.

It helped that, at his release, Las Vegas was undergoing tremendous expansion, with so many signature properties springing up on the strip that the town had come to resemble a cartoon landscape. The whimsy of the city had become wonderful, as long as you didn't take architecture seriously. The telescoped view down Las Vegas Boulevard revealed dueling pirate ships, a frothing volcano, an enormous pyramid, a castle. The New York City skyline was being erected, so as to block the view of Cheops's place. Also hard to see over the rising Chrysler Building would be King Arthur's Court. And yet this riot of shape and color was not, by itself, able to dependably produce enough sensation to reward customers for the casino's 16 percent hold.

Special attractions were required—something like a Barbra Streisand concert, something like a Tyson fight. "If you could bring the Super Bowl or the World Series to Las Vegas," said one industry worker, "that'd be great. They'd be one-two. But since you can't, you've got, in order of importance, New Year's Eve, Super Bowl weekend, and any Tyson fight. If Elvis came back, he'd be in the mix."

A big fight, of the kind that Tyson's return promised, could double and triple a casino's business for the night. The $6 million it might cost to market such an event would, under a proper deal, reap millions more. The casino's grinding math —that 16 percent markup on "fun"—would produce a bonanza for the bottom line, a tripling of the normal weekend's take. It was true, occasionally the whales (as the highest rollers were known) played well. But sending planes for the jumbos—the guys who bet $250,000 a hand in private parlors—was still the way to go, even though on a given night the high rollers might whack the casino; one Tyson fight night at the Las Vegas Hilton, back in 1989, left the casino with blood on its carpets when one player flew away with $3.5 million, another with $2 million. It happened, but not so much that the casinos stopped sending the planes.

Tyson, even beyond his being a boxer, was such a good fit for the casinos that it seemed he'd been invented just for their use. Nobody else aroused the desire for risk like him. Representing as he did the ultimate in menace, everybody's capacity for dread was ratcheted upward at his fights, and $1,000 hands became $10,000 hands. Now, as an ex-con, he was certified dangerous and doubly valuable. A bettor, his tolerances totally screwed up by the idea of so much peril, might be inspired to split jacks. Against the dealer's ten.

The MGM Grand was especially interested in Tyson, and King read their urgency with ruthless glee. MGM Grand owner Kirk Kerkorian, who'd once been a boxer himself, was wild to get the fighter. His nondescript property (not one moat) was distinguished by its massiveness, its desultory "Wizard of Oz" theme, and a theme park that nobody attended. At his direction, King's deals were solicited. Prestige would be obtained—at a surprising cost, though.

The deals King was insisting upon were wild beyond belief. Worse, over the three years of negotiating, every time the MGM agreed to a deal, King redid the figures upward. The fourth contract was so far out of the realm of possibility that officials more or less dismissed him, finally. But King came back later and reduced his numbers somewhat, and a deal was made.

Through all this there was no competition from the other casinos, no pretense of auction. Up and down the strip, other casino officials had already been burned by King or boxing and were too cautious to even entertain the idea. Only the MGM was committed to Tyson at these prices.

A Savage Business

It was, according to all who are in on the high-level gossip of Las Vegas, an atrocious deal. Besides giving King and Tyson a much-talked-about $20 million up-front—"For the privilege of doing business with Don," one operator said—it also ceded to King total control over Tyson's opponents. This was reckless. King and the MGM had earlier broken over just that issue; in 1994 the two were at such odds over opponents for Chavez that at one point King's spokesman said he wouldn't be doing business there anymore. And the MGM said it wouldn't mind if he didn't, since King's mismatches—Chavez's fight with Frankie Randall, to take one example, drew just 10,574—had been so poorly attended.

That was then and this was Tyson. There were other clauses that were much talked about up and down the strip. The deal was said to give King—give!—5,000 of the best seats in the 16,000-seat Grand Garden Arena to sell as he pleased. "They should get their expenses back," said one high-level official. "I mean, I hope they get their expenses back."

But this was Las Vegas, and nothing is ever as it seems. The buffets are not really cheap. The rooms are never free. The Mirage does not fire up its volcano for the Kodak crowd just because it's civic-minded. The MGM might—nobody knew how—get its money back if it played well. They had Tyson, that was what counted.

These were the dynamics at work in the spring of 1995, an incautious time, but an optimistic time. Maybe with Tyson headlining the property, the MGM would be hosting the likes of Australian Kerry Packer, a true Moby, a guy the Las Vegas Hilton had made special $12,500 chips for so that his $75,000 blackjack hands could be more easily paid. It might be worth anything to get his speed. It was easy to imagine the take from baccarat doubling on a fight night, plumping the fiscal quarter's take by as much as 40 percent—just for one night's play! Of course, it was much harder to imagine a

23

Kerry Packer, who did wander over to the MGM, taking them for $24 million, as he did (but not on a fight night, as it happened).

The promise of easy money had made everybody silly. In general Las Vegas has a relaxing effect on everyday standards of behavior; on fight night it is truly corrupting. Baseball great Pete Rose might return change at a diner if he was undercharged. But one fight night at the MGM, when Rose was playing high-stakes blackjack, a dealer fell asleep at the tray and overpaid him (so it was reported) by $10,000; Rose, seeing what happened, hustled the chips away to the cashier's cage and, no matter the entreaties of the pit boss, wouldn't give them back. It wasn't an atmosphere that seemed to elevate character.

This is a town built on the notion that you can roll in and get something for nothing. It's a form of legitimized theft, is what it is. The preponderance of pawnshops off the strip might suggest this is not so, that somebody besides city government is constructing the Brooklyn Bridge over Nevada dust. Indeed, players lose $6 billion a year at Las Vegas casinos. That's a fact. But no amount of evidence in the world can quash the gambler's feeling of anticipation, which in every sense provides the very electricity that lights the lamps above his head.

This same feeling works on the casinos themselves, though they are better protected from their bad ideas by the arithmetic of table games and the relentless compounding of profits from the slots. Still, they are occasionally led to ruin—and King had often been their tour guide—by their own greed. Boxing worked in Las Vegas, but not always at King's prices. He'd burned the Las Vegas Hilton (the night of the disastrous Tyson–Frank Bruno fight in 1989, the hotel was also hosed at the gate), and also the Riviera in years past. But there were always new hotels, new managements, and, at the MGM

Grand this time, it was no trick for him to conjure gold at the end of Dorothy's rainbow. *He had Tyson.*

Tyson himself would prove vulnerable to the idea of entitlement, the feeling that he was owed. To head off protests over his past behavior—even though he had served his time—he would spread $1 million around Harlem at a weird rally in New York some months later, a rally organized by Rev. Al Sharpton at which Tyson was introduced by King as "our son, our future." But the young man who had been boning up on socialism for three years got a whiff of capitalism and remembered that he liked it. There would be reports of colossal spending sprees in the Forum Shops at Caesars Palace, stories that he bought a $123,000 Mercedes over the phone, that he'd purchased four $320,000 Bentley Azures in Las Vegas, that he bought a Las Vegas compound.

It seemed perfect, so many needs being met by Tyson's release. It was a spectacular confluence of desires. Everybody was getting what they thought they wanted. Even the sport of boxing would be rejuvenated by his freedom.

Tyson hadn't been champion since 1990, hadn't fought since beating Razor Ruddock two times in 1991—and he might not have been great since 1988, when he knocked Michael Spinks out in 91 seconds. But what exactly had happened in his absence? What promoter, what fighter had taken advantage of his leaving? The most promising heavyweight, Riddick Bowe, had lost titles and credibility to Evander Holyfield, who in turn was upset by Michael Moorer, who in turn was floored by George Foreman. The division was in its familiar shambles, with successive champions of diminishing resolve and reliability.

It was only partly amazing that Tyson, whose popularity and skills would have to be reevaluated after three years in prison, was being hailed as the game's savior. "Without even lifting a glove," sniffed veteran trainer Emanuel Steward. "It just shows you the sad state of boxing, people looking to Mike to rescue the sport."

A lot of importance was being invested in Tyson, whether it was corporate enhancement or a sport's survival. The day he left the Indiana Youth Center, he was a bigger name than the day he'd gone in. He was richer, more famous, more interesting after his punishment. His reputation as a boxer had actually been restored just by his absence. A hundred million, the day he hit the street. It was a cruel idea: Raping a teenager had turned out to be a great career decision.

The innocents who stood in the Indiana corn, wondering about his rehabilitation, had reason to be concerned now that the pressure on him to perform would be greatly increased. His reading list had been impressive, and it never hurts to be able to drop a line from Voltaire on some skeptic. But, really, he hadn't been a complete person the day he'd gone in, and no amount of literature could integrate such a splintered character. The great stories—like the one about the old man and the kid—had been sad fictions; the legendary trainer Cus D'Amato, Tyson's inventor, hadn't survived long enough to have a finished product ready. There were signs that D'Amato, who'd plucked a 13-year-old Tyson from reform school and put him into his Catskills estate, had cut corners, had rushed his young heavyweight into action before he should have.

"He was unfinished business," said José Torres, another protégé of D'Amato's who'd transcended a hoodlum youth to become a champion. Tyson's teenage appetites for thuggery had appealed to D'Amato, according to Torres: "I swear to you, the worse a kid was, the more he'd like him." It was a teacher's arrogance, the idea that he could work a transformation toward citizenship, or at least championship. And Tyson, the mugger of old ladies from Brownsville, was perfect for D'Amato's teachings.

A Savage Business

"Plus," said Teddy Atlas, another early devotee of D'Amato's, "he could punch like a sonuvabitch."

Certainly D'Amato imparted many heartfelt and useful attitudes to Tyson. But he died in 1985, Tyson's first year as a pro, before his teachings—however compromised they'd become at his last chance for a champion—could be fully absorbed. "It would have been different," said Torres, even though he was no longer the D'Amato believer he used to be, "if Cus had been alive. Tyson wouldn't have been anything without him, but if he'd had him longer, Cus might have engineered and constructed him better. He ran out of time."

Kevin Rooney extended the D'Amato tradition for a few more years, calling out the numbered combinations from the corner just as his mentor, old Cus, had before him. But then Don King swooped in, took Tyson from Bill Cayton—the last man to do business with D'Amato, the link to those platitudes—fired Rooney, and cut all ties to the Catskills. The unfinished business could never be completed now.

It was the contention in the Catskills camp that Tyson's doom was foretold by his association with King, an association born out of Tyson's twin needs for money and love. "What he did," said Rooney of Tyson's switched allegiance, "isn't what Cus would have wanted. He chose to bite the forbidden apple."

When King was visiting him in jail and promising him fantastic amounts of money just for walking out a prison door, did Tyson ever harken back to those old musty sayings of D'Amato's? "You can't want too many things," the old man had once said. "The beginning of corruption is wanting things. You want a car or a fancy house or a piano, and the next thing you know, you're doing things you don't want to do, just to get the things."

Everyone around him as he was coming out of prison would encourage such notions now, the wanting of things.

King had an overriding respect for the power money conferred, if not for the money itself. And he had been careful to surround the fighter with men who had similar attitudes. Tyson's official comanagers, John Horne and Rory Holloway, were essentially highly paid buddies to Tyson whose skills were limited to the nursing of Tyson's fire, or what they believed it to be. They certainly weren't there to manage him in a business sense: "To say they were boxing managers," said one high-up casino worker in Las Vegas, "was like saying you and I were genetic engineers." King has said he took John Horne and Rory Holloway "through the University of the Ghetto and they graduated summa cum laude." Yet they did not participate materially in negotiations. All they really presented to Tyson was loyalty—which was no cheap thing.

Holloway, who hardly ever escapes description without being called pouchy-eyed, was just a kid Tyson met in Albany during the fighter's amateur boxing days, through one of Holloway's younger brothers, who was more into sports than Rory. Holloway and Tyson just hit it off. As Holloway was from upstate New York, he represented an improvement in society to Tyson, who mostly got into trouble down in the city. The same was true of Horne, an assistant manager at a shoe store in Albany in the mid-'80s; Horne met Tyson during one of the fighter's trips to the Crossgates Mall, and they too became friends. The two were an upstate upgrade.

They didn't become involved in Tyson's affairs until much later. Horne, who has said his "primary interest is entertainment," had forsaken shoes to try comedy in Los Angeles. Watching him glower at press conferences, this is a difficult image to wrap your mind around. He must have been like Eddie Murphy, only unrelieved by the possibility of laughter. But his ambitions, of which he had plenty, turned to promotion, and it was while he was putting together a slam-dunk contest in Las Vegas that he ran into the fighter again and asked him to be one of the judges. Later, Holloway and Tyson showed up for Horne's stand-up act and the bunch became a trio.

In 1987 they became more important to Tyson. That was when King began to insinuate himself between manager Bill Cayton and Tyson. The two younger men proved helpful, according to a book written by Tyson's former chauffeur, Rudy Gonzalez—although it's hard to tell whom they wanted to help most. According to *The Inner Ring: The Setup of Mike Tyson and the Uncrowning of Don King,* Gonzalez heard Horne exulting in the back of the limo over the deal to bring Tyson to King. "You believe that we just made the biggest deal in boxing history? We made it so fast and so easy. Can you believe he gave us one million in cash just to get him to the table?" (The three men have denied Horne's quote, and note that Gonzalez was later fired from Tyson's employ.)

Horne and Holloway definitely stood by their fighter as he served his prison sentence, and their loyalty, whether founded on money or friendship, has never wavered. But neither has the perception that they have been front men for King. They certainly never did much beyond keeping the fighter comfortable. Holloway's function turned out to be the running of the camp, from which he could report the grisly dispatch of various Tyson sparring partners. Horne insisted he was the man taking care of business, yet nobody involved in business deals for Tyson ever heard a peep from either. Showtime might depend upon Horne to deliver the fighter for interviews, but otherwise went straight to King when it came to money matters.

And they certainly didn't know anything about boxing. Their role was mostly to behave as a buffer between Tyson and the public (and King, who was at least one generation removed), and they seemed to believe the bigger the buffer the better. It was interesting that Horne and Holloway were upstanding family men, yet came across uglier than any of the downstate thugs Tyson might have chosen as his "managers." Horne in particular seemed a deep source of bitterness and distrust; watching him stand at Tyson's shoulder during an interview, you could actually see where Tyson's venom sprang from. There was a kind of puppetry at work.

Their one invention was the idea that Tyson would now move forward as part of a team: Team Tyson. Managers have always been allowed the traditional arrogance of the cornerman—"Go on in there, he can't hurt us"—but Horne and Holloway took this concept to a new extreme. Boxing is not anything like a team sport, and yet the comanagers would try to take equal responsibility and credit in the fighter's comeback. To everyone else, this was simply too aggravating, but Tyson didn't seem to mind. He seemed comfortable surrounded by the two. And King certainly liked it: Team Tyson was, after all, a way of isolating the fighter—from trouble, rival promoters, the press, you name it. How this would serve the fighter in the long run was anybody's guess.

"Tyson's pretty well surrounded," Rooney pointed out, "but he's by himself and he doesn't even know it."

On that March morning in Indiana, they were all Tyson had. Three years in prison had not bolstered his self-esteem, and it's doubtful he thought he deserved better. What was it Cus had said? People born round don't die square? Why shouldn't he leave with the people who'd brought him here? Had he changed?

The motorcade to the airport was a wild one, the helicopters barely keeping up. The flight to Ohio was short, and the drive past yellow ribbons (thoughtfully arranged by Don King Productions) to his estate located just 10 miles from King's didn't take long, either. What happened there that night was the subject of a few tabloid headlines, as it seemed the sheer newsworthiness of the day could not be exhausted.

A Savage Business

First reports were that King, in a massive misreading of Tyson's Muslim leanings, had prepared a welcoming spread of shellfish, pork, and alcohol—everything that might be offensive to a devout Muslim. Further, it was reported that Showtime had been on hand to film his homecoming for a documentary, but that Tyson had kicked everybody out. Until Tyson went public the following Tuesday with an announcement that King had remained behind—"The greatest promoter in the world, as we know"—there was fevered speculation that King had gotten the boot as well as the Showtime cameras.

According to Showtime's Jay Larkin, no such thing happened. They had simply gathered at Tyson's house—and, yes, there was a buffet, but, no, there wasn't any shellfish—to do some business. Showtime's contracts for Tyson's services required Tyson's signature for him to get the money. It had been a pleasant enough afternoon, Larkin recalled, even when Tyson, tired of so much freedom, tired of so much money, asked everybody to leave the room. King and the Showtime officials simply went out on the patio to finish their discussions.

They had left Tyson inside alone, was all. Larkin remembered looking back and seeing Tyson on the couch, balancing a plate of macaroni salad in one hand, a bottle of water in the other. His adventure was ready to begin. Tyson was staring straight ahead, expressionless, at his big-screen TV. He was watching X-Men. Cartoon superheroes, each with his specific powers, went about saving the day.

Chapter Two

"A mismatch of scandalous proportions"

In the uproar that surrounded Mike Tyson's first postprison fight, it was impossible to separate what was accidental from what was purposeful. In the absence of masterminds, neglect is usually the sport's operating principle, and whatever contrivance you've been led to believe in has generally been overstated. But the Peter McNeeley event, Tyson's ring debut, had a kind of genius to it all the same. There was evidence of planning, much of it aggravating, all of it calculating beyond belief. There were examples of intrigue and conspiracy. And there was, woven into the usual turmoil, a strict adherence to the promotional theme that less is more. In short, all the confusion seemed intentional.

For certain, Tyson's slow unveiling appeared deliberate. He appeared bit by bit, popping up in odd corners of the culture, revealing as little as possible. Snippets of conversation in a hip-hop magazine, generic cross-talk in a Larry King interview, bleached-out interviews in a few well-placed sports sections. It was an amazing promotional strategy, given that boxing is most often advanced at full volume with total access; it was especially amazing since King—the very definition of full volume and total access—is not given to secret campaigns. Yet here was Tyson, going against all tradition, doing a sort of striptease.

A Savage Business

It was weird, but mostly it was frustrating—especially to the media, who had been clamoring for Tyson's attention ever since he went away to prison. He, or rather Team Tyson, was blowing off all the old outlets that had so often served as advertorials in the old days, while the fighter remained sphinx-like through the prefight buildup. Those accustomed to more cooperation than this—and all of those who covered boxing for any part of their living were used to a virtual partnership in their work—were stunned and then outraged.

ESPN was told that Tyson would do no interviews with the sports network if its chief boxing reporter, Charley Steiner, was involved. Steiner's offense, as far as he could tell, was that he had been at the trial and reported the verdict. "I had him guilty, too," Steiner said. When ESPN countered with two other announcers and they, too, were found wanting, ESPN decided it could live without a Tyson interview.

Similarly, *Sports Illustrated* was told it would not be allowed any prefight access to Tyson, or even to Team Tyson. This was mostly because of its presumed alliance with HBO, another Time Warner property. Although Tyson grew up on HBO, they had since separated in bitterness, and King saw his enemy's influence everywhere he looked, even at *Sports Illustrated,* which shared nothing with HBO beyond corporate revenue. But *Sports Illustrated* had not enjoyed most-favored-nation status for some time, going back to the Buster Douglas fight; John Horne, the most visible element of Team Tyson, had complained before of both the picture and the text from that story, which depicted the once-great Tyson on his knees, "scrambling for his mouthpiece."

To the journalists who had to report the McNeeley fight, the intrigue over access seemed important. It reflected a paranoia that had always been there under King, but was now amplified to a strange and dangerous level under Horne. Horne seemed to enjoy having the upper hand, explaining time and again at press conferences that he was the gatekeeper. He made it clear that Tyson and his image would be better protected henceforth, and anybody who hoped to deal with Tyson in the future should begin by getting with the program. Mike Marley, King's spokesman and a former boxing writer himself, went so far as to tell *Sports Illustrated* that ingratiation might be the way to go: "We'll see how you do," he told the magazine, regarding its coverage of the McNeeley fight and its hopes for a Tyson interview down the line.

The journalists became preoccupied with their daily trials, examining this new quid-pro-quo way of doing business with incredulity. In the coverage of sports there is no greater sense of privilege than among boxing writers. Although, almost to a man and woman, they are the most combative writers in their sports sections, they enjoy a relationship with the athletes that would be unthinkable in any other sport. It was not out of the question, for example, to stroll down a hotel hall the night before a megafight and see Muhammad Ali, beyond his open door, crouched on his bed, examining the plans for a motor home he planned to buy with the purse from his Larry Holmes fight, and to be invited in. Even the hard cases liked the give-and-take. The night before one of his memorable fights at Caesars Palace, Roberto Duran allowed a group of writers into his hotel room. This was the rough equivalent of shooting the breeze with Troy Aikman the eve of the Super Bowl. Duran stayed under the covers of his bed, only his head exposed, but in this disembodied state he talked with the writers all they wanted.

So Team Tyson's approach was new. But if it was infuriating, it also happened to be shrewd. "This is very intelligent," decided Bob Arum, a rival promoter who does not often acknowledge proper cunning beyond his own promotions. "Selling the mystery instead of the fight. Brilliant." The writers stewed amid their pitiful pool reports, not seeing the larger picture. The pay-per-view operators grew anxious, as much for the lack of cooperation as for the fight date, during the reputed dog days of August. MGM clenched its corporate teeth. Yet this fight wasn't going to succeed in spite of the relative secrecy, it was going to prosper because of it.

Few appreciated the magic of Tyson's new image, actually enhanced for boxing purposes by the void of his inactivity. Arum was right, it was the mystery that would sell this fight. There was a built-in-anticipation; with Tyson being presented as an inkblot, public curiosity was reaching critical mass, and a fight that everybody agreed was the worst kind of walkover was now going to be one of those touchstone events: maybe not a moon landing, but pretty good box office all the same.

Here was the actual marketing genius: The public was forced to fill this empty vessel with meaning, to take his violent history, his horrifying successes and equally terrifying failures, and the perverse glamour of his prison term, and construct its own terrible attraction. Neither style nor substance was offered, only enough memory to provoke the imagination. Forgotten was Tyson scrambling for his mouthpiece or even struggling in fights with ordinary opponents like Razor Ruddock. Remembered instead was the spartan warrior—no socks, no robe, just a white towel with a hole in it for his sullen head—drilling his panicked opponents with pneumatic precision, producing sudden and breathtaking dispatches. The failures were not simply dimmed in the passage of time, but were replaced with the scary triumph of evil, the unrepentant rapist wriggling his handcuffs for the camera, mocking the solid citizenry, unbowed by justice or jail. These memories were a better sell than a Showtime trailer, making up a docudrama so thin it became practically interactive as the paying customers tried to project significance onto it. A ridiculous foe promises to wrap Tyson in a "cocoon of horror," and Tyson, sitting quietly nearby, only arches an eyebrow. It is funny, it is chilling. The empty vessel seems to fill with menace right before your eyes.

At times Tyson tried to present himself as a thoughtful and changed man. The jailhouse tattoos he emerged with were, after all, the curiously paired likenesses of Arthur Ashe and Mao Zedong. Of his prison belongings, the only things that returned home to Ohio with him were more than 20 banana boxes full of books—Voltaire, Maya Angelou, Machiavelli, Alexandre Dumas. He steadfastly refused to apologize to Desiree Washington, insisting their sex was not rape, but admitted at the same time that he belonged in jail for . . . something, a life of unexamined excess perhaps. "I don't know if prison was a blessing in disguise," he told the music magazine *The Source*, "but I do know I made it a blessing." Yet it was different to know if he was changed in a way that was any more profound than his mentor's prison transformation: Don King had also had a formidable reading list while serving time on a manslaughter charge, but critics believed the oft-quoted literature was only used to disarm his better-educated adversaries, and that he was no less vicious as a promoter than as a numbers runner.

When Tyson did speak, he said mostly reassuring things. In an interview with longtime boxing writer Ed Schuyler three weeks before the McNeeley fight, Tyson said, "I'm basically pretty stable at this stage of my life. I wish I was twenty and felt the way I do now. In life we're thrown curves, and sometimes we get a hit and sometimes we strike out. Life is not about having grudges and being bitter." He told Schuyler, the first white writer he had spoken to up to that time, that his natural arrogance had been tempered. "Can you imagine me, with my pride, being told, 'Get back in your cell, nigger, and count.' I know about humbleness."

Those who knew him from the old days were wary of these little nuggets. They played very well for a public that loves nothing better than a good rehabilitation story, but they weren't necessarily anything more than wishful thinking. Teddy Atlas, a fellow D'Amato disciple who broke away from that cult, having become Tyson's ex-trainer after holding a .38 to Tyson's head because the fighter had fondled Atlas's young sister-in-law, remembered a telling anecdote from his former pupil. "He used to tell how, back in Brownsville, he'd manipulate the people in the streets, act real polite, say, 'Ma'am, can I help you with your groceries?' then get them in the elevator and take their purses. Forget about him robbing these people; what stuck with me was the con job. He has no identity. He never had an identity." He was then, perhaps now, whoever he had to be.

It was a tantalizing idea, one that over the years had been often considered. After all, this wasn't Tyson's first reformation. His life with Cus D'Amato, his life with Jimmy Jacobs had promised him redemption, but—maybe because both men had died at critical points in his life—their stewardships were never fulfilled. Even while under their wings, Tyson would often escape into his past. The Tyson biographer and his onetime friend José Torres, one of D'Amato's first properties, remembered that D'Amato would often ask him to track the young fighter down, and he'd seek him out amid the porn parlors of New York's Forty-second Street.

Over the years, obviously, Tyson was unable to be true to D'Amato's teachings, although that was just as obviously a lot to ask of someone from Tyson's background. It was reasonable to wonder if Tyson, for all his reading and religious conversion in prison, was truly a humbled person.

It was all the more reasonable after a press conference outburst, a rare show of spontaneous behavior in which Tyson displayed a nice-sized chip on his shoulder. At the final news conference for the McNeeley fight, the only place Tyson could be counted on to face the press if not address them, he was asked to clarify a comment he'd made in a television interview, when he questioned the loyalty of "people closest to him." Greg Logan of *Newsday* wondered if he was talking about the people he'd eventually returned to. Tyson, who had reacted a little strangely when a provocateur in the crowd asked what he would say to his rape victim (he laughed, clapped his hands, and said, "Just enjoy the fight"), now went off the deep end.

"I said that because I wanted to say that, and that's the way I feel," he said. "And why I go back is none of your business. There are assassins who shoot people, but there are also other kinds of assassins." The writers in the crowd snapped to attention. So did King, sitting next to Tyson. King immediately tried to stifle him with some hah-hahing bromide, but Tyson waved the promoter away. "Please be quiet when I'm talking," he said to a startled King before going on. "They wait behind school buses and they wait for you to fall in the snow. They kill your character. They're character killers. That's what you are. You're a character killer. And that's the best thing that ever happened to you—I spoke to you, my friend." Logan and the rest of the crowd blinked in disbelief, not quite comprehending this public outpouring. But a lot of others elsewhere nodded smugly: This guy was still distilled anger, and his art as ever remained its commercial exploitation.

All these contradictions—he would quote Aristotle in one breath and Arnold Rothstein in another—made him a truly interesting man, which was valuable to the promotion because nobody was absolutely positive he was a great fighter any longer. Even before he went away he had appeared to be a boxer of diminished abilities. Such concerns were not useful in selling tickets, but they were there all the same. Especially troubling to Tyson's doubters were the persistent comparisons to Muhammad Ali, who had suffered a swerve in his own career. The doubters resented any suggestions that Tyson was going to remake himself Ali-style; to them it was a heresy.

It's true that Ali was in exile for a similar length of time, but there were few parallels beyond that. As Atlas pointed out, Ali was kicked out of boxing because of his convictions, and Tyson for his lack of them. This was an important point to raise at the press's pulpit, but arguably it was a dainty distinction to find in a sport increasingly run like some kind of gangster empire.

More to the point, though, was the fact that Ali—who was in exile, not jail—could spar as much as he wanted, while Tyson could not. And even more to the point was this: Ali was the classic upright boxer, who was devoted to craft and defense and improvisation in the ring, whereas Tyson was a robotic, straight-ahead presence who might not be able to adapt to the inevitable erosion of skills.

Ali, who was out of boxing from the age of 25 to 28, surely did change when he was allowed to box again. Once untouchable, he demonstrated in his comeback a horrifying ability—and even more horrifying willingness—to take a punch. "Rope-a-dope" soon went into the lexicon, although nobody knew for a long time how costly to Ali this new vocabulary would be. "But Tyson," said the veteran trainer Emanuel Steward, "his kind don't have long careers. Everything is instinct, do it, do it, do it. It's all aggression. He's more like Joe Frazier. And that kind of speed and aggression tapers off at twenty-six or twenty-seven. The ferociousness automatically declines." Tyson was a first-stage rocket, a sky-splintering missile long since spent, and all that was left was the orbiting shell of his celebrity.

Perhaps, though, the character issue would come into play. Is it possible that Ali, in sacrificing his athletic youth to his political stance, developed a moral authority that he could exercise in the psychological destruction of a young thug named George Foreman? Is it possible that he forged ahead with some notion of destiny, some idea of purpose, the correctness of which would be tested in the worst kind of adversity? Maybe he had dredged a reservoir in that exile from which he could draw, a source of strength when he peered from his corner in Zaire and saw "black lights." What about Tyson? His conversion to Islam and his new erudition did not necessarily square with the needs of the modern boxer; culture is counterproductive in the ring. He may have matured in prison, but up to that point he hadn't demonstrated—hadn't been able to demonstrate—any kind of improved character. It was a reasonable question: What about Tyson?

On the other hand, for all the hand-wringing anybody might do over Tyson's ability to pick up where he left off (never mind where Ali left off), there was this one crucial matter, one that obviated all concerns about Tyson's questionable condition, moral and otherwise: Whereas in his comeback Ali immediately fought a top-10 contender named Jerry Quarry, a rugged and fearless warrior, Tyson was paired with Peter McNeeley, a plugger of such specific suitability that he almost seemed to have been bred for the job.

McNeeley, an irrepressible lug of such suspect credentials that the world was set howling with the announcement of him as Tyson's opponent, was an example of genetic matchmaking. It was as if King, who had a pretty large pool of inept heavyweights to dip into for Tyson's first foe, was unwilling to trust in even their established incompetence. To be absolutely certain, he needed someone who manifested generational failure, whose very DNA predicted the loss. And Boston's McNeeley was his man.

McNeeley, delight that he was, happened to be one of those fighters who was born to lose. No getting around that. He was white (never a good sign), slow, and painfully artless. A

white heavyweight of even no ability is normally a highly
marketable commodity, but McNeeley, who enjoyed that lack
of pigmentation, was so frightful in the ring that promoters
actually fought to keep him out of sight. Bob Arum, who is
not above featuring artless and frightful white heavyweights
—a bald spheroid named Butterbean made him a lot of
money—was nonetheless so offended by the spectacle of
McNeeley that, in good conscience, he had to shun him.
"When we did shows in the Northeast on ESPN," he said,
"and the local promoter would ask for him, we'd have to
hide him from TV."

And if that didn't make him safe enough for Tyson, there
was his family tree. His grandfather, Tom Sr., a member of
the 1928 U.S. Olympic boxing team, was the one blight of
victory in the family scrapbook. His father, Tom Jr., is best
remembered as the heavyweight Floyd Patterson knocked
down 13 times, give or take a slip, on the way to a fourth-
round knockout to defend his title. The elder McNeeley was
so outclassed in that 1961 fight in Toronto that the sportswriter Red Smith reported it as "a mismatch of scandalous
proportions."

Then as now, matchmaking was the sort of social en-
gineering that didn't encourage much inspection. Tom
McNeeley, a football player out of Michigan State, was indeed undefeated going into that fight, but, in an eerie fore-
shadowing of his son's own grooming, had fattened up on
one unranked fighter after another—one of them, George
Logan of Utah, three times.

But he was definitely a friend of the promotion. As Peter
would prove to be, Tom was more colorful than accomplished, given to a decent quote and an obliging personality.
The week of the Patterson fight he dodged questions about
his psychiatric care—"The psychiatrist didn't treat me, he
just talked to me a couple of times"—and generally behaved

41

eccentrically. Speaking of Patterson two nights before the fight, Tom McNeeley said, "I hope he doesn't disappoint me and fail to show up."

Apparently, all McNeeleys have difficulty believing they are nothing more than fight fodder, even against all evidence. The only person who expressed any concern whatsoever over Tom McNeeley those 35 years ago was Patterson's manager, Cus D'Amato himself. Of course, with D'Amato the paranoia was simply reflexive; his charge that McNeeley was conducting nighttime workouts was not exactly taken seriously. To everyone else, though, he was a 10-1 underdog, and McNeeley had difficulty understanding this sentiment. Years later he said, "I actually felt bad for Floyd, that's how confident I was."

This bravado turned out to be congenital—every bit as much, it was presumed, as the inability to evade a right cross. Peter McNeeley, who had decided to call himself Hurricane some years back, stormed the promotion, filling the publicity void that Tyson had created. Everybody involved was grateful for his blue-collar charisma, but, given his pedigree, McNeeley was impossible to take seriously. His promise to wrap Tyson in a "cocoon of horror" was surely inventive, but the idea was as over-the-top as anything ever issued from a press conference dais, even one of King's.

Still, McNeeley did his part in filling notebooks. His tale was certainly Rocky-esque, the small-time scrabbler plucked for a pay-per-view assassination, and was attractive as ever in its underdog appeal. Even if Rocky only wins in the movies, the story line couldn't be ignored.

He was aided and abetted in this fantasy by his manager, the cat-hatted Vinnie Vecchione, a onetime mobster with a .22 bullet still in his shoulder and dreams of a big score in his bald head. Vecchione was one of those guys made to be in boxing, the sort of character who pops up from time to time to refresh the sport. At the age of 50 he remained capable of creating entire mythologies for his fighters; neither his own history, nor that of the lugs who stumbled into the South Shore Boxing Club in Whitman, Massachusetts, held any predictive value for him. The big time was always around the corner.

And sometimes, of course, it is; the hardest part is recognizing it. That was Vecchione's genius in this affair, seeing McNeeley for what he was, a story. Vecchione had been schooled by a local promoter called Subway Sam Silverman, a fellow who understood the importance of the press. Vecchione was once startled when Subway Sam intervened on behalf of a sportswriter. "Are you crazy?" Silverman said. "That's a newspaper guy." Vecchione slowly came to understand that the power of a story was paramount in the type of promoting he'd be condemned to doing. He wasn't going to come across many fighters who were going to blast their way into the nation's living rooms on the basis of their talents; he was going to have to develop novelty acts, and hope for the best.

So, in 1990, in walked Peter McNeeley, a meaty, impulsive Irish brawler with so much back-story Vecchione would have to parcel it out to reporters a paragraph at a time. Here was a kid, Vecchione learned early enough (or said he learned), who had decided to become a boxer at six, the day he was killing time in the attic of the $23,000 house his father had been able to afford with his Patterson purse of $40,000, and found a picture of him on the cover of an old *Sports Illustrated*. The specifics of this highly unlikely tale were not gratuitous; Vecchione had learned from Subway Sam long ago that if God isn't necessarily in the details, good press always is.

In fact, McNeeley was not driven into the sport by any sense of destiny, real or imagined. He was floundering at Bridgewater State College—"a victim of partying"—and became convinced that a return to sports might help his grades. Boxing had always been in the back of his mind, although he had been more devoted to football in high school, and he thought to finally give it a try. It had been a long time since Tom had taken him and his brother Snubby (Bryan) to the CYO to "learn how to take a jab to the puss," but what the hell. How hard could it be?

When McNeeley showed up at the South Shore gym, he was sporting an amateur record of 15–6 and was somehow keeping the Olympic selection committee at bay. Vecchione, meanwhile, was not standing in the tall grass himself. He was handling the comeback of Paul Pourier, a former middleweight who had quit the game 10 years earlier to join the Jehovah's Witnesses and was now campaigning as a heavyweight. So when McNeeley showed up to spar, looking rugged and wild and little else—"He couldn't box a lick"—Vecchione was nevertheless able to find room for him in his stable.

Vecchione was in love with the kid's story and recognized a certain promise in him. He told people that McNeeley had "a fire in his belly and a chip on his shoulder," and didn't believe either was compromised by his higher education, a traditional drawback in this game. Downplaying the college credits, Vecchione often said of McNeeley that he was "just smart enough to be a fighter." McNeeley never proved him otherwise.

To get McNeeley from the South Shore sweatbox, where neither windows nor fans were operational, to the airiness of the MGM Grand would take more than attitude. McNeeley would need a record. And he got one, in a tradition that goes back to the beginning of boxing. Few beginning fighters are matched over their heads, but Vecchione's handling of McNeeley was protective beyond even the good conscience of boxing.

A Savage Business

When the particulars of McNeeley's record were exposed, the fight world was set bawling with laughter. Everybody seemed to be using his own arithmetic, and it got a little confusing, but there was no getting around the obvious conclusion: McNeeley's opponents were a joke. *USA Today* figured his opposition's record at a combined 148–436, adding a provocative aside: At the time of their fights, a full third of his opponents had never won a single bout. Even at that, McNeeley was not unblemished: He was 36–1, and the loss came the first time he fought somebody with a winning record.

It was an expensive buildup. Vecchione was putting McNeeley into fights that earned him little or no money. Six months before the Tyson fight, McNeeley made $190 for a bout in Arkansas. But fighter and trainer both recognized this part of McNeeley's career as a kind of loss leader. They were fronting promotions that had no purpose except enriching McNeeley's record.

If McNeeley was making no money, he could hardly be accused of shortchanging his fans. Still, some of the bouts he engaged in ought to have attracted the attention of consumer groups. He once fought Lorenzo Boyd, who was fresh from a four-year prison term. He fought Ron Drinkwater (one of the chosen few who actually had a winning record), who had been retired for 15 years. It reflects more on their specific abilities as opponents than on McNeeley's punching power that neither ever fought again.

It is impossible, among so many, to single out the most lopsided pairing. All the matches Vecchione made were remarkable in their own way, but fighting John Jackson, who had an 0-10-1 record at the time, might have been the worst. Or maybe it was one of the three fights with Jim Harrison, a 37-year-old warhorse with a 6-32-1 record, who might have been better if he had not just come out of drug rehab. Or was it the fight just before Tyson, when McNeeley blasted Frankie Hines in one round? Hines, 36, had been knocked out 49 times and had lost 11 straight.

This exaggerated grooming was not overlooked by the local press, which dogged the two mercilessly. It was hardly fatal to their campaign, though; Vecchione took the criticism in stride. When the *Boston Globe* accused McNeeley of avoiding anyone without a toe tag, Vecchione began answering his phone "Coroner's office." In any event, the record of a white heavyweight is beyond criticism. It is a marketing tool, boxing's *Good Housekeeping's* Seal of Approval. According to Vecchione, Arum sufficiently overcame his repulsion at the sight of McNeeley to offer him $100,000 for a fight with Tommy Morrison. They turned that down, as well as a $75,000 offer to fight Joe Hipp and a $50,000 payday for Jorge Luis Gonzalez. The worst of these purses was five times what McNeeley had ever earned in the ring.

Vecchione's restraint in the face of these offers was nothing short of miraculous. For these two, $100,000 was the big time. Yet Vecchione, whose dream had become the buyout of his brothers in the purchase of the family home where he still lived, was holding out for a bigger jackpot. Maybe a title, even. Well, he overplayed his hand there: The World Boxing Council proved a little more discriminating than the average boxing commission, and the idea of McNeeley meeting WBC champ Oliver McCall went nowhere.

But Vecchione didn't downsize his dream. He told Don King's matchmaker, Al Braverman, that he'd take Tyson instead. Braverman, who reportedly received a $100,000 finder's fee for bringing this Boston pair to King, was interested. Somebody would have to take Tyson. Two months before Tyson's release, King called to say, "You got him." Vecchione argued the price for about five minutes, he remembered, then agreed on a figure of $540,000. "He's playing chess, everybody else is playing checkers," Vecchione said in admiration. King got him a few quick opponents and a sudden and bewildering ranking. He went from 20 all the way to 7 in the WBA's estimation. The Frankie Hines fight must have been the one that did it.

The real miracle, though, was how at home Vecchione and McNeeley made themselves in the big time. Amazingly, neither was intimidated by the size of the promotion. "I been in plenty of life-and-death situations," Vecchione said. "Nothing really shook me up." As for McNeeley, he turned out to be made for just this kind of event—the promotion of it, anyway. Camera crews came from Norway and Japan to his mother's house in Medfield—where he still lived—just to film him walking the neighborhood with his dog, or his brother, Snubby. And he loved it. "One night you're fighting at the Foxboro Raceway," he said, "the next you're in the MGM Grand. Why wouldn't I love it?"

While Team Tyson brooded silently in its version of a buildup, the McNeeley Group was consolidating its various talents in Medfield. A neighbor two houses down composed McNeeley's ring walk, the music that precedes the fighter—McNeeley called it the "angry song"—and it could still bring tears to his eyes a year after the fight. A high school buddy gave him his "cocoon of horror" line. Other buddies—a former roommate who became a city councillor, another friend who was a lawyer—agreed to form his entourage. "I kept it pretty local," McNeeley said.

Throughout he remained agreeable and available, social aspects that did not affect Las Vegas wagering but that did give him an appeal that contrasted starkly with the surly and reclusive Tyson. "Who sold that fight?" McNeeley asked. "I sold that fight. As far as the legwork, I did it all." His "cocoon of horror" strategy was a good invention, inasmuch as it promised a certain amount of activity, if not necessarily competence. There'd be some awkward hurly-burly in the ring and then Tyson would bring the sledge home. It was an evening out, right?

The idea of McNeeley swarming Tyson was actually the only sensible plan; as Vecchione pointed out, "What nobody thought was, how about if my fighter gets lucky?" Well, nobody really thought that, and at times McNeeley's confidence got a little aggravating. At the final press conference, when his swagger drew more sniggers than applause, McNeeley bellowed into the crowd, "Keep laughing, keep laughing. Real funny, huh? If anyone doesn't respect me for going against this guy . . ."

Sadly, nobody did. The odds were 22-1 against him and not even Vecchione was exuding a lot of confidence. Although he believed that his fighter had a great shot, getting Tyson first after this layoff, and had the capacity to "hurt him, get in a position to dominate him for a while," it was clear that his long-term thoughts did not extend all the way to victory. In fact, he had given quite a bit more consideration to the possibility of defeat. "No problem," Vecchione said a couple days before the fight. "He's twenty-six years old, he's got a great future, he will have lost to one of the top fighters in the country. Probably within four to five months, he'll fight back in Boston. I'll be sure to get him the right opponent, probably move on from there."

Tyson as stepping stone. A fresh idea. Vecchione even had a shortlist of opponents, all upgrades from Frankie Hines. There was Axel Schulz, Oliver McCall, or Francois Botha, a fellow McNeeley disliked enough to have slapped at a press conference. "He'd have a shot at the world heavyweight title within a year."

All McNeeley had to do was live the night. As more than 16,000 assembled at the MGM on August 19, 1995, that seemed problematic. Vecchione took his 19-year-old son

Shane into Tyson's dressing room to inspect his wrapping before the fight, and the boy was shaken by what he saw. "Dad, I want you to watch out for Peter, he's in big trouble here." For that matter, once McNeeley glimpsed Tyson inside the ring, his own formidable resolve finally weakened.

A year after the fight, McNeeley agreed to collect his impressions. "Tyson came into the ring with this kind of thuggy song, and I wasn't prepared to be scared. I had been checking him out in all the press conferences, and he ain't that big, not in street clothes. If you go back to the film, you'll see I stood in the corner with my back to him. That's not where you want to get beat, staring at your opponent. I was just going to look at his belly button when we got to the middle of the ring. Well, Pandora's Box, I have to take a peek. He's all pumped up. He's so wide! His lats are gigantic. His neck, his cranium. He's a fierce-looking individual. I winked and blew him a kiss, but I was scared."

The moment was huge, as big as it gets in sports. Financially, of course, there had never been anything like it. Besides the live gate, there was a record tune-in from 1.4 million homes. The gross revenue from this single event was going to be another record, $63 million. All this money, to see Tyson's half-sneer, to hear the roar as he strutted across the canvas for the first time in four years. To feel what it was like to be in the ring with this killing machine. That's what this was about, right, to absorb McNeeley's fear secondhand? What a jolt, a scene like this, to be victim by proxy.

That was the idea, to enjoy McNeeley's fright. It was wholly reasonable that he would have some, too, as ill equipped as he was for certain slaughter. Yet, despite all this collected adrenaline weighing against him, he still wasn't afraid enough—or perhaps sensible enough—to throw out his fight strategy. McNeeley was still emboldened by his recent Hines fight—"Knocked the guy out in six seconds, had it down to a science"—and didn't figure he'd ever need anything more than his "cocoon of horror." Actually, he didn't have anything in his repertoire beyond that, and it was way too late to develop something more.

Seconds after Johnny Gill's rendition of "The Star-Spangled Banner," McNeeley was upon Tyson. The result was an awkward entangling that in its brevity and lack of composure from all corners was anything but satisfying. Nobody was going to feel cheated by a quick stoppage; not even the plungers who had paid $1,500 for a ringside ticket, or $39.95 for the pay-per-view, expected more. But this? After McNeeley pushed Tyson to the ropes, catching him off guard, Tyson brawled back, a little wildly, and flash-floored McNeeley with a right hook. This was in the first six seconds, roughly the time it took McNeeley to dispatch Frankie Hines. But McNeeley was up quick enough, and for another minute he crowded the confused Tyson. Tyson, missing a lot, connected with a right uppercut to down McNeeley again. And once more McNeeley was quick to his feet.

But, amazingly, as referee Mills Lane was pushing McNeeley back for a mandatory eight-count, the ever-hatted Vecchione was climbing into the ring—in that short time he had not even gotten to the bottom of the steps after sending out his fighter—to force Lane to stop the fight. In 89 seconds, a minute less than Johnny Gill's anthem, the fight was indeed over.

The MGM Grand fight floor was immediately awash with confusion, and then a growing disgust. Tyson had done what he could, what he had to, without raising the veil on his own mystery. He had finally fought, and still nobody knew how good he was. It was entirely inconclusive. The subject of his comeback—and the source of another promotional bonanza —was still open. Perhaps sensing that nothing good beyond that was coming his way, Tyson quickly skedaddled, stopping briefly at the postfight press conference to admit, "I've got a lot to learn. I have to continue to cultivate my skills." As for Vecchione's interference, Tyson, who had thrown fewer than 10 punches, didn't seem to mind. He acknowledged the inevitability. "You know me," he said. "I'm a blood man. I'm glad they stopped it."

McNeeley likewise seemed unaware of disgrace. He welcomed his mother and father and girlfriend into his corner, kissed them all with relief, and refused to join Mills Lane or the Nevada State Athletic Commission in any second-guessing of Vecchione's action. Whereas Lane said, "In my opinion, he could have gone on," and whereas the commission decided to withhold Vecchione's $180,000 share of the purse, McNeeley was decidedly unapologetic. Taking his turn at the press conference, McNeeley first called, "Let's have order here!" then yelled, "Look at the films! Look at the films! I came to fight. I talked the talk and walked the walk."

As Harvey Araton of the *New York Times* wrote, he also "swooned the swoon." Nobody else was quite as forgiving of Vecchione as McNeeley, as it turned out. Even King tried to put distance between himself and McNeeley's corner. "Blame the manager, not the fighter," he screeched, the fans' chants of "bullshit" having penetrated the promoter's professional deafness after all. "The man came to fight. The manager, for some reason, jumped in and stopped it."

For some reason, all right; Vecchione said the reason was simple enough, that his fighter was about to get vaporized. "When I saw Mike Tyson in a track stance," he said much later, clinging to his humanitarian thesis, "and the guy has that kind of punching power, well, if you think he wasn't going to crawl all over my fighter . . ." In truth, with a three-knockdown rule in effect, the fight wouldn't have likely gone much longer anyway. McNeeley wasn't going to see Round 2, no matter what happened.

But the whole premise of the evening, the entire entertainment package, was based on McNeeley's willingness to reflect Tyson's danger for the rest of us. Just how horrifying was Tyson, after all this time? McNeeley's job, whether he understood it or not, was to register the amount of terror Tyson remained capable of, just so we'd know. With Vecchione calling the deal off before blood or brains were spilled, Tyson's menace remained unknown. McNeeley was safe, yes, but who cared?

Worse, Vecchione's interference had a premeditated feel to it. Suddenly it appeared that he was leveraging this event for McNeeley's career, and had meant to all along. Forget Tyson. This whole thing had been done to establish *McNeeley's* identity. He would lose, of course, but to the most feared fighter of his generation—no harm there. And by saving McNeeley from the inevitable pummeling, Vecchione had preserved his fighter in the moment—unmarked, unbowed, and still bellowing away.

It was a breathtaking concept: Vecchione and McNeeley had worked the con, not King and Tyson.

Vecchione vigorously denied any motives beyond his fighter's safety, solemnly invoking the memory of the dead fighter Jimmy Garcia, a recent Las Vegas fight victim, whenever he was questioned about his role in the stoppage. Still, he seemed more than poised to capitalize on McNeeley's 89 seconds of fame in the aftermath. Once he got back home he made a few calls to New York advertising agencies and, within 14 days, landed two national spots, one with America Online, the other with Pizza Hut. Both featured McNeeley as a horizontal lug, constitutionally unable to remain upright for minutes at a time; in the Pizza Hut ad, he was rendered unconscious by the business end of a crust.

The two of them got $110,000 from Pizza Hut and $40,000 from America Online to reenact their embarrassment, decent paydays that were not subject to the boxer's normal tariffs—finder's fees, training expenses, you name it. That was it, though. More bonanzas failed to materialize, and even McNeeley, the guy in the ring, seemed to sense that Tyson had not been a stepping stone after all. He may have recognized that immediately; right after the fight, while the Tyson party raged in the MGM Grand's theme park, McNeeley gathered his buddies in the casino's Betty Boop bar, where the loyal entourage drank Bud by the case: "Does this mean," he said, throwing his arm around a friend's shoulders, "I'll be back at Foxboro?"

McNeeley's career as white-contender-who-frustrated-Tyson (a little) did indeed stall shortly thereafter, and so did his status as celebrity pitchman. His talents, it turned out, were so specific to the needs of this particular promotion that he was henceforth unemployable.

There were a few more fights—including one in which he was pelted with pizza crusts—and talk of meeting Butterbean, but when you got right down to it, he was just not very good, and ultimately, despite his rise in the rankings, this proved to be a handicap. A year later, fighting on small cards for what Vecchione called "short money" (no more than $7,500), McNeeley was once more a struggling heavyweight with iffy prospects. Not only had Butterbean lost, spoiling the curiosity that match might have provided, but so had McNeeley: "Asleep at the switch," said Vecchione, who had taken his fighter to mile-high Denver to fight somebody named Louis Monaco (whose ring profile to that point had been supplied by the aforementioned Butterbean, who had stopped Monaco in one round). It was all a matter of altitude, they said. "A fluke," McNeeley reported, "even though I fought five vicious rounds."

As the noise of Tyson's continuing comeback roared about him, McNeeley sank into his former obscurity, his story briefly recalled during a sporadic series of small-time adventures: a bar brawl, some driving errors. Late in 1996 he made the news wires once more when he was scooped up off a table inside a Medfield sandwich shop; it was reported as pneumonia, then the flu, although it wasn't really either. McNeeley said it had more to do with spending time in the cooler the night before after being rear-ended while driving without a license—speeding tickets, parking tickets—and, in the subsequent investigation to untangle the mess, may have gotten "some germs out of the cell."

At that time, "after a very tumultuous year," he figured he had about $130,000 left from the fight and its financial fallout, as well as a used Audi Quattro he had bought for $5,000 and a newly totaled 1983 Porsche, which he had also bought for $5,000, "some threads," and some nights out on the town. But he refused to admit defeat. He said he would be back; Butterbean was waiting for him down the road, and there is no denying a white heavyweight with a pugnacious nature.

Today, still living in his mother's house, where the Tyson poster hangs, he has reapplied himself to his boxing career. You can be updated daily on the Hurricane Hotline, his answering machine, which provides some homemade sound effects (McNeeley doing a whistling wind) and information on his record and any upcoming fights. "The Hurricane will be back better than ever in the coming months," you're told. Then the sound of wind again, right before the beep.

Chapter Three

"The spirit just came right from the heavens"

The McNeeley fight didn't encourage anybody to think that either Tyson or big-money boxing was back. Though a commercial success, one that left cash registers ringing as loudly as McNeeley's ears, it nevertheless had the stink of a con, a quick hit, a one-time scheme after which the players would slink away and count their money somewhere in the Bahamas. Yet Team Tyson, which meant King, knew they weren't even close to the really big money. With McNeeley, the bonanza had hardly been realized; King would have to work fast to convince consumers and co-conspirators that he was in this for the long run.

So he quickly announced that Tyson's next fight would be beyond Showtime's exclusive purview, the land of the $50 minute and a half, and would be restored to the people. Tyson's follow-up feature, scheduled for November 4 with the marshmallow-fisted Buster Mathis, Jr., would be on free TV. King had persuaded Showtime to step aside and allow him the chance to sell this fight to Fox. No cable operators to call, no descramblers to buy out of the *Popular Mechanics* classifieds. Just dial up Fox on the high end of your VHF dial and settle back with John (Boom!) Madden and Pat Summerall for the small-screen annihilation. The popcorn was on you.

It was a PR masterstroke, a brilliant move to repair Tyson's contract with his fans. King had always believed that Tyson would require two tune-ups before he reentered the championship fray, tune-ups that would allow him to demonstrate his historical fierceness without jeopardizing his safety in the least. But shouts of "Bullshit!" were still resonating in King's huge head after the McNeeley bout, and he was certain that another catastrophe such as Vecchione had orchestrated three months earlier—to this day he lays it on Vecchione—would damage his campaign beyond any possibility of reclamation. Besides, it gave King, a multimillionaire who effectively presents himself and his millionaire fighters as economically and racially oppressed, a chance to try out a new and politically double-edged slogan, a shrewd play on his property's recent incarceration: "Free Tyson."

There was something else about the Mathis fight, an otherwise nondescript event, that elevated its headline size. In an industry where it was difficult to distinguish business decisions from acts of outright revenge, King was scheduling his freebie on the same night as the pay-per-event on TVKO (HBO's pay-per-view arm) featuring Riddick Bowe–Evander Holyfield III, the poor man's Ali-Frazier. It was most curious. Was boxing so big that it could accommodate the game's three most important performers this way—same night, different cards, different casinos, different channels?

It wasn't, of course. Though he would argue otherwise, King's move was a preemptive strike on rival HBO, particularly its president of sports and his enemy, Seth Abraham. When you sorted through all the issues, it came down to this: Despite all these millions of dollars, all these companies listed on the New York Stock Exchange, all these men in suits—Rupert Murdoch, Time Warner, Viacom, ITT Sheraton—this swing in corporate fortunes all came down to a grudge. It was another of boxing's strange lessons: It's always business, and it's always personal.

A Savage Business

TVKO had the marquee event here, no question, and it had it first. Caesars Palace had blocked out the date for TVKO in the spring, about the time Tyson was first stepping out to espy an Indiana cornfield. No other casino would, on its own, seek to interfere with that date, since to do so would be as much a self-inflicted wound as an offensive strike. But here was King, willing to split boxing's fragile market in two, apparently just for spite, and taking his own sponsor down with him. It was absurd. Would he damage the Bowe-Holyfield fight? Of course. Would he, in his insistence on sharing the date, damage his own? Of course. Was it worth it? Well, this is boxing.

It was, one casino executive said, "suicide." It was worse, really, more like a murder-suicide. It was as if King had decided to set himself (or rather his business partners) on fire just so his enemies would be inconvenienced by the heat and be forced to loosen their collars. Nobody could figure it out. King would claim that this particular pact was unavoidable and asked that nobody take it personally. It was just business. But it was not a kind of business anybody else was used to conducting, even in Las Vegas.

To be fair, there was an argument to be made—although not a very sound one—for these dueling dates. Neither the MGM Grand nor Caesars is truly free to schedule events of this magnitude whenever they want. While the seemingly obvious solution to a dilemma of this sort would be to move one fight ahead or back a week, in Las Vegas this is not always possible. Indeed, in any three-month period, there may be no more than two possible dates for a pay-per-view-level event.

An early week in November is often the only time that makes economic sense for the fall. A lot of big fights have been held that exact week—Ali-Holmes, Leonard-Duran, Foreman-Moorer, the two Bowe-Holyfield fights—and it is no accident of scheduling. It falls after the World Series and before the annual Comdex convention (the city's largest), and is spaced just far enough away from New Year's Eve, the town's single biggest night of the year, so that gamblers won't feel their seasonal pilgrimage has become a commute. It really is the casinos' only window of opportunity. The date is no whim.

And Caesars had it. Rich Rose, Caesars World Sports president, had first penciled in Foreman for that date earlier in the spring. When he finally made the Bowe-Holyfield fight for November 4, the only Tyson date on the books was the August fight with McNeeley. A conflict of dates didn't seem possible.

King, however, claimed that he was under the same seasonal pressures as Caesars, and that his were even more intense: He had to squeeze one more Tyson fight into 1995 to set up the championship timetable for 1996. It was an argument, but few bought it. The MGM was stuck, having given King free rein in its contract with him; otherwise, it would never have allowed this conflict, no matter how choice the weekend was. The casinos, in events like these, are forced into cooperation—they share their high rollers, or else all those $1,500 seats would never get sold—and enjoy a give-and-take when it comes to the bigger attractions. By itself, the MGM would not enjoy marketing this event for a return that would be severely diminished by a competing, and better, event. Not only would their favored patrons be frustrated by the inability to see the fight at Caesars, but MGM would be denied the spending power of Caesars' best customers at their own fight. The fact that the two fights would run one after the other that night—with 15 minutes between the end of the Caesars show and the beginning of the MGM main event—was no economic balm. For both properties, it was a lose-lose proposition.

But King continued to insist on the date, even after the

MGM, which has an indoor arena (Caesars at that time did not), offered him spots later, in December. What did it matter to King, though? He had insulated himself, if not his partners or his fighter, from any kind of financial failure with his stunning Fox deal. The move eliminated any carping from fight fans who felt stung by the McNeeley fight, protected him from the inevitable erosion of ratings from a competing pay-per-view telecast, and allowed him to tweak HBO.

This startling development was not part of the original plan. King had been initially emboldened by the numbers from the McNeeley fight, and although he filed for the date with the Nevada State Athletic Commission days after the Bowe-Holyfield promoters, he had assumed that TVKO would cave and that Showtime could present the fight undisturbed. But criticism of his matchmaking was fierce; Mathis was a professional fighter, but he was not much more dangerous than McNeeley. Besides, HBO was showing no signs of caving. Abraham had quickly signed agreements with Viewers Choice and Request TV, the two major distribution networks, to give him the entire cable universe. He clearly meant to compete with King, at whatever cost. Abraham even hinted that this was the start of an all-out war. Would he launch fights involving such HBO stars as Pernell Whitaker, Roy Jones, Jr., George Foreman, Bowe, and others against future King cards? "That's a pretty interesting silo of missiles," Abraham said, thoughtfully. "I would do it."

Even against these threats, King and Showtime could have conceivably forged ahead, but cable operators, anxious about this divided market, were trying to talk King into an alternate date. That's when he experienced the epiphany that would not only save himself but, almost better, punish his enemies.

Explaining his sudden contract with Rupert Murdoch's ambitious Fox network, King said, "In searching to do things, you are led spiritually by God, and I found Rupert. . . . I was riding on the Concorde to America. It's thirty thousand feet high, and the spirit just came right from the heavens."

His competitors would charge that King was communing with authorities in a more nether region, and there was no denying the devilishness of his solution. Although his partners, Showtime and MGM, would be left out if not hurting, King's bacon and his date were saved, and he could afflict his HBO nemesis while he was at it. No wonder the programmers at HBO called him "Blackiavelli."

Of course, in a shootout like this, there are bound to be some losses suffered in friendly fire. For sure, Tyson took a bullet. There were immediate reports that the fighter wasn't as thrilled as his promoter with this little swerve. Tyson's purse, provided out of Fox's fee, was just $10 million—unfathomably huge for a free-TV event, but still a pittance compared to his pay-per-view rates.

There would be lots more blood on the water later, once King's business partners could survey the full casualties, but when he signed the deal on September 14, Fox was certainly ecstatic. More seasoned King watchers might have likened Fox's brash sports president, David Hill, to one more sucker being led into the tent, but the network, with Hill guiding its expansion into sports franchises, was nothing if not ambitious, aggressive, and bold. It had become hard to discount Fox. Its virtual piracy of the NFL contract the year before was no folly. The NFL, however costly it was to Fox, delivered the fledgling network one of television's richest audiences. And, marketing it with a savvy cool that was seemingly unavailable to the older and stodgier networks, Fox appeared ready to translate its growing sports franchise into a significant windfall.

A Mike Tyson fight would be a similar loss leader. The network did not hope to recoup its $10 million in ad sales. Rather, the fight would continue to give it championship cachet and, more to the point, launch a November sweeps period—during which ratings establish new advertising rates—that would bulk up the bottom line down the road. Fox was calling it Knockout November. It spent millions more in promotional collateral to set up the whole thing.

Fox may now wish it had been better educated before investing in Don King and boxing. It might have wondered, for example, what had become of King's previous business partners. Did Fox ever stop to ask why it was in the middle of a war between King and HBO in the first place? Did Fox, whose major contribution to sports television to this point had been a glowing hockey puck, somehow believe it was going to survive a relationship that nobody ever had before?

Theirs was an arrogance that did not permit small doubts. A more reasonable, or wary, outfit might have more fully investigated the collapse of King's relationship with HBO, a hugely profitable partnership for all parties that had dissolved in a thoroughly mystifying tiff, just when Tyson was about to sign a contract that would have made him sports' first $100 million man.

That had been in 1990, when such contracts were not yet the language of the daily sports section. HBO, which had nursed Tyson through his championship apprenticeship, was reaping magnificent rewards with each Tyson telecast. Tyson, for his part, had been granted a tournament of HBO's devising that unified the title and created the opportunity for its winner to turn the sport into his own virtual bank. It was a happy, if apparently unholy, alliance that had lasted for years to the benefit of everybody's retirement account.

If Fox thought it could enter the boxing arena with similar success, it should have considered the model a little more closely. HBO's Seth Abraham, who had steered the pioneer cable company into boxing way back in 1979 (partly to strengthen his own position in the company, which up to that time considered volleyball and man-vs.-shark its commitment to sports programming), did not exactly take the game by storm, even by his own reckoning. Among Abraham's early negotiations was a fight between WBC welterweight champ Wilfred Benitez and Harold Weston, a fight whose scant publicity in the New York papers could be explained only one way: "I had bought a fight that didn't exist!" he said, still amazed by his naïveté.

Abraham had better days, specifically a 1979 heavyweight match between champion Larry Holmes and a late-blooming, well-muscled Mike Weaver. Weaver had an 18–8 record and was not creating much anticipation over the Madison Square Garden production. King, who was promoting Holmes back then, wanted $1 million for the fight. ABC, which had an active schedule in those days, wanted to pay $750,000. Abraham called up King and offered $125,000. King said, "Who are you, anyway?"

King eventually bit; the fight was a rousing success, earning an important (for HBO, anyway) sanction by Red Smith in the *New York Times;* and King and Abraham entered a long and strange partnership. Any partnership with King is bound to be odd, but as much can be said of Abraham, a meticulous man who ought not to seem so happy in so messy a sport. Even King seemed to be surprised to find so prim a man in boxing. "He's got these big rimmed glasses! He wears suspenders and he enunciates!"

They were, at first glance, a beyond-odd couple. Yet they were equals in their fascination with the state-approved buccaneering that boxing had become. And they were near equals in their love of the public hurly-burly, the private deal making, the number crunching, the gamesmanship. And one was as theatrical as the other. King, as the boxing writer Phil Berger once wrote, treats everybody like a paid admission. But Abraham, with little bombast in his repertoire, was something of a spellbinder, too, delivering his anecdotes to the press in copy-ready paragraphs studded with particulars that were guaranteed to see the light of day in tomorrow's newspaper. Inasmuch as his stories invariably began with a restaurant address, the menu, and the tab, Abraham seemed more out of *Zagat* than *Ring*. The residue of that night's deal, however, would in Abraham's telling be juicier than King's New York steak.

Their negotiations were vigorous—such as the time in an early negotiation when King sprang at Abraham, stopping just short of contact—but even-handed and, normally, entertaining. Abraham loved to tell stories of their deal making. Once he tried to make a match between Larry Holmes and the South African Gerrie Coetzee, and had to meet King in a Cleveland rib joint—Winston's—where white faces had not been seen since "before the war, and I mean the Civil War," according to Abraham. His two aides, also white, hunkered down in their car outside the restaurant until King's limo arrived and everybody went in and ate smoked whitefish and ribs until 5 A.M.

That particular fight never happened, but lots more did, including a seven-fight, two-year $22 million series to unify the heavyweight division. Abraham claimed he got the idea while watching the 1985 World Series between Kansas City and St. Louis. King had been badgering him to buy a fight between WBC heavyweight champion Pinklon Thomas and Trevor Berbick. Abraham had been resisting. King visited Abraham at his home in New York and badgered him some more. Abraham, looking up from the World Series they had been watching, came up with their own World Series. "You really want to make history?" he asked King. Seven games, seven fights. A boxing world series. Afterward, according to Abraham, they had lobster.

It was King's genius to wrest promotional control of Tyson

away from his managers of record, Jimmy Jacobs and Bill Cayton, who were reluctant to enter their novice fighter in the tournament. But once King got Tyson enrolled, the fighter blasted through it, beating Berbick, James "Bonecrusher" Smith, Thomas, and then Tony Tucker all in 1987 to gather the three crowns unto himself, legitimizing the badly fragmented division in the process.

The year that Tyson won his third title, HBO discovered that neither Tyson nor boxing was a sideshow for the network; a 1987 survey showed that 40 percent of the men who subscribed to HBO for the first time did so because of boxing. The short kid with the lisp was, in particular, the engine behind this success. Tyson fights were guaranteeing HBO a 35 share of HBO subscribers, with some shows doing a 55 share. No wonder HBO re-upped Tyson following that little tournament, with a new eight-fight contract that paid him $26.5 million.

Their relationship might have continued into a new contract extension had Tyson and his cronies not taken increasing umbrage at the questioning of one of HBO's announcers. Larry Merchant, alone among the broadcast mob, had more than a tux and a haircut; he had a journalist's training in newspapers, and his postfight probings, one of the features of the HBO broadcasts, often anticipated the viewer's actual curiosity, whether the fighter was comfortable with that or not. With Tyson, he had become more and more interested in the fighter's apparently wavering loyalty to what was left of the management team that had taken him from a juvenile detention facility in upstate New York to untold fame and riches.

Starting with the Tyrell Biggs fight in 1987, Merchant began addressing the rumors that Tyson was jettisoning the D'Amato team, meaning Jacobs and Cayton and trainer Kevin Rooney. With Jacobs's death in 1988 the rumors intensified, and Merchant kept up the nagging line of questioning following Tyson's fight with Larry Holmes. What would Cus have said? Merchant wanted to know. No reply. Merchant didn't let go. Still no reply. King, hovering in the ring at Tyson's shoulder, told Merchant the man had no comment.

It was mild stuff by any measure, especially as Tyson actually was in the process of dumping all the old gang—they'd be gone after the Spinks fight six months later. Yet it stuck in Tyson's craw. He began communicating to HBO, through King, that all subsequent contracts would be sans Merchant.

Nobody took this too seriously. In 1990 King and Abraham were finalizing a contract extension for Tyson that would have made the fighter the first $100 million man in sports, and the Merchant issue seemed more or less dead. The proposed contract was for 10 fights, for $92 million, with space in the contract for one pay-per-view fight, which surely would have provided the magic number. The two shook hands on it in October, ending 16 months of back-and-forth, although King was still dutifully bringing up Merchant's role, though not in any deal-breaking kind of way. Abraham has always insisted the broadcaster's role was a "nondiscussion," and lawyers went ahead in the drafting of documents. "Fool that I was," Abraham said, "I thought it was over."

The deal was done—over dinner in New York's Chinatown—and at 11 o'clock that night King hustled from there to Atlantic City, where Tyson was training for his December fight with Alex Stewart. The next morning Abraham and King talked on the phone, congratulating each other, and then Tyson entered the conversation. "Thank God," Tyson told Abraham, "I won't have to deal with Larry." Abraham suddenly realized that King had not informed his client that a codicil barring Merchant from Tyson telecasts was not in the fine print. King, it turned out, had simply hoped that

Tyson would forget. As Tyson hadn't, the congratulatory phone call quickly degenerated into a 45-minute screaming match, with John Horne coming on the line to present their absolute right to an "Eddie Murphy clause." Murphy, Horne told Abraham, could insist upon a favored director; similarly, Tyson could very well insist on an announcer. King couldn't back down in front of his most important client. Abraham refused to sell Merchant out, and the deal unraveled right there. King and Abraham never got back together again, with King suddenly cast in dangerous waters as a free agent and HBO without its single best piece of sports programming. It was a development both parties nursed into a full-blown conspiracy theory, and things in boxing were never the same.

None of this history seemed to worry Fox in 1995. Too bad about HBO, too bad about Caesars. Fox had a knockout month coming up. A year before, the same evening, Fox got a 6.8 rating for an episode of *America's Most Wanted*. This, King's critics might have opined, was basically the same show, but Fox expected a ratings boost to 11.4.

Others besides Fox were somewhat more concerned. While Showtime tried to put a good face on it, its president, Matt Blank, saying, "Putting Mike Tyson in front of ninety million households will turn him into an even more valuable asset," it was considered just an exercise in damage control. For that matter, King's insistence that Tyson was happy to fight on free TV rang a little hollow. "Tyson backs this as an investment in his career," King said. "He feels he always wanted to do something special for the fans and the sport. It's not a sacrifice; it's an investment." It was, comparing his $25 million purse for McNeeley with his $10 million purse for Mathis, a $15 million investment, at least. "It will pay for itself tenfold," King assured.

HBO, while relieved that King hadn't tried to insist on a competing pay-per-view show, was going to be hurt bad;

each of the two Bowe-Holyfield bouts had produced about 900,000 buys, and this one was likely to be reduced by at least a third because of Fox's November 4 presence. Its new marketing slogan, "Buy one, get one free," might appeal to the hard-core fan, but the rest would likely get their fill with the free one.

To outsiders, this mindless collision of promotions did have its appeal. This one major intrigue seemed to hatch dozens of smaller ones, and each was as much fun as the last. Abraham, who admits he sometimes goes to sleep wondering what King might do next, was allowing for additional sabotage. Although the fights were supposed to go consecutively, Abraham got it into his head that King might introduce some delay into the Tyson-Mathis fight so it would run over into the start of the Bowe-Holyfield bout. He even ordered that such contingencies be entered into the TVKO production book. "Like Frank Bruno getting into the ring and shouting, 'You're next, Mike,' and a melee starts between Tyson and Bruno." Abraham apologized for the extremity of his suspicion, but explained, "The way I do business, unfortunately, is to try and get into Don King's head." And that is a very busy place.

In any event, things do happen. Keep in mind, somebody once parachuted into Caesars' outdoor ring, interrupting Bowe-Holyfield II. That was not something most programming executives might have put in their production books.

Let's just say the atmosphere the week of the Double Hitter was more than a little redolent of paranoia. "Awash" is another word. There was also a sense, however small, of injustice being done. This had more to do with an inevitable media slant than reality; journalism is not horribly objective at these events, especially one where convicted felons working in tandem are the principals. Sports columnists, who make up a disproportionate amount of the fight coverage these days, are of course free to write more opinion than news, and many of the more influential New York columnists, despite more or less growing up with Tyson, had come to be in any camp but his. This was especially true the week of these two fights, when the alternative bout featured boxing's two most likable lugs.

To be sure, Bowe-Holyfield III was the better fight. It wasn't close. The first two fights had been wars, exemplifying everything that could be right about boxing. For that matter, the two boxers exemplified everything good about the sport, both of them having risen from hardscrabble circumstances to become, at different points, champions.

Bowe in particular was a favorite of the fight crowd. He had survived Brooklyn's Brownsville neighborhood in a way that Tyson hadn't, seemingly unmarked by the violence that so affected his boxing brother. He was so full of good cheer that you would never have guessed he'd shared the same dismal type of childhood as Tyson.

Bowe's brother died of AIDS, and his sister was stabbed to death while resisting a crack addict's attempt to steal her welfare check. Another brother was in and out of jail, yet another was a crack addict. When people interested in the young amateur went to visit him in his housing project, they had to step around people guarding stairway landings with automatic weaponry. Yet Bowe was positively incapable of putting anything but a good face on it. "Oh, we had a lot of fun," he once said of his apparently horrific childhood. Much richer and much older, he said, "If I could just go back to being between ten and sixteen, I'd never grow up."

He would endure criticism later on, and he would pull enough chuckleheaded stunts so that he wasn't always easy to cheer for, but few could root against a guy who, in the same neighborhood that Tyson was terrorizing, would walk his mother one and a half miles to her job at a plastic-housewares factory every night, pouring out his dreams to her, telling her how he'd be a champion someday and buy her a house. Dorothy Bowe, who was given to wearing shirts with BIGDOT on the back, always said, "Just don't go to jail."

That never seemed likely. There was a decency in him that seemed to preclude that. And as he moved through his Brownsville youth, he seemed strangely safeguarded from the violence around him. Maybe he was just oblivious to it. Did he remember Tyson, the bully at Public School 396? "About all I remember," he said, "is that he was big for his age and he always had a bag of cookies with him. Good old Mike."

Of course, Bowe was flaky to a fault, which would eventually prove terminally frustrating to his veteran trainer, Eddie Futch. But it was endearing, too. Once, after he floored Bert Cooper—"Good old Bert"—in an important fight for contention, he spotted Bill Cosby at ringside and, while the referee was attempting to raise his hand in victory, began jiggling his head like a dashboard dog, the good old Cosby gesture. He was, at 6'5" and 230 pounds, with the limber moves of a middleweight and the temperament of a standup comic, the Clown Bomber.

His ever-contentious manager, Rock Newman, also exhausted a lot of goodwill in his exaggerated attempts to keep Bowe independent of King and other promoters. This was fine as long as Bowe kept winning, but it would be disastrous if he lost. Newman, whose side job was consulting for embattled Washington mayor Marion Barry, even after Barry's cocaine arrest, obviously liked going against the grain. He was less politic in his dealings with boxing authorities, and you got the feeling that his high-minded efforts to get Bowe his title and millions were really just another way of acting out. You could respect Newman's determination on the one hand, but then have to turn away from whatever ugliness—a ringside brawl, say—he'd instigate on the other.

Three Novembers earlier young Bowe had outmuscled Holyfield, winning the undisputed championship on points on the strength of an unforgettable 10th round, three minutes of back-and-forth savagery that were considered the finest in heavyweight history. In the rematch the next November, with Bowe having learned of life's finer things and ballooning to 280 pounds at one point before the meeting, the indomitable Holyfield decisioned Bowe to win back the International Boxing Federation and World Boxing Association titles. That fight was distinguished by "Fan Man," the paraglider who sailed into the ring during the seventh round, causing a 20-minute delay and sending Bowe's pregnant wife, Judy, out of the arena in a faint.

Nearly a million people saw each of those two fights, honest wars both, but neither fighter could translate that popularity into long-lasting success. Bowe, whom Newman had prompted to dump his WBC belt in a garbage can following his 1992 victory over Holyfield (he was refusing to make a mandatory defense against Lennox Lewis), was stranded in defeat without a political alliance. All the people Bowe and Newman had estranged on the way up were now jubilant in his downfall. Whereas Bowe might have made great hay in Tyson's absence, he was instead fighting Mathis, Larry Donald, Herbie Hyde, and Jorge Luis Gonzalez. His enemies were giddy at the relative humiliation. Bowe, the lone heavyweight with talent and personality—and just one loss—was unranked by the three major governing bodies.

"Herein lies an immigrant," explained King at the time, "who is capable of treasonous activity. So he was deported." King admitted the obvious, though, that it was just a matter of payback. "Any sane man knows he's one of the best. But he's got this manager, here's a guy who burnt every bridge and then set dynamite under them."

Holyfield hadn't been faring any better. He lost his titles

shortly after Bowe II, when the tortured Michael Moorer decisioned him. Moorer, a reluctant warrior, had been prodded by one of D'Amato's protégés, Teddy Atlas, in the upset. After the defeat, doctors revealed that Holyfield had a congenital heart defect; his retirement would take effect immediately.

That the two fighters survived these travails to make a third fight was miracle enough. In Holyfield's case, "miracle" was the actual word. At first he insisted that the faith healer Benny Hinn, in a laying on of hands, had cured him of his heart problems. Other times, when he was dealing with an incredulous Nevada State Athletic Commission, for example, he'd say it was simply a misdiagnosis. A battery of tests at the Mayo Clinic finally did convince Nevada officials that he was sound.

Bowe, for his part, had the advantage of being young and available. His recent demolition of Gonzalez had been encouraging. He remained for HBO a potent and sometimes reliable missile in their anti-Tyson arsenal.

Even though the two would not fight for one of the major titles (Bowe held the dimly recognized World Boxing Organization title), a rarity in a title-happy age, their bout was widely hailed as the real deal, while the MGM fight a 15-minute walk away was a novelty act, an exhibition. The visiting media left no doubt where they stood on this issue: "This battle's for the fans," screamed a New York *Daily News* advance (the paper was offering the winner its own championship belt).

The bias was evident as well in the fine print, where boxing notes observed with a nearly obscene glee that Bowe-Holyfield III was beating the pants off King's promotion. Advance ticket sales at Las Vegas fights are hardly a good indicator of fan interest, inasmuch as everything that happens in the town is governed more by impulse than rational thought. Still, as casinos must buy blocks of tickets for their own gamblers, there was something worth noting in the numbers: Three days before the fight there were reports that the MGM had sold no more than 1,500 of its 16,000 seats, while Caesars was hoping to sell 9,000 tickets in its 15,000-seat outdoor arena. (The MGM insisted it had commitments for 7,000 to 10,000 tickets.) Casino owner Steve Wynn, according to one source, had spent $1 million on Bowe-Holyfield tickets for his Mirage, Golden Nugget, and Treasure Island customers—and none on Tyson-Mathis tickets.

That fight, which might have been perceived as a dud on its own, was losing what little luster it might have had with every comparison to Bowe-Holyfield. It began to seem more and more presumptuous: How dare King promote this exhibition against Bowe-Holyfield, a fight of enough importance that the lack of a title exchange was considered irrelevant? Caesars had the real goods; the MGM was merely serving as Tyson's parole officer.

It's not likely King could have reversed this spin, but he was largely distracted in any event. While Team Tyson was pumping ticket sales in Las Vegas, King was undergoing cross-examination in a Manhattan courtroom, trying to survive a federal wire-fraud trial in which he was accused of taking $350,000 in insurance money from Lloyd's of London. It was an old case, going back to a 1991 contract with Julio Cesar Chavez, the longtime champion who had bolstered many of King's cards in Tyson's absence. King was accused of forging a clause in the contract that made Chavez's training expenses for a canceled fight nonrefundable. But the government, despite testimony from King's former accountant, Joseph Maffia, could not prove the case; eventually it was declared a mistrial, after the jury became "irretrievably deadlocked."

That amounted only to a reprieve for King, as the prosecution intended to retry him on the charge. His defense costs would double, but, worse than that, he was losing promotional time on the Tyson-Mathis fight. As refreshing as his absence was to longtime press-conference sufferers, there was no denying his ability to garner news space, whether in print or, more likely, on the local newscast.

Team Tyson, to nobody's surprise, had zero skills in this area. Their idea of enterprise was to open a Tyson workout at the Golden Gloves ring to the press five days before the fight. It was too little, too late—and, even at that, it wasn't very reassuring. Sparring just three rounds with the 6′7″ Clevelander Tyrone Evans before holding up his right fist and signaling the workout's end, Tyson was short of overwhelming. At moments, burying a left hook into Evans's ribs, he made four years disappear. But mostly he looked confused, rusty, and surprisingly overweight. His fists were quick but his combinations were wide, and those old fundamentals of defense, the crouch and the side-to-side bob, were long gone.

Whether it was a last-gasp attempt to galvanize ticket sales or just time to answer a question or two, Tyson lingered in the ring afterward to speak to a few reporters. Or rather, as a Tyson aide proclaimed, "Mr. Tyson has graciously consented" to an interview session.

That formality aside, the talk was fairly casual, the old give-and-take that he used to enjoy. What was with his hand? they wondered. He admitted he had hurt it, but no problem: "I'm okay," he said. "It felt a little strange today. It's just a precaution."

That was not promising, but the development was overlooked as Tyson relaxed and spoke of life after prison, articulating a disorientation that, against higher odds than Mathis was facing, humanized King's monster. With Holloway and Horne looking imperial at his shoulders, Tyson admitted, "I've just been out a few months. I'm confused."

With his hands safely on his knees and his sullenness dissipated in the ring's heat, he seemed a sympathetic figure, without bravado or much purpose. "I wish I felt as good as all my guys think I do," he said. "I'm still pretty much confused over what I want to do in boxing in general. I'm back in civilized life and it's difficult." He likened himself to a college grad— "cum laude and now has to go out in the real world." He was 29, had just bought two $3 million homes, was planning to marry Monica Turner, a medical student who was pregnant with his child, and had a schedule, more or less chiseled into stone, that would return his three heavyweight titles in a matter of months. And there he sat. Confused.

There would, the next day, be plenty of confusion to go around. Everybody would have their share. They might have been tipped off at the workout, which had been scheduled for eight rounds before Tyson called it quits. Certainly, Vic Ziegel had a clue six hours after that. Ziegel, the New York *Daily News* sports editor and columnist, was checking into the MGM Grand that night when he ran into Tyson's trainer Jay Bright at the elevator. How was Tyson doing? he wondered. Bright mentioned the thumb. "It was giving Mike real pain," he said. Ziegel wondered if it was serious. "It's in the doctor's hands," he said.

That's never good, but plans were still proceeding for the fight they called "Tyson II: The Road to the Championship," a fight that didn't even require mention of an opponent. At Tuesday's press conference, which would be the last glimpse of Tyson until Saturday's fight, Carl King hosted the festivities, indulging himself in a 90-minute preamble that might have made his stepfather proud. At one point he informed the dais that the MGM Grand was also hosting the American Ambulance Association and that "there'll be enough stretchers for all of you."

As usual, Tyson was silently smeared by the bad taste of his coworkers. It continued to be his unhappy fate to reflect everyone else's ugliness, whether he had any to contribute or not. In fact, Tyson could hardly contribute anything. "I feel great," he said when it was his turn to speak. "I'm happy. Everybody knows I'm gonna do my thing. Not much I have to say, except I want to give praise to God every time I have a chance to. I'm looking forward to this fight and I'm gonna burn."

At the traditionally unproductive Q&A, Tyson said his right hand was "sore but okay." Later he snapped back at a reporter when he was asked how it felt to fight with King absent. "Don's around," he said. "He's just dealing with a slight adversity at the moment. It's not as if he's no longer on this earth. He's around . . . very close." The panel, all of them dependent on King's ability to produce their income, applauded. Tyson joined them, not quite clapping, but tapping his left hand on the table.

At 4:10 P.M. that day, two physicians who identified themselves as Tyson's doctors notified officials at the MGM Grand that Tyson's right thumb had been fractured and that the fight was off.

Chapter Four

"Put some bass in it, baby!"

For those whose taste runs to chaos, which includes everybody in the boxing industry plus a lot of the sport's fans, this latest development was a godsend. It was proof that no matter how much money was thrown on boxing, no matter what institutions became involved, it could never be legitimized or made trustworthy.

It was reassuring in a way, inasmuch as its appeal remains largely antisocietal. Boxing should be unpredictable, somewhere beyond the reach of all things appropriate, standard, and wholesome. After all, those who appreciate and encourage the lawful assault and battery that is boxing cannot similarly expect the conforming effects of sponsors, league offices, and all the other smoothing influences of American culture. Tyson's injury, if indeed he had one, was proof again that no amount of economic pressure—society's last resort in the rehabilitation of troublesome enterprises—could reform it. If anything, as the stakes grow higher boxing becomes even more unstable, more and more prone to surprise, less and less accountable to normal business principles.

It was natural to look for a commercial convenience in Tyson's broken thumb. Boxing, so riddled with competing agendas and so suffused with the consequent paranoia, does not suffer coincidence lightly. Wasn't it strange that the star of a failing production, with just the flash of an X-ray, was able to cause the fight's postponement and rescue his management and sponsors from certain critical and financial defeat? You had to overlook the fact that Tyson's and King's paydays were guaranteed to find grounds for suspicion in the low ticket sales; a flop meant nothing to them. Nobody suggested that the MGM ordered the injury to save itself the embarrassment of empty seats; but wasn't it interesting that Tyson pulled up lame days before his fight, a bout that was inviting scorn simply in contrast to Bowe-Holyfield III?

For that matter, where was this X-ray? The *New York Post* had, as always, a good feel for what you might call the supernatural. It was a knee-jerk headline, but it did speak for a lot of doubters out there: "Prove it, Mike," the *Post* demanded on its back page two days later. The *Post* reported that Tyson had failed to come clean and show the paper the X-rays, "fueling speculation that the fight was called off because of a lack of interest."

In fact, there wasn't much doubt that Tyson had suffered an injury. One of his two physicians, Dr. Gary Marrone, told reporters at a hastily arranged press conference on Tuesday night that Tyson had reinjured a thumb that had been broken three weeks earlier at a workout in Orwell, Ohio—an injury that, while unreported, had been the talk of boxing's grapevine for a while.

Marrone said, "Mike came to our office approximately two weeks ago. The injury is basically a break in the thumb between the main joint of the thumb and the tip of the thumb. Our feeling at that time was that we weren't sure whether three weeks would be sufficient for Mike to fight. But Mike wanted, under any circumstances, to be able to fight and not have to cancel this. So we gave it three weeks."

Marrone said Tyson's camp had called him earlier in the

day to say he had hurt the same thumb in sparring the day before. "In the X-rays taken," Marrone said, "the fracture that had already started to heal had basically rebroken. At this point, there was no way we could medically release Mike to fight."

Tyson, who also appeared at the press conference, was not blithe, but neither was he any more animated than usual. He admitted, "It was a pretty serious setback as far as the continuation of my comeback." He said he had been looking forward to going up against the Bowe-Holyfield fight and hoped he could "sneak it through. I wasn't thinking professionally. It's not my job to think as a doctor. I'm paid to fight. But the pain became too intense to do that."

He added, in a way that seemed to confuse Nietzschean philosophy with his standard of living, "It's not going to kill me, and it's not like I'm hurting for money or anything."

The Nevada State Athletic Commission, which counted itself among the hurting because of $250,000 in lost tax revenues, was not happy, yet it was satisfied that Tyson had truly been injured. By Thursday those mysterious X-rays had been made public, and a commission doctor, Flip Homansky, said Tyson must have been in "excruciating pain." In general, the idea that the injury was bona fide was not that hard to swallow; after all, Tyson had postponed fights before. Perhaps this was one more thing Fox should have looked into: The indestructible Tyson was actually an extremely fragile figure when it came to fight night. Between 1988 and 1991 Tyson had forced four postponements. An auto accident in 1988 put off his September fight with Frank Bruno until February of 1989. Pneumonia destroyed a November 1989 fight with Bruno; a cut eye moved a September 1990 meeting with Alex Stewart to December; and a rib injury postponed a November 1991 fight with Holyfield, a fight that subsequently got lost when Tyson entered prison.

A Savage Business

Fighters do get hurt. But they often fight that way, too. Floyd Patterson won the heavyweight title against Archie Moore with a broken hand, and Larry Holmes won his against Ken Norton with a torn biceps, a muscle that rolled up his arm like a window shade. For that matter, said Steve Lott, an associate of Cayton's and a friend of Tyson's before King gained sway, Tyson the fight historian knew full well that Beau Jack once won a title fight on a broken leg.

As far as that goes, Riddick Bowe was saying the day after the Tyson fight was postponed that his own hand had been injured in preparation for Holyfield III. Which one? somebody asked. "My good hand," Bowe said, ever coy. And even Holyfield was chiming in with war stories. "I fought Michael Moorer with a sore shoulder," he said. "Maybe I'd still be champ . . ."

So rumors swirled. John Horne tried to dampen them, saying, "Mike Tyson is the one missing the payday. We had ten to fifteen million in foreign sales. Ticket sales had no relevance on what we were being paid. The reason we're not fighting is because Mike's thumb is broken." Horne further protested that, if their operation was as diabolical as everyone thought, they'd have played it out until Friday and then called it off. Those wonderful intentions aside, rumors swirled all the same: Tyson wasn't in shape; he was upset with the deal King had gotten him with Fox; Tyson's kid handlers were instituting a power play to distance King. More realistically, would any of this have happened if King were in town, with attention undivided by his insurance-fraud trial?

Any and all of these rumors were plausible, made more so by the Tyson camp's curious decision to stage that public workout—sparring!—five days before a fight. "It was a setup," said veteran trainer Lou Duva.

Up the street at Caesars, where the Bowe-Holyfield fight

was now uncontested, dignity reigned, sort of. Rock Newman, who had told *USA Today* in September that he had "an
eerie feeling that their fight won't come off," showed up at
his fighter's Wednesday press conference wearing a swami's
turban. "We know all, we see all," he said. Seth Abraham,
who had suffered Tyson postponements himself at HBO, was
sympathetic. "Unfortunately," he said, "injuries are a part of
boxing, and I'm sure Don already has prepared his Lloyd's of
London claims."

In other words, it was a great day in the Roman Empire. A
very stupid thing had not happened after all, admittedly no
thanks to the men in suits. Abraham confessed to a damaging
willfulness when he likened the rival promotions to *Dumb
and Dumber*. "I'm in there somewhere," he said. Still, bullets
had been dodged. Caesars was now hoping for a sellout.
TVKO, which was projecting pay-per-view sales of 500,000,
was now hoping for 750,000, with some officials hoping for
much better. Abraham thought it would be an "easy hit" to
convert some of the 100 million Fox households after so
much publicity. "This is like a double-play combination," he
said, eager to exploit the controversy. TVKO's chief, Mark
Taffet, thought Bowe-Holyfield III might eclipse the first
fight's numbers of 950,000 homes, and perhaps challenge
Holyfield-Foreman's record 1.4 million buys, even though
some pay-per-view distributors had lightened up on their
marketing because of the Fox show. For certain, the fight was
now going to get the attention it deserved.

The only person under Caesars' tent who seemed the least
bit ambivalent about the postponement was Bowe, good old
Bowe, who said he had been looking forward to the competition. "If his arena is half full," he said, "and our place sells
out, that just proves that the public feels Riddick Bowe and
Evander Holyfield are going to put on another great show. I
wanted them to see who was the better fighter." This, presum-

ably, was before he consulted with his bean counter, who might have informed him that he was entitled to a larger percentage of the pay-per-view proceeds than Holyfield; his guaranteed $8 million could swell by two million more in pay-per-view dollars, thanks to the sudden lack of competition.

The media, however, did not have mixed feelings about this development. Their attitude had been somewhat superior through the whole affair; they wanted to pay attention to the better of the two fights, yet they knew that their readers and viewers, who were sadly not as knowledgeable as themselves, might prefer nuggets about the lesser fight instead. This produced an irritability that was evident in their initial coverage, and then, once Tyson-Mathis went away, a similarly transparent jubilation.

"No hype, no fuss, just a real fight" was a headline in the *Newark Star-Ledger*. "The only game in town" read the *New York Post*. And ESPN, which had planned to devote most of its prefight coverage to Bowe-Holyfield in the first place, was, like a lot of folks in Las Vegas, simply relieved that the Double-Hitter had been Halved. "The Tyson fight is an exhibition," ESPN's Charley Steiner said. "A pitbull vs. a poodle." In Bowe-Holyfield III, everybody's fur was going to fly.

As the rightful anticipation for that fight mounted, the Tyson card down Las Vegas Boulevard was being dismantled at frightful expense. The promotional costs had been staggering for MGM, but at least the postponement spared the hotel the possible embarrassment of empty seats and tables. Fox could not afford to be so sanguine. This was more than a matter of canceling travel arrangements for series stars Luke Perry, Heather Locklear, and Christina Applegate, who had hoped to preen at ringside and cross-promote through their very presence. It was more than a scheduling snafu, forcing Fox to ram reruns of *The X-Files* into the fight slot, opposite

HBO's combative decision to premiere the blockbuster *Forrest Gump* on its own channel. It was more than a production inconvenience, more than the cancellation of its helicopter (TVKO had hired one in reply, offering rival producers the chance to laugh about warring gunships).

It was millions of dollars down the drain—not including Tyson's $10 million—is what it was; that and a huge programming opportunity during sweeps, all lost, forever. "It cost us millions in promotional collateral, in business plans," said a Fox executive. "We were not pleased."

A company that puts out a 31-page press release celebrating its coverage of an event might safely be considered humiliated when said event is canceled. That was certainly the tenor of the company's announcements henceforth. There was a lot of ego involved for Fox, which had fancied itself an assured marauder, set to teach its rivals how boxing is really covered. This irritated Ross Greenburg, HBO's executive producer, who told one reporter that "David Hill has given me a little bit of a . . . I don't know how to describe it. David Hill is someone I admire, but I just want him to know who has been covering boxing for over twenty years."

And now Fox had nothing but some reruns and a chopper for its Halloween night festivities. "It was trick-or-treat, and we got tricked," said Hill, an Australian who was becoming a fast study in American holidays and its less predictable sports. "All the marketing we've done, all the promos, you can't recall that. We were totally burned."

Buster Mathis, Jr., was left twisting in the wind, too, although for a boxer this is more or less a permanent condition. Told that Tyson's hand was sore, he initially said he thought Tyson was faking it. Yet when the fight actually came apart, he seemed pretty much accepting, even sympathetic ("My prayers are with Tyson"), and immediately began assessing his immediate future. Though still under contract to fight

A Savage Business

Tyson—sometime, somewhere—Mathis more or less kissed his $700,000 check good-bye. The contract, as his promoter Cedric Kushner pointed out, was vague and one-sided. King could hold Mathis to fight Tyson, but Kushner couldn't hold Tyson to fight Mathis. Mathis, in any event, seemed wiser in the ways of boxing than David Hill: "Hopefully," Mathis said, "you will see me again." He didn't seem to be asking anybody to guarantee it, though. "Maybe I can get something out of this, like a title shot. I have to look on the bright side."

It was hard to know how Tyson was looking at it; his comments were cryptic at best. A lot of other people, however, looked at the fight's disappearance and Tyson's apparent lack of disappointment and decided he was without his old resolve. "I don't think he wants to fight," said trainer Emanuel Steward, "not when he says, 'I've got enough money.'"

Tyson was shooed out of town with a few parting shots like that one, a columnist here and there wondering about his "fire in the belly." But attention soon turned to the fight at hand. Credential requests for the Caesars fight jumped another 150 up to 1,200, 150 timid souls who had doubted their ability to cover crosstown fights. Problems of transportation now solved, reporters had grown intrepid. Plus, it was natural that excitement would grow; Bowe-Holyfield III was as sure a thing as there was in the unpredictable world of boxing—a cashed ticket, even in Las Vegas.

Going in, it was a pleasant affair, notwithstanding their history of 24 brutal rounds. Bowe and Holyfield were not without bravado, but their instincts for low blows outside the ring were poor. They seemed physically incapable of badmouthing each other. Maybe 72 minutes of each man's trying and failing to impose his will on the other had produced respect. Or maybe it was just their temperaments. The worst thing Bowe could say about Holyfield, whose appearance does lend itself to easy caricature, is that "he still looks like a

83

gargoyle." But, he added, "it was nothing personal, just an opinion."

Holyfield had been bothered before their second fight when Bowe made that comparison—"bad words," he said, as if those were the worst he'd ever heard—but remained just as respectful as ever, refusing to liken Bowe's wide-eyed and jiggling head to, say, a dashboard doll. He even applauded his opponent for his recent fatherhood. "He makes sure he's going to be there for his kids," said Holyfield, who himself had announced his engagement, a frequent prefight strategy of his. "I do admire him for that."

Yes, it was possible to ballyhoo a fight without ugliness, Holyfield's mug aside. "I think I'm starting to like you," Bowe told Holyfield. And it was true, these two were becoming coupled in a comical matrimony, their relationship almost domestic after so much time together. In a face-to-face appearance on ESPN to analyze their previous meetings, Holyfield petulantly accused Bowe of low blows and hitting after the bell. While Holyfield continued to scold Bowe, the big man apologized and covered his smirk with his huge hand. *Those guys.*

But, considering what had gone before and what was almost certainly ahead, it was a horrible intimacy. Each fighter had been made by the other. Until their first meeting, Holyfield had been considered a bulked-up cruiserweight whose championship was accidental, whose box-office power was similarly serendipitous; he happened to fit into the plans of people like George Foreman. Bowe, for his part, was a goofball of questionable courage and achievement. But the first two fights, up and down across 24 hard rounds, ennobled both, certifying Bowe's guts and Holyfield's heavyweight skills. They, and everyone else, knew there would be no coasting through a third fight.

Holyfield promised to knock Bowe out, which was so uncharacteristic of him that even Bowe was surprised. "He said that?" he asked. Bowe, the 3-1 favorite, decided Holyfield was just asking for it. "He wants to be stretched," he said. "Most of 'em don't give up until they get a bona fide butt whipping." The camaraderie of these two warriors, who had visited each other's houses and played pool together, would not last beyond their ring introductions.

The fight went off without a hitch, no airborne fight fans interrupting the action, and it did indeed produce a memorable meeting. A Tyson-Mathis fight would not have survived any critical comparison, that was for sure. Mathis would not likely have presented Tyson with either Bowe's ability or Holyfield's heart; in fact, this fight could only remind Tyson's fans that no one in his past ever had.

Bowe, his desire or desperation at least suggested by his weight (240 pounds, six less than in the last meeting), decided to do this the hard way, abandoning his plans for a boxing fest and turning slugger instead. This was okay with Holyfield, who nearly always allows himself to get drawn into wars, usually against the better judgment of his corner. For seven rounds they muscled each other around the ring and an astonishing truth became evident: Bowe would beat Holyfield at his own game.

"In my mind," Holyfield said, "things were going pretty bad for me." He was leading on the scorecards through those rounds, but fight people sensed something surprising. Emanuel Steward, the gun-for-hire who had trained Holyfield to his upset of Bowe but who dropped out after Holyfield offered him just a small increase for the third fight, said, "Evander was bone-tired from the second round." Steward thought he knew why. "You know, they do all these exercises, StairMasters, have these contests climbing ladders, but it's not the same as muscling a guy around, bone on bone, that you get in sparring. He doesn't like to box. He was conditioned for exercises, not boxing."

Holyfield was in such bad shape, flat-footed and unable to

raise his arms, that he actually thought about quitting in the fifth round when Bowe lifted him off the canvas with—what else—a low blow. "An easy way out of there," he thought. Of course he didn't quit, never does and never would, and somehow found the strength in the next round to flatten Bowe with a lunging left hook. Bowe, who had been eyeing Holyfield for signs of fatigue, could hardly have been more surprised to find himself on the seat of his pants. "I thought, that ain't right." He was in obvious trouble. He arose at the count of seven, staggered back against the ropes for support, and prepared for his certain extinction. But Holyfield, in an impotent flurry that would affect matchmaking and betting in fights to come, was unable to finish him off. Bowe's condition was so dire, ringsiders thought, that the slightest wafting punch might end the fight. "He taps him on the shoulder," Steward estimated, "he knocks him out." Holyfield could not even tap him on the shoulder.

Instead, after using the seventh round to collect himself, Bowe charged back in the eighth and walloped Holyfield with a right hand to down him. Holyfield got up at the count of nine, and subsided for good seconds later after two chopping rights to the head. The knockdown had every appearance of finality; referee Joe Cortez didn't even pretend to count. Their brutal marriage of convenience was at long last over.

If the fight seemed to retire Holyfield, the game's grandest warrior, it still was a celebration of sorts. The fight was a rare triumph for boxing, the actual delivery of goods, and it encouraged fans to think that if the game's ritual and corrupting artifice were removed, there would occasionally be something to cheer for. For Bowe-Holyfield, no synthetic titles were at stake, no phony rankings. Their fight was not a political premise, as Tyson's would have been—a sly maneuvering into some jackpot down the road. It was just an honest display of character, character stripped so bare in the overhead lights that people could see the bones of bravery. They might, for their $39.95, marvel at a certain kind of manhood, prehistoric perhaps but awesome all the same. A lot of people think this kind of opportunity is a bargain at any price.

This lesson was lost on Team Tyson, an outfit that remained mired in its fighter's own arrested mythology and committed to the most cynical forms of capitalism. It was quickly determined that Tyson would keep his payday with Mathis and Fox—at reduced rates for everybody but Tyson —but the date would be December 16, who knew where. The determination to stick to a championship timetable revealed their total lack of interest in the Mathis fight. On such notice, it was sure to be a jury-rigged affair, its purpose having less to do with competition or entertainment than the disposal of obligations. The fight had to be gotten out of the way. As King hustled to place the bout, it took on all the significance of a nagging afterthought.

The matter of location for a pay-per-view–level event is not ordinarily left to the last minute, as it was here. Huge site fees cover a significant portion of the costs, which is why casinos are the last remaining players in this field. Only casinos can safely advance $20 million jackpots to promoters; only they have the advantage of high rollers who are expected to subsidize ticket sales—high as they are, they alone don't make it worthwhile—with gaming losses. For King to still be trying to find somebody to accept this risk at this late date was almost foolhardy.

Las Vegas, because of the timing, was not a proper site. Nor was anywhere else where gambling was conducted on a significant scale. The New Jersey Casino Control Commission was adamant about upholding its 1994 ban of King, instituted when he was originally indicted for wire fraud. Donald Trump wanted to put the fight on in Atlantic City, where his Trump properties have often sponsored events in the Boardwalk's convention center. Despite King's trial's ending in a hung jury in November, New Jersey wasn't swayed by the reprieve. Even though King had yet to be proved guilty the prosecution promised to retry him, and the state still refused his business.

King was largely unmoved by the rejection by New Jersey. "Atlantic City didn't hurt nobody but itself. No one else is hurt. The tragedy is for Atlantic City, not for Mike Tyson and Don King." King once more was forced to consult the deities. He turned to his staff and "told them to cast the net. As God would have it, Philadelphia was sitting there, pristine and proud."

A fight twice-blessed by divine intervention ought to have been held in a cathedral. Indeed, the miracles just kept coming. Philadelphia's 18,000-seat CoreStates Spectrum, booked for a performance by the Red Hot Chili Peppers, was suddenly available when the group's drummer broke his arm and the band's tour was called off. So King was now able to extract favorable terms in Philadelphia, where seats might be priced more aggressively than pews. Maybe too aggressively, though: King was using the scale he had set up for Atlantic City, and the old prices didn't seem to fit with the new location. At $500 for ringside, Mayor Ed Rendell said, the promotion didn't have a prayer.

Moreover, there was no chance that Philadelphia was going to give King the tax abatements he reportedly sought. City officials later said that King had not asked for any tax breaks, and questioned whether he had really asked for 1,000 free hotel nights for his fighters and staff. King's staff admitted they did seek some free rooms and meals at the downtown Marriott and Bellvue, but no more than any convention might expect for providing them with so much additional business.

For King, who plays the victim with over-the-top gusto,

these charges were manna from heaven, allowing him to stage his familiar set pieces of aggravated injury. For King, the entire purpose of the event may have been the opportunity to dress in an Uncle Sam costume for a TV ad (a historical reenactment that was refused by two of the three local stations), and describe the constitutional guarantees that had once again been abridged in his case. It was wonderful. "Any lesser man would have been destroyed," he exulted to Mike Bruton of the *Philadelphia Inquirer.* "He wouldn't have been able to survive this. I just keep going and keep winning, not just surviving. So they can't stand a wild-haired nigger looking them in the eye, saying, 'I'm a man and you're a man.'"

He was wallowing in injustice, and he loved it. The promotion, renamed "Presumption of Innocence," clearly had more to do with his trial than his fighter's. In reality, King was performing a kind of miracle, restaging a broken fight in just six weeks, during the holidays, in noncasino territory that was turning more and more hostile as officials kept learning just what they'd invited into town. Few promoters have King's determination or work ethic when it comes to solving problems like the original postponement. Perhaps he was entitled to pout a little in the press.

But his sulk, however deserved, wasn't diverting attention from the sheer unworthiness of the fight. Philadelphia wasn't buying it; three days before the fight, less than a third of the arena had been sold, making it unlikely that King would lift the local blackout. Mayor Rendell kept needling King about ticket prices, saying the scale was way too rich for his citizens, who weren't very likely to get "comped" as they would in the more typical casino environment. "I'd like to make more of those twenty-five-dollar tickets available so the average working guy can come and bring his family," Rendell said. King hinted he would make discount tickets available, then quickly backed off. "It would be difficult to put someone who paid the full price next to someone who got in later at the lower price," he said, reasonably.

However, he had already cut one deal, as Fox had forced him to renegotiate the TV contract. King told everybody that Fox, which no longer had the imperative of a sweeps-month broadcast, had been allowed to buy the fight for just $4.5 million. A Fox executive laughed at that figure. "It was less than four and a half million," he said. "We let him get away with saying that." Mathis, meanwhile, did his part, agreeing to a new contract of $600,000.

Although Fox still expected a ratings bonanza, it knew it was essentially pointless without the benefit of sweeps and the ad rate increase down the road. You could tell the network had cooled to the whole enterprise; of their series stars, only Thomas Haden Church, of the marginal show *Ned & Stacey*, was being sent forth.

At that, the only personality of less wattage than Church at the fight would be Mathis, a fighter who at this stage of his life invited more pity than fear. Like McNeeley, Mathis was the son of a heavyweight contender, in this case inheriting only his father's genetic propensity to flab. Unlike McNeeley, who maintained a fighter's bravado, Mathis refused to act threatening. It was beyond him, physically and mentally. Certainly vocally. Whenever he opened his mouth to speak, an unfortunate high-pitched squeak came out, causing passersby to stop in their tracks. At a press conference, when it was Mathis's turn to talk, members of Tyson's entourage jumped all over him—"Put some bass in it, baby!"—even though their own man, truth to tell, sounded more like Barry Gibb than Barry White.

Mathis didn't have that much to say, anyway. Although he was 20–0, with bona fide boxing skills, he had no reign of terror to advertise. In a way, he was as soft-spoken in the ring (six knockouts?) as outside it. He was one boxer whose fists did not do the talking. Outside, he was, by the colorful standards of his sport, practically mute.

The way Mathis told it, he was not just the dullest man in boxing, but the dullest in Grand Rapids, Michigan. He didn't party, drink, or do drugs. He lived at home with his mother. "I'm a big-time mama's boy," he told his public.

In other words, he not only didn't belong in the ring with Tyson, he didn't belong in boxing. His father, who had fought well in losing efforts with Ali and Joe Frazier, must have sensed as much a long time before, pushing him to become a doctor, anything but a fighter. Yet once the young Mathis, a 300-pound source of ridicule as a teenager, learned of his father's brief celebrity, he became determined to plunge into the sport and seize some dignity for himself.

He was a typical kid, thinking he had none. But his situation really was worse than most. He was one of two blacks in an all-white high school (the other was his sister), grossly overweight—"big and fat," by his own reckoning—and constantly teased. In his mind, nothing was available to him but boxing.

He didn't learn of his father's career, he says, until he was 12 and one of the networks broadcast the Ali biopic *The Greatest*. In one of the film's fights, he was startled to see a portrayal of his own portly father, fighting the greatest. "Which one are you?" he asked his father. "The one on the floor" was the answer.

Nevertheless, the young Mathis had increased importance in the school halls the next day, even though the Mathis name had one more connotation: loser. "I saw your father get knocked down by Ali," his classmates reported. Still, there was a grudging respect; you could get knocked down by worse. "I tried to use that as an advantage," Mathis said. "I tried to get girls off that, but it didn't work out."

That he finally persuaded his father to take him under his

ample wing and train him for boxing set the stage for another collision of coincidence, this one great enough to provoke investigations into the hereafter. In the Tyson-McNeeley fight, there had been some weird resonances in the fighters' histories, with the legacy of D'Amato popping up in odd corners. But in this one, the links between the fighters— D'Amato again—became downright eerie.

Buster Sr. had in fact been part of D'Amato's stable, and the old man's sway over the fighter, though it could never extend to his diet, was nonetheless considerable. When Tyson, created entirely by D'Amato, stepped into the ring that Saturday night, he would be facing a fighter whose middle name was . . . D'Amato.

He would also be facing a fighter who had just lost a parent (another Buster had once used the loss of his mother to inspire him to boxing's biggest upset). Buster Sr., whose weight had reached 507 pounds at one time, had been in poor health for years. He'd had two strokes, two heart attacks, and had lost two toes from diabetes complications. In addition, he had to undergo regular kidney dialysis.

Buster Sr. had, in the recent years of his son's development, faded from active involvement. When Buster fought, his father would wait at home for postfight calls to learn the news. He had high hopes for him, even though he recognized there were DNA hurdles that wouldn't allow abs of steel ever to become part of his son's physique. But he thought his son's hands were even faster than his—"and that's saying something."

Toward the end, when Buster Jr. was preparing to fight Bowe in a bout that would end in disqualification (Bowe would smack him in the head when Mathis was on a knee— good old Riddick), the father's influence had become entirely motivational as he imparted Cus-isms over the phone, telling his son, for example, that the fight would be easy but that the ring walk—"going to the lion's den with pork chop underwear"—was always the hardest part.

On September 6, while Mathis was preparing for the November date with Tyson, Buster Sr. died of a heart attack and stroke. He was just 51.

Joey Fariello, another D'Amato disciple and onetime trainer of Big Buster, allowed himself to be drawn in as Mathis's trainer. He was reluctant at first, watching him work out and saying, "This guy's terrible." The fighter was 250 pounds at the time, out of shape and without any firepower whatsoever. But Fariello had learned loyalty at D'Amato's hands and couldn't walk out on the memory of Big Bus, a guy he had sent into catastrophic action with Joe Frazier almost 30 years before. So he dove in and tried to do what he could with another generation of genuine grace that was almost comically encased in blubber.

He wasn't by any means predicting an upset—"The bad thing about Buster," he said before the fight, "and everybody knows this, he's not the biggest puncher in the world, he's a bit of a slapper"—but he had retained enough of the old D'Amato mumbo jumbo to reserve the possibility of success for his fighter.

Fariello admitted that "Cus was nuts, in a funny way," but that a lot of his ring psychology was basically sound. The old man's understanding of fear and need was still an important weapon in a cornerman's arsenal. "Fighters are hungry for different things," he said, "and Tyson doesn't have that anymore. He's living like a millionaire." His thought was that Mathis might frustrate him during those dangerous first four rounds and "reinforce that negative thinking." Tyson's appetite would be gone, and who knew what would happen after that? Then again, he said, thinking it over, "he's got bombs and my guy's got BB's."

Mathis was also sizing up Tyson for mental collapse. He

said he felt sorry for Tyson, who had once been his hero, and wondered if he was still into his sport. "He doesn't seem happy," Mathis suggested. "I'm going to use his insecurity against him." Then, perhaps recalling some Cus-ism, he added, "Fear the man who has nothing to lose."

And yet nobody feared Buster Mathis, Jr. By the time the fight moved to Philadelphia, he had become a 25-1 underdog. For all his success, for all the prominence he was promised in this bout, he was becoming once more a subject of ridicule, a fat boy with a squeaky voice. His hometown manager, Bruce Kielty, sensed the tenor of the promotion and, in the days before the fight, sequestered his fighter from the media. He found objectionable such characterizations as "stiff" and "boiled chicken wing." Kielty finally said, "I think we've about had it."

Once-in-a-lifetime paydays exacted certain trade-offs, even beyond the opponent's ritual beating. Humiliation, apparently, was one of them. Mathis was an adult in a very grown-up business, and it was hard to feel sorry for him. And yet Kielty was right in understanding that Mathis's victimization went beyond the likely ring thrashing. A certain level of ugliness was needed, it seemed, to satisfy the promotion's requirements. Cruelty and contempt were in the air.

The Philadelphia press conference three days before the fight was the usual King burlesque, with a Benjamin Franklin imposter on hand, as well as several Minutemen (not McNeeley impersonators, but rather drum-tapping, stocking-legged, tricorner hat–wearing American Revolution hobbyists). The point of their presence was not clear, although the sight of Franklin reminded King of meteorological events, and thus Mathis's chances: "He could catch lightning in a jug," he suggested. In addition there was the usual Tyson entourage, led once more by Steve Fitch, a.k.a. Crocodile. Dressed in his guerrilla fatigues, an unintentional updating of the Minutemen's garb, he moved about the room, yelling, "Fight time," and "Pound for pound," and any other phrase for which volume could be made to substitute for sense.

And the flunkies hollered for Mathis to put some bass in it.

At Thursday's weigh-in, the atmosphere was similar. Tyson, appearing indifferent, took off his PROPERTY OF ALLAH sweatshirt to reveal a chiseled abdomen. "Cut in stone!" King exulted. "Adonis!" Mathis tipped the scales at just 224, but no amount of work would ever remove his softness, a doughiness that would have been obvious beneath a suit of armor. "Take your shirt off," the flunkies hollered. But he kept his T-shirt tucked into his pants.

Mathis had more to worry about than comparative physiques. Tyson appeared to be working on more than his body in the fight preparation, and accounts of sparring partners being disabled in training were coming with growing frequency. The news was that Tyson had knocked out 20 different spar buddies in all. It couldn't be discounted, since media members at an open workout had watched him floor Nate Tubbs after he'd already had him out on his feet. Another report had him sending Leroy Seals to the hospital with a huge gash on his jaw.

Michael Spinks, who hadn't had it as good as even Nate Tubbs in his meeting with Tyson, thought Tyson must be "sick, sick, sick," and that he had become an insecure bully. On the other hand, reports that the fighter's brutish instincts had returned encouraged others. Nobody was buying tickets to see Tyson needlepoint. People were showing up to see a train wreck.

As with the McNeeley fight, this evidence of ill humor, however scant, was all Tyson was going to provide the promotion. His public appearances were typically brief and sullen. Asked at the press conference how long the fight would last, Tyson said, "I'm not a predictor, but I'm going to give you something Philadelphia will never forget." When he was pressed, he asked the questioner, "How long have you been covering my fights?" Told it was the first time, Tyson sniffed, "You'll see."

In the one interview he did before the fight, he told Bernard Fernandez of the *Philadelphia Daily News* that success had failed to live up to his expectations and that, although "fight night is fun," hardly anything else was. "I thought it would be more exciting than it turned out to be. I didn't realize it would be boring sometimes. Right now, I'm a little bored."

He acknowledged, in a way, that the promoter's agenda was partly responsible, but didn't really see how it could be otherwise. "The public isn't going to put up with me fighting ten or fifteen nobodies before I fight for the real title," he said. "There is a great deal of pressure on me to get some things done right now. People want to see Mike Tyson in big-time fights. And I have exclusive contracts I have to honor. Those contracts pay too much money for me to come back slow and easy. It's business, big business. All those people care about is that I'm in the ring and making them money."

Well, it wasn't like he minded so much. City fathers had been trying to assure themselves that the fight would have roughly the same economic impact as a medium-sized convention, albeit one where the convention-goers forgot to attend all the presentations. However, they failed to factor in Tyson's own spending power. Though Tyson would have to go some to put a dent in his $10 million purse, his Philadelphia shopping sprees were impressive nonetheless. After his Wednesday press conference, Tyson and his entourage—nine bodyguards were in attendance—swept through Stanmoor's Just Hats, where everybody bought as many as two "Godfather" lids apiece. Then it was off to Via Shoes, where Tyson, Holloway, and two others dropped $1,900 on suede shoes and boots. One more stop: Vizuri, where Tyson and Holloway managed to spend around $20,000 on Versace and Moschino sports coats.

As fight night came upon the city, it became clear that the haberdashers were the only ones making a killing. Ticket sales continued to sputter, stalling at 6,000 two days beforehand. It seemed to have finally dawned on Philadelphia that the event wasn't going to be quite major league, that they'd been involved in another sucker play. Philadelphians were certainly not reassured when King, who is normally shrewder than this, began predicting a short and noncompetitive fight.

"How long?" he said. "Not long." This, however, did not mean Tyson had taken Mathis cheap. "He's working strenuously for this round. Or two rounds." One round? Two rounds? Asked if that sounded like $500 well spent, King said, "It's not about how much time, it's how the quality is. A masterpiece don't go on for hours and hours."

This was clearly not about art, though, and was never meant to be. This was all about Train Tyson, another metaphor King had stumbled upon. "Once Tyson starts rolling," King said, "he doesn't want to stop. You have to keep Tyson going before he derails." Philadelphia was a whistle-stop, a place to pick up some hats, shoes, and $10 million. And then Tyson was going to steam right out of town, back to Las Vegas.

The only real anticipation was about who was going to be onboard. King had gathered the three heavyweight champions then under his control at ringside so that they might appear to be contesting for Tyson's favor. Indeed, to see them there fight night made for an interesting tableau: champions as supplicants, each hoping to still have his title by the time Tyson got to him, conferring the millions of dollars at his promotional disposal upon them.

It was widely understood that WBC champion Frank Bruno, whom Tyson had stopped nearly seven years before, was up first. Though it hadn't been announced, the date was penciled in for March 16, back at the MGM Grand. The other two champions, WBA king Bruce Seldon and IBF titleholder Francois Botha, would fill dates on June 22 and November 2, probably in that order, with perhaps another fight for Tyson in September. This was all being laid out one day before the Mathis fight, the latter's apparent insignificance so obvious that nobody thought twice about outlining Tyson's timetable nearly a year beyond the next night's event.

"This is Mike's era," said John Horne of his fighter. To him, all of boxing was at Tyson's mercy. "Possibly Lennox Lewis will fit in somewhere. Bowe is totally at our discretion." Holyfield? "The worst thing Holyfield did in his career was not taking advantage of his two opportunities to fight Mike Tyson before Mike went away. I don't know that it will ever happen now."

Wasn't he sounding a little imperial? "That's the way it is," he said. "It's like when Elvis was here."

As it turned out, if Tyson had bought blue suede shoes at Via's, Mathis wasn't going to be the one to step on them. Fight night at the Spectrum, where about 8,000 finally braved the bitter cold to attend (King lifted the Fox blackout in Philadelphia at 5:30 that afternoon), was every bit as anticlimactic as Tyson's attendants had suggested it would be. The action was foreordained and lackluster, the result entirely predictable.

About all you could say of Mathis's performance was that he wasn't scared. This, as later opponents would demonstrate, was no small thing. But there he was in his dressing room before the fight, having sat silent for 45 minutes, finally looking up at Kielty and saying, "This could be one helluva good fight." He seemed to Kielty to have no apprehension whatsoever.

A Savage Business

Certainly he wasn't cowed in the ring. He bored in at the bell, choosing the safety of an inside game, hoping his busy hands could score points with the judges. Kielty was somewhat surprised at the strategy his fighter developed. "Here he was throwing bombs from the beginning," Kielty said of his man. "He made Tyson look so bad, Mathis being a very tough guy to nail clean. But I never thought he'd be as aggressive as he was. Too bad he moved the wrong way."

That would be in the third round, when Tyson, who may not have connected even once in the first round, unloaded one of his own bombs from the right side and followed it with an uppercut that landed flush on Mathis's cheek. Whichever way Mathis had moved, it was wrong. Two punches more and Mathis was scattered across the ring.

"When I looked up," Mathis recollected pleasantly, "the referee was at five. I thought, Damn, this man is counting fast." Referee Frank Cappuccino, not counting that fast at all, got to 10 before Mathis could formulate further action. The evening was over.

A lot of folks there found the event inconclusive, even though Tyson did manifest power in the stoppage. All those wild right hands were not encouraging. Tyson, appearing afterward in his Philly duds (black double-breasted suit, black homburg with a red feather in the headband), said that he had been "lullabying him." He playfully suggested that the missed punches were "all a plot, all a setup. Just like this society." He seemed very pleased with himself for finding a metaphor in so meaningless a fight.

As this would be Mathis's last appearance in the glare of appreciable light, it is worth noting that he behaved rather eccentrically after the fight. Coming into the interview room, he seemed more undone by the fashion that was on display before him than any damage that had been done to his person. Seeing Tyson's entourage—all in their Stanmoor's tops

(10 were counted), looking for all the world like a bizarre secret service force—Mathis was obviously stunned. He finally turned to the similarly skimmered Tyson, said, "You okay?" then, in a strange homage, added, "I like your hat, man." And then he was gone.

Mathis would disappear even quicker than McNeeley had, not even stopping off for the loser's parting gift. Much to Kielty's disgust, Mathis never landed a single endorsement. "He got not one penny," he said much later. Of course, the idea that Tyson's victims deserved ancillary income was still new; it may have been that McNeeley was unique in that respect, and that most losers didn't actually gain earning power in their defeat. Poor Mathis, all he got out of his fame was a Grand Rapids auto ad, and the use of an Oldsmobile Aurora for one year.

For Mathis, it was all downhill after that, one thing after another. Fariello suffered a stroke on Christmas Eve and died three nights later. Mathis plunged on under the direction of Kevin Rooney, another former D'Amato disciple, and had two more fights until losing to Lou Savarese in a fight Mathis was born to win, or so everybody thought. His strut across this grand stage had not amounted to much, just a payday, a car for a year, and a cultural footnote. Not long afterward Mathis asked Kielty if he'd be disappointed if he retired. Kielty said not at all. Actually, nobody minded. Nobody even noticed.

More than a year later Mathis was still living in his mother Joan's house in Grand Rapids, with plans to study business at the University of Miami. He said he had started up his own management company and might even promote some fights of his own. For that matter, once his mind had cleared after the deaths of two father figures, he didn't rule out a comeback. "I just might get back into it," he said, in that high piping voice of his.

Chapter Five

"What's the name of that junkie I got?"

Looking back, King's Philadelphia Story is fairly easy to understand. The city was just a staging area, makeshift at that, for Tyson's upcoming championship parade. The Mathis fight itself was pointless; everything about that evening, it turned out, was pointless, incidental to the promotion's real purpose.

It even dawned on Fox, which at least had the appearance of a huge winner, that it had been used and abused in the service of King's greater good. Fox did get the ratings it had hoped for, gaining an incredible 29 share of the audience, its highest-rated night ever, for the two-hour-and-15-minute show. The Tyson bout itself drew a 20.6 rating and a 34 share during its half-hour duration. Of course this wasn't the sweeps-week kickoff Fox had hoped for, but how could they complain about that? Ratings were ratings.

But it wasn't too long before Fox understood to what extent it had been duped. As part of the Tyson contract, Fox had, according to King, agreed to a 12-fight deal, monthly King cards, beginning in January, that Fox would carry throughout the year. In truth, the 12 fights were Fox's option; they were bound only to show three of them. As it turned out, that's all they broadcast, thanks to the caliber of fights

King supplied. A Fox executive said they were the three sorri-est cards ever provided national television, and that out of six hours of programming, "there were probably two minutes of action. They were terrible. People were getting knocked out in four seconds. We kept complaining and King kept saying, Don't worry, I'll take care of it. He never did. Let's just say that Don King screwed his last network."

Philadelphia wasn't exactly enriched by the experience, ei-ther, but at least it wasn't embarrassed or otherwise plun-dered. Team Tyson did spread a few bucks around, and the fighter and King did engage in their annual holiday turkey giveaway. So maybe the bonanza failed to materialize, but some poor got fed and it was a good week at Stanmoor's. What would the Red Hot Chili Peppers have done for the economy? They mostly wear socks.

But for King, this wasn't meant to be about Fox or Phila-delphia; they were just bit players in a stopgap promotion. This was about a Tyson send-off into big-money boxing, into a unified championship where fortunes would be banked like a franchisor's fee, regularly and easily. Once Tyson held all three titles, all of boxing would bow to him; no heavyweight could fight for true gain beyond his realm. Once Tyson ruled the division, there would be no more pirate contests, like Bowe-Holyfield, for big money and no championship. Any-thing that was to be credible, or marketable, or at all desir-able would have to go through him.

That was why, just in case there was still somebody so dim as to be confused by King's plan, the promoter assembled "his" champions at ringside in Philadelphia. Was there any-body who still didn't get it? King arranged them, in all their plumage (did Stanmoor's have the fight concession?), like ducks in a row. Given that King had just spent a day handing out turkeys, the poultry imagery was perhaps unavoidable. It seemed to some folks that if there had been just one more duck in that row, Tyson's fights would have to be sanctioned by the Fish and Game people, not a boxing commission.

The three champions—Bruce Seldon, Frank Bruno, and Francois Botha—were rendered all the more ridiculous by their necessary subservience. They were champions, but at the same time they were really just hopeful challengers, angling for some of that Tyson loot. They could poor-mouth Tyson as postfight convention required, but they couldn't go too far in offending him. They were there, after all, at his pleasure.

Bruno, who was next up for Tyson, seemed the boldest of them, perhaps because he had already fought Tyson once, getting stopped by him in 1989 in a try for the undisputed title. His familiarity with Tyson bred at least a little contempt, which Tyson hadn't minded reflecting right back at him. Leaving the ring after the Mathis fight, Tyson pointed at his pectorals and mouthed "I'm Number One" to Bruno, but the WBC champion pretended to be unimpressed.

"I was confident before tonight," he said, "but now I'm even more confident. I saw some weaknesses but I'm not saying what they were. I won't get caught up in the hype, but I believe I will knock Mike Tyson out."

Was there any chance he had said that before—say, six years ago? "I'm totally different now. I'm bigger, stronger, more experienced, and one and a half stones [21 pounds] heavier." Moreover, he said, "Tyson's not Superman. He's been out of the ring for four years. And now, he doesn't look right."

Before dispatching his little audience, Bruno concluded, "He will not live with me."

Seldon and Botha were far more respectful. They hung around the interview area, listened to Tyson try to describe his knockout combination ("It manifest itself. I can't articulate the particular science"), and acted equal parts courteous and blasé. Seldon, the WBA champ, thought Tyson's timing might be off, but he was too polite to say more. He had already made peace with his station in life, telling everybody how happy he'd been to defend his title on the undercard of Tyson's fight with McNeeley. And Botha, the so-called White Buffalo from South Africa, simply disappeared from the heavyweight herd.

They were not the most impressive bunch to sit at ringside and cheer, however ambivalently, for a heavyweight challenger. Even taking into consideration the dilution of greatness that the existence of three organizations guarantees, this was as lackluster a group as could ever be convened. There were not too many men on the street in 1995 who could have identified these three titleholders. There were a lot of people in boxing, for that matter, who'd have to think a good long while to remember just how they had become champs. Just whom did the Buff beat to wear the IBF belt, anyway? Axel Schulz? And Schulz got the title how? By losing to George Foreman?

The lineage of these three kings did not survive much investigation. Theirs was a low-rent royalty, gotten painlessly and without much public attention. They were mail-order champions, with all the rights and privileges of Kentucky colonels or Tahitian ambassadors. All the influence, too. These titular figureheads, who would only become commercially important once their synthetic titles were put up for grabs in Tyson fights, were in almost every sense Don King inventions, single-purpose creations of no known provenance and absolutely no future beyond their inevitable prostration before Mike Tyson.

That there would be any ducks at King's disposal, much less three in a row, was King's real achievement in Tyson's comeback. The work, the manipulation, the conspiracy that was required for this setup could only have been performed by Don King. Nobody else had the gifts for this kind of enterprise, nobody else had the perseverance. It was a masterpiece of grit and guile and perhaps, as his critics complained, corruption, too.

Keep in mind that King didn't even have a feather in his cap, much less a duck in his yard, when Tyson went away. Julio Cesar Chavez, the Mexican legend who had forestalled his decline with a couple of questionable decisions, was King's only draw during Tyson's prison term. Although King staged some memorable promotions with Chavez, the fighter had not become the cross-over star King had hoped for. In any event, Chavez was not a heavyweight (though he'd grown past his lightweight legacy), and heavyweights, as bad or as good as they might be in any given era, controlled the public's interest and wallets.

Nobody understood this better than King, whose entrée into boxing had been Muhammad Ali all those years ago in Zaire. Remembering the box office power of Ali, whom he had egged into that memorable Foreman fight in 1974, he steadfastly made the heavyweight division his power base, even when men like Sugar Ray Leonard, Marvelous Marvin Hagler, and Roberto Duran were glamorizing the smaller weight classes, and his own heavyweights were stinking up the game. King knew that the charisma of these little men was fleeting and that America's fascination would always return to the contest for heavyweight champion—the chance to see the biggest, baddest man alive. Even when the champions were mediocre, as was often the case in the 1980s, the division was a reliable moneymaker for those willing to promote there.

During that decade, King ruled the division with his usual combination of hard work, intrigue, and coercion. These were skills that had served him—up to a point—as a young numbers boss in Cleveland a lifetime ago. That little career had come to a close in 1967, more or less, when he was convicted and imprisoned for pistol-whipping and stomping a man to death. But there is strong evidence, unearthed by Jack Newfield for his 1995 investigative biography *Only in America: The Life and Crimes of Don King,* that many of the furtive abilities King refined in boxing's backrooms were always at hand. The best deal he ever cut may have been the one that, somehow, modified his second-degree murder conviction so that he served a far lesser penalty—just four years in Ohio's Marion Correctional Institution—than he probably should have. Years later, according to Newfield, King produced Ali to campaign for the same judge, Hugh Corrigan, when he ran for a court of appeals position.

In any event, then as now, King had a shrewd appreciation for the heavyweight's natural ascendancy in inner-city evolution: His victim, who had owed $600 in gambling debts, weighed 100 pounds less than King. The last words he spoke were "Don, I'll pay you the money."

During the seventies and eighties King made everyone pay, everyone who wanted to conduct business in the heavyweight division. Using his enormous charm, his ability to relate to the black athlete, and the usual intrigue, King was able to sign up virtual top 10s. Indeed, in 1978 he wrote a letter to Madison Square Garden offering the services of no fewer than seven of the division's top-10 boxers. With this kind of inventory, he was able to hold an economic gun to boxing's head.

Such a monopoly, and that's what it was, guaranteed him the most important title in boxing, no matter who won or lost. There was little anxiety on his part, watching one King fighter batter another. Who really cared who won or lost? Sadly, as it turned out, not even his stable of fighters cared very much; as a group they had become so demoralized over their enslavement that defeat, and the possibility of freedom, had actually become cause for celebration in some cases.

A Savage Business

Poor Tim Witherspoon, who had been forced to pay King's stepson Carl a 50 percent management fee to remain on a championship track, was made more and more miserable by his success. When he defeated one King-controlled fighter, Tony Tubbs, for the WBA crown in 1986, he expected to become wealthy. But when, in defense of his title, he knocked out Frank Bruno in London and received a check for just $90,094 (Bruno, the challenger, had gotten $900,000), Witherspoon snapped and fell into a career swoon from which he never really recovered. He lost in his next defense to the King-promoted James "Bonecrusher" Smith and said later, "I didn't care. Losing meant Don was out of my life."

Witherspoon's story was not unlike those of many of the other King-controlled heavyweights—seven-year champion Larry Holmes often complained of underpayment—who had been forced into mysterious contracts just for the privilege of performing on King's cards. Witherspoon was different only in that, in 1987, he sued Don and Carl King for $25 million, claiming fraud and conflict of interest. The suit, settled six years later for $1 million, was mostly important for the exposure of King's ritual contract rapings, where his attention to detail could either be taken as shrewd business practice, or as utter contempt for his fighters.

A lot of people have thought this over since then. Maybe it's the careful man who, in addition to deducting 50 percent of the fighter's purse for the manager's share, subtracts $98 for the boxer's protective cup. Maybe the need to stiff Ali— Ali!—of more than $1 million, as Newfield details, was the reflexive behavior of a born accountant. The penny pinching, in the shadows of such excesses, might even have been recreational, the sport of numbers crunchers.

Or perhaps it was just the work of a bully, who seeks his punitive amusement in the sly language of contracts, from behind his big desk.

Critics, and even his own boxers, took King on from time to time. But he discovered early on that he could insulate himself from most insult simply by playing the fool. His hair, his wild oratory, his malapropisms, an almost deliberate mangling of literary references—these all made it easy for him to deflect any serious challenge. "One of his best defenses," sighed Abraham, "is that he's great copy. Everybody in the media says they're tired of him and his press conferences, but they all go. And as nefarious as he is, particularly to his fighters, he's just a cartoon character to most people. And so they indulge him, let him get away with a lot of crap, fail to take him seriously, and hold him to a much lower standard."

During this time, though, King's inexhaustible ramblings were largely unnecessary to his purpose. King, aside from his dealings with Witherspoon, had found he could pretty much do whatever he wanted with his fighters because, in the heavyweight division, in the 1980s, he controlled the product. It's instructive to note that Bonecrusher Smith, who had become heir to Witherspoon's crown, was a disaffected King fighter himself. Smith had been jumped into the title fight only after agreeing to drop his own suit against King and to make Carl King his manager. It was a lesson a lot of the heavyweights had learned. Even the most unsophisticated fighter could realize how desperately foolish it was to try and remain independent.

But King's men didn't have much strength, except in their numbers. Apart from Holmes, who had a seven-year reign for King, none was a reliable champion. Witherspoon's title tenure was far more typical of the group than was Holmes's. Consequently, there was no lasting legacy, nobody to withstand the terror unleashed by the teenage Tyson, a talent that was all the more fearsome to King because of his free agency.

It was inevitable that King would eventually enlist the destroyer of his realm, the kid who'd gone through his inventory—Trevor Berbick, Bonecrusher Smith, Tyrell Biggs, Holmes, Tony Tubbs—so systematically that it didn't make a bit of sense to think of additional product without first acquiring Tyson. King was able to do this in 1988, when Tyson was being buffeted by his manager's death, and his own divorce. D'Amato was long since gone from Tyson's life, and there was no longer anybody left who could relate to him. King could.

So Tyson became the inventory. Once King seduced Tyson, wooing him away from Bill Cayton and Kevin Rooney after the Spinks fight in 1988, King no longer needed the leverage of quantity. Now he had a fighter who was considered unstoppable, and his place in the division was more secure than ever. All the other fighters would have to come to King and give up future promotional considerations in the application to bank at his money machine—Mike Tyson.

Besides, by then, perhaps noticing how churlish and litigious his ungrateful fighters had become, King had decided to rely on the goodwill of more reasonable men, the folks who determine the rankings (and therefore the challengers) at the major boxing organizations. Their cooperation had always been vital to the promoter and even, at times, comical. Who could ever forget the morning in 1990 when Buster Douglas plunged King's empire into disarray with a 10th-round knockout in Tokyo—and the WBC president, José Sulaiman, was prodded to stand up in front of the press assembled there and say, more or less, that it had never happened?

Sulaiman, swayed by King's insistence that Tyson had actually knocked Douglas out in the fourth round (King: "The first knockout obliterated the second knockout!"), did finally declare Douglas the champion, but only after he was at some remove from the shouting and blustering promoter. Sulaiman felt so terrible about his obvious misreading of the situation that he offered to resign. Even so, the incident reminded everybody in boxing just how influential King could be with a governing body.

King's enemies alleged corruption, then and now, citing the ever-friendly ratings. But corruption, either with him or with rival promoters, was never proved. And even though it's more or less assumed in the boxing industry—HBO boxing chief Lou DiBella says, "If it talks and walks like a duck, then . . ." —it still can't be nailed down. It can be winked at, though. It almost has to be winked at. To do otherwise would be to agree that Peter McNeeley had been promoted into the top 10 through his ability and hard work. Such stupidity would be unforgivable. Better to assume institutional depravity.

In the end, corruption in boxing is the same as a lot of people's faith in a god: You either believe or you don't; in any event, there's no paper on it.

What is certainly the case is that, perhaps through sheer diligence, King had gained a stranglehold on all the sanctioning bodies, not just the WBC. His influence with the WBC had always been a given. People remember King attending a 1988 WBC convention and sitting on the dais with the WBC officials while other promoters sat with guests. To this day, he is a fixture at their gatherings, taking out full-page ads in their programs (which invariably list him as promoter of the century), and generally remaining supportive.

But, said DiBella, what changed was that "there used to be a system of checks and balances. King had the WBC, Bob Arum had the WBA, and Duva had the IBF." It was true that each of the three major promoters was considered to be allied with his own personal sanctioning body. But Arum, who promoted at Top Rank, and the late Dan Duva, who had begun Main Events, had decided in the nineties to direct their energies elsewhere. Their relationships with the so-called alphabets became less meaningful. Arum, for example, began promoting Oscar De La Hoya and discovered that the organizations were suddenly irrelevant to his drawing power. "It opened my eyes," he said. "We got him the WBO title, and then when Oscar became big and everybody realized he was a superstar, the WBC was much easier to work with. But up to then, it wasn't worth my time."

The consequence, DiBella said, was that "King then got all of them."

King has never denied his advantages with the sanctioning bodies, claiming it has always been simply a matter of adhering to their guidelines. "I worked the system," he has said. "I played by the rules. I went to all the conventions the sanctioning bodies ran." And if Arum and Duva and others did not? "My opponents went to sleep," he said.

The result, as he was able to boast after the Mathis fight, was that "I laid out the table for Mike to sup." His attention to detail large and small, coupled with some luck large and small, gave him three champions for Tyson's dining pleasure. It was, as King bragged, his "crowning achievement," considering he had had as few as none only a year earlier.

A little history: The undisputed title that Tyson lost to Douglas in Tokyo in 1990 might have remained in King's grasp had he not behaved so badly on Douglas's behalf. Douglas and his manager, John Johnson, felt King had, you might say, "obliterated" their former promotional agreement by trying to nullify his victory. King didn't give up easy. He tried every angle on Douglas—gifts to Douglas's estranged father, a media campaign in Douglas's hometown of Columbus, and finally a lawsuit—before he was willing to let it all go. In the settlement, King got $7 million for himself and Donald Trump (who had hoped to partner with him in the rematch), but lost Douglas and promotional rights to the title.

The title began a series of turnovers, fragmenting in the process. From Douglas it went rather quickly to Evander Holyfield, a Main Events fighter at the time. Douglas lost whatever drive had propelled him to sports' greatest upset and showed up for the weigh-in at Steve Wynn's Mirage in Las Vegas at 246 pounds. People who were in the room at the time were knocking over chairs to get out to the Mirage's sports book, where the odds had been even money. Newly established at 8-5 in favor of Holyfield, they were still badly skewed; Holyfield knocked the bloated Douglas out in the third round.

Then, in 1992, Holyfield lost it to Riddick Bowe who, in a misguided show of independence from the governing body, quickly ash-canned the WBC portion of the title. So when Holyfield beat Bowe in the rematch in 1993, it was only for the WBA and IBF championships. The WBC was up for grabs. And very soon, thanks to George Foreman, they were all up for grabs.

Michael Moorer upset Holyfield for the two titles the next year, and he in turn was upset by big George. And that's where the fabled championship lineage—"I beat the man who beat the man"—was again interrupted. Foreman, who in 1995 refused to fight either Tony Tucker or Bruce Seldon, two King fighters, let the WBA title fall away. Then the IBF took its title from him when he refused to give Axel Schulz a rematch following his controversial decision in the spring of 1995.

According to Arum, who promoted many of Foreman's comeback fights, "Foreman let it go because King was using his influence to make his life miserable. And George wouldn't allow us to sue, which I wanted to do. That's George." But Foreman was notoriously picky about his opponents and his purses. It wasn't all politics; there was a little personal survival thrown in, too.

Even with Foreman proving to be a dithering champion,

the complete disintegration of the heavyweight title in just one year could not have been predicted. Yet it was as if King had anticipated just such a turn of events. By the time Tyson got out of prison there was not a single champion who had won his belt from another. By manipulating a rather mediocre cast of characters up and down the rankings, King had already recaptured control of the WBC title, would have the WBA champion no matter who won or lost, and had a similar chance of securing control of the IBF title. Was Tyson going to sup or what? Coming out of prison he needn't have worn much more than a napkin.

To some, steering Oliver McCall into the WBC title in 1994 really was the masterstroke. Even if McCall didn't hold it long enough to hand it directly to Tyson, this was the key play, giving King reentry into the heavyweight division when all doors had been locked shut. Without McCall's victory over Lennox Lewis, whom King did not control, the WBC title would have been circulating among the enemy HBO fighters, perhaps even Bowe.

For sure, McCall's surprise emergence as a contender and then champion was an example of how little King left to chance, and how invisibly he worked. It was an example of King's vision, the wicked ability to see into alternate futures.

McCall, who'd had his share of drug problems and had never risen beyond the status of Mike Tyson's sparring partner (for nine of Tyson's title defenses), was not an obvious vehicle for King's drive back to dominance. Going into the London fight for Lewis's WBC title, McCall was 24–5, having lost to the likes of Orlin Norris and Tony Tucker. He was a huge underdog. The fight was little more than a tune-up for Lewis, who had already agreed to meet Bowe for a "real" championship fight.

A year after McCall's upset, King was still flush with the memory, although he couldn't quite remember the man who made it possible. "What's the name of that junkie I got?" he wondered. "Oh, yeah, Oliver McCall, the junkie." In King's recollection, the fighter had been less instrumental in Lewis's defeat than he had. "I cleaned him up for that fight, dechemicalized him and detoxified him. I fired him up that night, singing 'Yankee Doodle Dandy.' Nobody could have beat him."

Some in attendance thought the outcome mysterious, even beyond the use of George M. Cohan as master motivator. Citing a quick stoppage by Mexican referee Lupe Garcia, who had been handpicked by Sulaiman, the conspiracy theorists had more than their usual ammunition; Garcia got to the count of five before waving Lewis off, and some already hyperactive imaginations went right to work.

In reality, McCall's upset probably had more to do with trainer Emanuel Steward, brought in for that one fight, than King's crooning. Steward had calmed the normally nutty McCall with his own paternal influence, the kind of total involvement that makes some fighters call him Pops. As far as any singing goes, it was probably McCall's that did the trick. Steward, mindful of McCall's nocturnal adventuring, dressed the fighter up and planted him in his nightclub, where the fighter passed his historically turbulent nights singing "Unforgettable" to the patrons. "He's a good singer, man," Steward said. "I don't mean good for a fighter, like Larry Holmes. He's a good singer."

The fight itself was no theft. But if there was a crime, it had happened much earlier and before far fewer bystanders. The miracle was not that McCall had stopped Lewis—Lewis, for all his gifts, was a typically unreliable British heavyweight, and he was catching McCall on the night of his life —but that he had ever been ranked high enough to force Lewis to fight him.

HBO's Seth Abraham, who has worked with and against

King long enough to believe in miracles of all kinds, was trying to initiate another heavyweight tournament back in early 1994 when he first ran into the McCall phenomenon. That was when Holyfield held the IBF and WBA titles, Lewis the WBC, and Michael Moorer was in the mix as the IBF's top challenger. It was a simple plan: Holyfield vs. Lewis, Moorer to fight the winner. It was not only fair, it was attractive. And, as King was entirely left out of the promotional picture, it was one that might be made to work.

Abraham got into his car during the worst snowstorm to hit New York City in 25 years and inched his way to IBF president Bob Lee's offices in East Orange, New Jersey. Lee would be leaving town for Italy soon, and Abraham was anxious to cement the agreement. The only sticking point was that Moorer would have to step aside as Holyfield's mandatory defense for the IBF half of the title and allow him to fight Lewis first. HBO was going to make it worth Moorer's while, paying him $4 million for that consideration plus a guaranteed shot at the winner for $6 million. Everybody was happy.

"It was all agreed," remembered Main Events' Dino Duva. "We had the deal."

But when Abraham made his way through the snowstorm, reached Lee's office, and visited with him in one of the conference rooms—"We had Dunkin' Donuts, as I recall"—the deal collapsed under the weight of King's unseen influence. Lee was suddenly unexpectedly sympathetic to the IBF's No. 2 fighter, Oliver McCall. He told Abraham the plan was unfair to McCall. Abraham remembered thinking he had just entered the Twilight Zone. Lee went on to explain that, according to the rules, if Moorer stepped aside as the No. 1 challenger, the mandatory defense should go to McCall as the highest-ranked available contender. But the point of allowing a fighter to step aside, Abraham argued, was to preserve his status, wasn't it? No, Lee told him, he had to protect McCall's rights for a mandatory defense.

"I am not normally a reflective man," said Abraham, "but maybe because it was such a long, slow drive back, I had time to think. And it occurred to me that this was just a microcosm of what was wrong in boxing."

As it turned out—and this may be the most impressive little detail—McCall never did fight for the IBF title. Under Lee's ruling, Moorer simply went ahead and fought Holyfield, won, and set a number of other events into motion. The only real effect, although an important one, of McCall's sudden importance to the IBF was the scuttling of an HBO tournament that might have made it impossible for King to gain a heavyweight reentry.

In his attention to the IBF, King was merely covering all the bases. By the summer of 1994, McCall, although he had beaten nobody of note but Francisco Damiani more than a year before, was the mandatory defense not just in the IBF, but in the WBA and WBC. King had somehow positioned him as No. 1 in the other two organizations as well. "If your guy's Number One," Abraham pointed out, "you'll always be one fight from the championship."

McCall, one fight from the championship, was King's guy. And, dechemicalized and full of marching songs, he beat an HBO fighter, Lewis, on enemy turf. In doing so, he plunged HBO's other attraction, Bowe, even further into the earth. Bowe, a little more humble than he'd been a year before, had been looking forward to the Lewis fight as his chance to rejoin the establishment. He'd even hammered out a 65/35 split of revenues with Lewis. After McCall's great night, Dan Duva surveyed the wreckage and said, "Bowe is in a deep, cold place right now."

And King was in business again, the result of incalculable intrigue, hard work, and vision. "Nobody can see into the future like Don," said Abraham. "He's a genius. Then, so was Al Capone."

As for McCall, his junkie, King never did hide his plans for him. "Oliver will make two or three defenses," he said, "and by that time Mike Tyson will be out of prison."

King was similarly poised within the WBA, where he staffed the No. 1 and 2 positions with Tony Tucker and Bruce Seldon. King had a little luck, of course, when Foreman surprised Moorer to win the WBA and IBF titles and then refused to defend against Tucker—or anybody, actually. The WBA was well within its rights to strip Foreman of the title and put the vacant championship in front of Tucker and Seldon, both King-promoted fighters.

By then, King didn't have as much to work with in the IBF, the last organization with a true champion in Foreman. Tucker, as the WBA loser, would fall from his No. 2 spot; McCall had already been removed from the IBF top position after winning the WBC title; and Seldon, the new WBA champ, was now gone, too. The only fighter left with King ties—signed to a long-term contract by 1995—was someone named Francois Botha, well down the rankings. And deservedly so. He was so bad, according to HBO's DiBella, that the network refused to use him when "George was looking for his stiffs to fight."

And yet, like McCall, Botha had acquired an institutional momentum that was impossible to explain. Number 10 in the IBF's July '94 rankings, Botha had soared to No. 1 in less than a year. How mysterious was this? Botha had never beaten a fighter in the top 30, and now he was ranked ahead of Riddick Bowe, Evander Holyfield, Lennox Lewis, and lots more fighters. That wasn't the only mystery: The No. 3–ranked fighter in the IBF had been Moorer, yet when the top two fighters, Tucker and Seldon, were removed, leaving Moorer the next in line, it was Botha who somehow leapt to the head of the class. "They said," recalled Moorer's manager, John Davimos, with a nearly straight face, "that Michael had been inactive."

In fact, Moorer had been among the quickest fighters to return to the ring after a loss (just five months after getting knocked out by Foreman) and had already scheduled another fight in May. In the same period, Botha had struggled to an eight-round decision over Willie Jake.

Things were certainly falling King's way, because Foreman was about to be stripped again. His victory over Axel Schulz in an IBF title fight had been so controversial that he was ordered to appear in a rematch. Foreman, throughout his comeback, had been brilliant in picking his opponents, and if he occasionally made a mistake, as he had with Schulz, he wasn't likely to repeat it. No way he'd fight Schulz again. It was just a matter of time before the IBF title would be up for grabs.

To have a chance at it, Main Events filed suit against the IBF on Moorer's behalf, a complaint that offered a little boxing reality for the rest of us. According to the complaint, Botha had gained his ranking "in conformance with the plan of Don King" and IBF president Lee had "solicited bribes and/or extorted monies" to effect that plan. Lee suddenly agreed that Moorer was a worthy challenger and ordered the new IBF champion—the winner of the Botha-Schulz fight—to give Moorer first shot. (And the lawsuit was dropped.)

In December 1995, Botha won a decision against Schulz, and King's stranglehold on the division was complete. Although Brit Frank Bruno had unseated McCall for the WBC title, King retained control of the new champion, and his empire, however fragile, was intact. So the night Tyson climbed out of the ring in Philadelphia, King was able to produce three titles at ringside for his fighter to behold. They were Tyson's, just for the taking.

A Savage Business

It had been up to King to provide them and it would be up to him to keep them available, which would be no small matter, considering the fighters' marginal abilities. Botha would come under additional attack when a drug test revealed that steroids had been in his system the night of his Schulz fight. To King and the IBF, the only fair remedy was to fine Botha $50,000 and order him to meet Schulz in a rematch; Moorer could wait a little longer. But after another lawsuit, it was decided that Botha would vacate the championship and that Moorer would fight Schulz for it. The winner, it was understood, would fight Botha, the White Buffalo, the last of the great Don King fighters.

But that was later. As 1995 drew to a close King had regained his heavyweight monopoly, setting the table for his hungry fighter, turning his enemies away hungry. It was quite an achievement, "mind-tingling," he admitted. Most of his enemies ended the year sputtering, fuming over his new control and their own missed chances. There was, after all, some truth to what King said: "If all these people stop and reflect —they gave it to me." He had outworked them, outspent them, outmaneuvered them. Possibly it was infuriating to his rivals to hear him boast afterward, "If you follow the rules you will not clash with the groups that sanction boxing." There are rules? But they really had given him more chances than he usually needs. They relaxed, they grew tired, they became confident enough to throw belts into garbage cans. King, then 64, scrambled behind them, salvaging the scrap he'd need to construct his own awful dominion.

To watch this unfold was at once disturbing and impressive. Moorer's manager, John Davimos, besides being involved in the suit with the IBF, had once gone after the WBA in a lawsuit, where he testified that the WBA's counsel, Jimmy Binns, had suggested Moorer's career might run smoother if Binns were given 5 percent of the fighter. Davimos took the suggestion for granted; what made him angry, he later said, was that, at the beginning of Moorer's career, Binns had told people the fighter just wasn't any good. See, in boxing there's hypocrisy, and then there's hypocrisy. But even though Moorer's promoter had come out on top in both lawsuits, and Davimos would continue to keep Moorer in place for a title fight, he was discouraged by King's unlimited energy, his apparently amoral appetite for success.

"I don't believe I can manage again," he said. "There's only two ways you can be successful. You can make the deals you have to make or you'll have to end up burning all your bridges in representing your fighter."

When Tyson became champion, as he surely would, his power over the organizations would grow. The alphabets grovel before the sanctioning fees, suddenly willing to work with Bob Arum, say, because 3 percent of De La Hoya's $10 million purse comes to $300,000 on top of their expenses at Caesars Palace. With Tyson as their champ, they would be accepting fees in multiples of that. There was no stopping King now.

King had recognized this many months earlier, before Tyson's title package was gift-wrapped. Attention should have been paid to his strange exuberance before the McNeeley fight. What did he know that nobody else did? Simply that every worthy fighter had been placed in a purgatory of his own design, that ordinary fighters had somehow been deputized by him, maneuvered into championships they didn't deserve. The system had been rigged; the few watchdogs that were left to guard the consumer had been completely worn down by King's preternatural energy. It was now too late. Maybe when he explained that he had been buried in the "media cave of death" for three years, until "the master came to the cave . . . and said, 'Don King, come forth,'" his rivals ought to have been more alert.

A Savage Business

"I rose from the death pallet of the media," he said one day before the McNeeley fight, standing beside Tyson on some dais at a press conference, most everybody tuning him out. "I serve the master who sits beside me." Tyson, the master, stared grimly ahead.

Chapter Six

"I'm expecting a jubilant life afterwards"

Business was better than ever. It was booming. Tyson was going to earn $30 million to challenge Frank Bruno for his WBC title on March 16, 1996, a tenfold raise from 1989, when he exploded the same poor Brit inside of five rounds. Historians would certainly puzzle over this arithmetic in the years to come, looking for some missing multiplier, that absent factor of 10: Tyson had been the undisputed champion then, and worth $3 million; now, seven years older and without a title or one credible victory, he gets $30 million.

Of course, nobody who'd been following this comeback was so naïve as to pretend Tyson's value had been plumped by anything as wholesome as athletic attraction. More sinister and cynical forces were at work here. It was depressing to realize that jail time had a little more to do with Tyson's 1996 purse than the rate of inflation.

Where else but in boxing? Going to prison for three years is not a marketing ploy many other athletes would ordinarily consider. It's an intriguing idea: Michael Jordan breaking rocks for a couple of seasons before returning to the Bulls. You might pay to see what he'd do against the Knicks right out of the box. But you'd have to figure Nike would have downsized its Air Jordan campaign in the meantime, and maybe Jordan is no longer up for the part in *Space Jam II.* The paying customer might be newly suspicious of Jordan's high-priced fragrance as well.

But, as historians would have to conclude, this is boxing. The dread that Don King was manufacturing, even if it hadn't up to this point produced anything more dangerous than a scowl, now came at a higher price than ever, and satisfied a lower longing. The appetite for destruction and whatever other dark forces as could be mustered on pay-per-view TV, or any TV, had never been keener. It was odd, perhaps peculiar to these times. The statistics all said dangerous crime was going down, yet Americans seemed to revel in the idea of violence and destruction all the more, lapping up shows on "scary" police chases, "wild" animal fights, "deadly" weather events. Professional wrestling, which slyly mocked the country's cultural divisions (teams of arm-raising black activists were set off against biker bumpkins), had never been more popular or, to judge by the listings, more available.

Tyson's career now seemed similarly contrived, as cartoonish and inauthentic as anything seen on Fox's "reality" shows or TNT's wrestling programs. Consider: Since that first fight with Bruno, Tyson had made just one more successful defense before losing to Buster Douglas, had fought four times before his rape conviction and twice more since getting out of jail. He'd not provided one genuinely athletic moment, one memorable performance in all that time. And now, because he was the hooded avenger with an unclean past—in other words, someone Vince McMahon might have created if Don King didn't hold the copyright—he was going to make $30 million.

For that matter, Bruno had gotten a fivefold raise of his own and now was going to earn $6 million. The basis for this pay hike was easier to understand: Yes, he'd lost to Tyson, but in doing so he had demonstrated the ability to throw a punch (one, anyway). Also, after a campaign in which he'd invariably come up short against any champion (three and counting) and every American (he'd also lost to Tim Witherspoon, in 1986), he'd finally nailed himself a Yankee titleholder, holding off Oliver McCall for a decision. His reputation as a boxer was not much enhanced by the victory, but it did accomplish two things: It made him all the more popular in England, where he'd been permanently installed as a lovable loser, and it made him absolutely necessary in the United States. He now had a title.

Showtime, which was hoping for as many as 1.4 million buys, even in competition with the NCAA basketball tournament, was not trying to justify the occasion, chills-and-spills-wise, or even to insist that Bruno's title made this that much more important than the Mathis fight. Since the fight would be essentially a replay, that would have been too much to ask. Showtime knew exactly what business it was in, and it wasn't sports broadcasting. "It shows," said the company's vice president, Jay Larkin, "that Tyson is a compelling TV event no matter who he fights."

The ability to generate these sums without even the pretense of presenting a good contest had meanwhile made King gaga. He truly had arrived in the Promised Land where the actual sport was a slim premise, and cartoon caricature was what sold the show. King was obviously suspicious of Tyson's remaining ability; otherwise he wouldn't have insisted on two preliminary bouts, then title fight number one against a familiar foe. So it was absolutely exhilarating for him to discover that Tyson's remaining ability, whatever it was, had no effect on his box-office pull.

King must have been doing the numbers in his sleep, because they began to have a dreamlike quality. Noting that Tyson had finished 1995 atop *Fortune* magazine's list of the highest-paid athletes in the world—$35 million for his 10 minutes of "work"—King was predicting his fighter would soon become sports' first "Mr. Billionaire." You could understand his euphoria. Baseball's Ken Griffey was tops in his game with a six-year contract for $34 million, Deion Sanders was making $35 million for seven years, and even Jordan was probably going to make no more than $30 million in endorsements. (For that matter, Sylvester Stallone was setting the pace among action heroes with a three-picture deal for $60 million. For Tyson, the equivalent was McNeeley, Mathis, and Bruno. Probably Stallone would work harder.)

So King might have gotten a little carried away when he predicted, "Tyson will be the first billion-dollar athlete the world has ever known." Counting the $70 million he'd made before he went to jail, that meant Tyson would need 30 more Bruno-type fights to make that prediction come true. Not very likely.

Still, the money that was real was astounding enough. King was on firmer ground when he said, "From the day this man hit the streets, one hundred million was there." And as long as he kept winning, and it apparently didn't matter against whom, the money would keep rolling in. While $1 billion might be a lofty goal, there was every reason to expect Tyson's rates to keep inching up. "There's two businesses in boxing," King explained. "There's the Tyson business and the championship business." For two fights King had only been in the Tyson business and had still earned his fighter a quick $35 million. Now that he was about to be in the championship business, too, everybody but Bill Gates could watch out.

Oddly, this talk of money seemed to please only King. Tyson seemed increasingly dour, if that was possible, afflicted with a melancholy that was theatrical in its proportions. The opportunity to demolish Bruno anew didn't seem particularly exciting to him, even for $30 million. As that fight neared, he seemed to get even more depressed.

Three days before the fight, at the usual press conference, the only one that Tyson would attend, the dais was so gloomy that Jay Larkin thought to observe "how somber this is. I've seen more levity at a funeral. There's so much money here," he said from the podium. "If I was getting this much money, I'd have a grin from ear to ear." This drew exactly zero laughs from the Tyson camp.

When it came Tyson's turn to speak, it was clear that Larkin's stab at levity had not improved his frame of mind. His remarks were clocked at 11 seconds: "I'm happy to be here; I'm in great shape; I'm fit and ferocious as ever. I look forward to a good fight and being victorious and champion of the world. I'm here to work. I'm ready to get it on."

But when a few questions were allowed from the floor, he revealed an even deeper funk than his opening remarks suggested. Asked about his fan support, Tyson shrugged. "I never dwell on who cares about me. I think no one cares about me. My main concern in life is to try to do the right thing in God's name. I've had so many mistakes. I'm trying to do my best to do the right thing, but I always fall short of my mark."

But wasn't he about to fight for the championship of the world, about to win it, as far as anybody could tell? "I look forward to winning it," he said, expressionless, nothing like a smile anywhere near his face. "I'm expecting a jubilant life afterwards."

It was strange to see such sadness play out, to see "Mr. Billionaire" square himself to face a world of indifference, as if that was all he could ever hope for. Around him was the usual high-pitched chaos, King filibustering ("I liken the three belts to the Father, Son, and Holy Ghost"), Steve "Crocodile" Fitch bellowing ("Pound for pound!"), and John Horne complaining about "lies and innuendos" in the media ("Ninety percent of what you guys do is not real, not fair, not right").

126

And Tyson sat quietly in the gloom of his own making. "My objective," he said, "is to think no one cares about me, and I guess that makes me the person I am."

All this self-pity on display caused a lot of people to remember it had been a while since they'd seen Tyson smile. For some reason, thinking back on it, this headlong drive toward fame and fortune had not been accompanied by much visible pleasure on Tyson's part. All his public moments, such as they were, had sounded more like cries for help.

A Q&A with Tyson that *Ring* magazine published in its March issue read like a suicide hotline transcript. Although *Ring* editor Steve Farhood said Tyson didn't seem particularly depressed at their meeting, Tyson's words certainly suggested a problem with self-esteem that surely was unique among billionaires, or even millionaires on the make.

Though Tyson insisted that when he was "right, there's no one can stand a chance, even at this stage of my life," he was also doubtful of his impact on boxing. "When you think about it," he told Farhood, "even though I'm a fighter, I've never really done anything with fighting. You see me on the rag magazines or some other kind of magazines, but I've never done anything or offered anything to the sport to give me the stature that I have now. I've never really done anything tremendous for the sport."

And he didn't feel he was doing that well out of the ring, either. He pledged his allegiance to King, but elsewhere in the interview suggested he was wary of those closest to him. "Sometimes I feel like everyone hates me," he said. "It's like that phobia, paranoia. I don't like to be around people, and I think everyone has a motive, an agenda that's not in my best interests."

He added, "I sometimes lose a high opinion of myself. You just don't feel cool . . . in retrospect you deal with what happened but you lose a lot of self-esteem."

Farhood tried to steer Tyson onto boxing topics, but then

shrewdly realized that he had a fighter on the couch, not the canvas. Farhood asked him about the possibility of fear in the ring and got this: "I find myself more nervous now than in the beginning of my career or when I was champion. Maybe it's a slight insecurity. Even in training, I find myself taking that last breath. I don't know if it's good or not. I know what to do, but you have those doubts. I guess that's what pisses you off—you have those doubts about yourself even though you've been successful for so many years."

Asked about losing to Buster Douglas, Tyson went off on a rant that, in cold print, seemed more melodramatic than anything else. "People say, 'Look how much money you have.' But I've been through a bunch of dysfunctional evaluations. I just can't imagine anybody being jealous of my life. If they had to go through what I went through, they'd probably kill themselves."

Tyson finished that thought off by relating how he fought off his demons, barely. When the fear that he had finally snapped hit him, "I almost died. My hair started turning gray and falling out because I was thinking of these things. . . . I could've snapped then but instead I just got out and just went and ran all day. I just went and ran. I just went and ran in place in my room. . . . I'd get in the shower and then, boom, it just hits you again."

Tyson was on a roll, as if he didn't often get to discuss his anxieties. Would Horne and Holloway countenance such disturbing thoughts? "I just expect the worst of things to happen now," Tyson continued. "If good things happen, I enjoy them. But I expect the worst things to happen. I expect to be dumped on all my life."

But what about Bruno, what about pounding him senseless? Won't his life be improved then? Tyson thought so. Hoped so. "I just need to get my confidence back," he said. "After I have that fight with Bruno and I have the belt around my waist, there's nobody who could beat me. My confidence will rise to the sky, to the stars."

Had he ever sounded so confused, so vulnerable? Farhood, who had gone into the interview hoping for a boxing-oriented piece, ended up leaving pretty down himself after so much fatalistic conversation. "I took the Amtrak home," he remembered, "and I was feeling very depressed. All I could think as I was leaving there was, I'm glad I'm not Mike Tyson."

Only Tyson, among all his money-counting associates, apparently realized the unpopularity of his campaign. The money was rolling in, but affection and respect were being withheld, and Tyson felt their absence like a blow to the liver. Indeed, many of those blows were decidedly below the belt, and they were being inflicted without penalty. He seemed to have realized early on that he was more likely to be harassed than cheered. This from a questioner on a national media conference call: "Mike, is there any truth to the rumors you've got some eye injury and, if so, is that from the effects of all those years of Mace during sex?" Tyson said nothing.

The boxing hadn't been there, and the charisma was a reverse one—the whole comeback had been a falsehood that just provoked more ridicule and further humiliation. There were no long-lasting rewards to his awkward pummeling of McNeeley and Mathis. Victories just aroused more doubt. Only the savage beating of Bruno could possibly correct this. It was the only tool for redemption at hand.

This was not Bruno's take on the subject, although he was pleased to hear Tyson's desperation. Bruno's idea after all this chitchat was that Tyson was confused, which is exactly where he wanted him. "I'm going to do Mike Tyson a favor," Bruno announced the week of the fight. "I'm going to take him out and take him away from all this. He's bored and frustrated. He doesn't want all this."

Forgotten, as was most history whenever Brits returned to

American soil, was Tyson's state of mind for their first meeting in 1989. If Bruno thought Tyson was out of it for this fight, then the knockout had removed a significant amount of his memory—at least everything he'd learned about Tyson to that point. Tyson, somebody in Bruno's camp should have recalled, was a genuine mess back then.

In the year before their first meeting, Tyson had created a time line of self-destruction that, to this day, seems harrowing enough to support even Tyson's most alarming comments. Yes, some people probably would kill themselves. Or at the very least, their hair would turn gray.

In that time he had married actress Robin Givens, been humiliated by her on national TV when she told Barbara Walters that her husband was a violent manic-depressive, gotten divorced. He'd broken his hand in a street fight with Mitch Green over . . . nobody was really sure what. He'd gone to Jimmy Jacobs's funeral, suffered the hounding of King, fired Bill Cayton and Kevin Rooney, signed with King. He wrecked a BMW on the lawn of Cus D'Amato's property, the single-vehicle accident becoming a suicide try in the tabloids. He'd become fat—260 pounds—and was often drunk, by his own sorry admission.

It was quite a turbulent time, in addition to the usual excesses of his youthful career, the high-speed, wee-hours trips to Los Angeles during training in Las Vegas, the long nights in the Crazy Horse Saloon where the girls provided lap dances, no strings attached, G or otherwise. If there had ever been a fighter who was bored or frustrated, this was the guy. Had Bruno taken him away from all this back then, Tyson might truly have thanked him. Alas, it was Buster Douglas a year later, during a time when Tyson had upped the recreational ante and was jetting from Tokyo to New York to club-hop during training, who provided Tyson the relief Bruno might have given him.

A Savage Business

Bruno was hopeful all the same, saying he was better prepared to give Tyson his emotional freedom this time around than he'd been before. "As a fighter," he said, "I'm nastier than I was when I came here to challenge him. I'm the champion and I've been working regularly, while he hasn't taken a proper punch in four years. The sparring partners he's got are scared of him. Well, I'm not scared of him and he'll be taking punches from me. I really believe I can knock him out."

Bruno was a pretty transparent fellow, but there was this one area of mystery within him: Who knew what winning the title would mean to Bruno? One of his strange and admirable qualities was that repeated failure didn't particularly daunt him. He remained as positive as ever, even after one title loss after another—Tim Witherspoon, Lennox Lewis, and of course Tyson. Coming back to England in 1989 he told a throng of fans at Heathrow Airport, "I proved he's only human. He can be hurt."

This determination had made him a national hero way out of proportion to his accomplishments. The British fans loved him. Following his loss to Tyson, the airport crowd he had tried to reassure broke through police barricades to get to him, cameramen climbing on each other's backs to snap pictures of the bruised Brit.

His failings in the ring—his lack of stamina, his stiffness, his poor chin—were offset in his countrymen's minds by his power and strength. Also, his good-natured affability; he was, in fact, a national treasure in England, appearing in commercials and Christmas productions called "pantomimes." Perhaps it wasn't so much that England loved a loser as that the country was simply used to having one. There hadn't been an English-born heavyweight champ since the turn of the century, after all.

The fact that Bruno became one was due more to King's

desperate need to sew up all the contenders than Bruno's actual desirability as a heavyweight fighter. "Frank Bruno was in no-man's-land," said his promoter, Frankie Warren. "He had gotten beat in three title fights and this would be his last throw of the dice." Bruno and Warren were absolutely delighted to give King the rights to his next four or five fights, should he beat McCall. "He was out in the cold," Warren said. King, for his part, was up-front about it: "Whatever happens," King told Bruno in London, "I'm the Mike Tyson man. I'd like to see McCall beat you, but I want Tyson to win the title." In other words, King could care less who kept the title for him.

When Bruno survived Oliver McCall's two-round rally at the end of their fight more than a year earlier, he naturally achieved an Olympian prominence in Great Britain. According to Warren, they had "pilfered" the title. Warren had installed two of Bruno's loudest stablemates, Naseem Hamed and Nigel Benn, at the ringposts in Wembley Stadium. "They got McCall's attention," Warren boasted. "As we've seen, McCall is not very focused in a fight. He's not got great concentration." However they worked it, England couldn't have been prouder of them. Bruno still wasn't the country's best heavyweight—the Canadian-raised Lennox Lewis was more highly regarded and he was about to go to court to force a deserved title shot—but he was its champion.

The effect Bruno's win had on England, though, was probably nothing compared to what it did for Bruno. Having gone through every champion's rite of passage—seeing Don King discard one fallen champion in the ring, walk over, and anoint the winner as "My man!" (and promise delivery of a red Bentley for his new loyalty)—Bruno was the picture of confidence. "I don't want to be flashy or cocky," he said, "but I'm the champion. I hope you realize that—the champion. It's one hundred years since a British heavyweight, Bob Fitzsimmons, won it in the ring." In case anybody didn't understand his reference to Lewis, who had been awarded the title after Bowe trashed it, he added, "I emphasize that—won it in the ring."

Bruno was at such ease the week of the fight, bolstered by the plane loads of supporters who were flying in, that he had begun addressing whatever Americans he saw as "Bob," usually trying out some accent on them. "I have very superior confidence," he explained. "You don't get them sort of championships at the sweet shop or the supermarket. I've been working sixteen years to get that, Bob."

It was as if he'd forgotten all about their 1989 meeting, after which Tyson had been so disdainful of his competition; following the Bruno knockout Tyson had said, "How dare they challenge me with their primitive skills?" Amazingly, the experience had been totally lost on Bruno, and he was now swaggering about Las Vegas promising to do the country a much-needed service.

"Nearly every single American I meet wants me to teach him a lesson," Bruno said. "The American people want me to do a job. They want me to do Tyson a favor and wipe him out."

And he thought it should be easy. Having looked into Tyson's eyes at one of those staged confrontations to announce their fight in December, Bruno was surer than ever. "I didn't see positive," he said. "I didn't see balance and focus. I saw blinking. He don't want to be here. He's coming out of prison, and he's made his money."

This talk reassured him greatly, made him increasingly bold. "He can't answer a question straight," Bruno continued. "Is he here? He doesn't seem here. He seems spacy. Well, he'll be more spacy when this [his left hand] or this [his right] gets him. There'll be more stars on the American flag that night, I'm telling you, Bob."

Bruno had become so confident that he had begun taking umbrage at Tyson's top billing. Even though he was a 10-1 underdog among bettors, Bruno thought his place as title-holder should have earned him more respect than the promotion seemed to be giving him. "The Championship Part I," as King called it, did not suggest to Bruno that his new Bentley-giving friend expected him to be around much past the national anthem. Shouldn't the champion be on the top floor, Bruno wondered, "like Tom Jones, Mike Tyson, and Don King"?

Also, he didn't much care for Team Tyson, which as usual provided the routine ugliness. Several weeks before, Horne had said, "Frank Bruno couldn't beat Mike in ten years. He might end up dead. I hope not." Bruno made it clear he didn't hold Tyson responsible for the remarks. "He's probably a nice guy, but he's got some amateurs and naughty people around him."

King was delighted Bruno was willing to help promote the fight and had to agree that he "grows on you like a tooth-ache." King was also pleased at the British turnout Bruno was producing—between 3,500 and 5,000 transoceanic fans. And he couldn't fail to profit from England's first-ever pay-per-view event, Bruno's popularity assuring sales even for a 4 A.M. showing. But King insisted there was no surprise, that he could have predicted the attraction, having himself seen Bruno in the middle of Trafalgar Square, "the pigeons forming a halo and descending on Frank Bruno." It must have been an extraordinary sight.

Tyson, again, was refusing to carry any part of the load. It was left to his two young comanagers to stir the pot, although Holloway wasn't much of a pot stirrer. His contribution to the international debate had been to inform the press that Tyson was home at his "training house," as opposed to his "nice mansion," by 6 P.M. every night, had an evening work-out, and was in bed by 9 P.M. Not too many writers fashioned a story out of that nugget. But anything more, Holloway insisted, would be "biographical stuff."

Holloway did allow that Tyson had become freshly interested in "family values," which was predictable since he was now 29, had been engaged to Monica Turner, and on Valentine's Day had become father to the eight-pound, 10-ounce Rayna. "Mike is most ecstatic about his newborn child," Holloway said. "This is a pivotal time in Mike's life. He has a new sense of family values."

Except for saying that boxing was second in his life, "next to my children," Tyson could not be made to comment on his personal life. Or anything, really. For this fight, Holloway became the spokesman, but less about the "biographical stuff" than about Tyson's typical demolition of the sparring staff.

This talk was occasioned by a bulletin in the New York *Daily News* that quoted sparring partner José Ribalta as saying that Tyson was very hittable. Not really, said his camp. "I can truly say this," Holloway said. "We started out with fourteen sparring partners and there's only three left. They can't stand up! Mike's utilizing his jab, his footwork, he sees everything coming and he has a dead calm about him. He doesn't waste energy like he used to. Like yesterday, he wanted to work. He knocked out two sparring partners. Before this, I've never seen him destroy guys like this. They're leaving in the middle of the night. They won't even collect their pay."

Unfortunately, the press was as likely to be able to confirm this awful carnage as they were to see pigeons form a halo above Bruno's noggin. Such bloodshed, however instructional it might have been, was kept behind closed doors. Holloway was asked, if Tyson really was wasting his staff again and if he really did look that wonderful, why the workouts were closed. "We have our reasons," he said.

Short of scanning the obits, there was no way to ascertain

the sparring partners' true well-being. But there was one definite casualty, and that was trainer Jay Bright, the lone holdover from the D'Amato dynasty. Just over a week before the fight Bright told some writers that Tyson was a little sluggish and that he had ended his sparring after four rounds. "He was a little off," he said. "He just wasn't picking himself up. He was just flat. It was a flat day. He has looked a lot better. I think he could have done a lot better."

That was the last thing anybody heard from Bright, one of the few nonthreatening workers in Tyson's camp. From that day forth, Bright wasn't allowed to discuss Tyson except with the permission of Horne and Holloway. He'd been gagged. This was a rather amazing development to everybody but the rest of Team Tyson. "How do you criticize your fighter days before a fight?" said Howie Evans, who operated the lower tier of Tyson's nonpublicity offices.

Bright had never been a high-profile part of the team, not even taking the dais at the press conferences. Crocodile, by his presence at these ceremonial occasions, occupied a place of more importance. Bright simply lurked about, sometimes sitting among the rabble in the back of the room.

He was not thought to be doing that much for Tyson anyway, except perhaps as keeper of the flame. Only he and Tyson were left from D'Amato's Catskills school, both having joined the old man in their early teens. They were nothing alike, of course. Bright, six years older, joined the complicated household in 1973 after the death of his parents and became another son to Cus—another disciple, really. "He's the best person I've ever met in my life," Bright has said. Bright's interests, though, were more domestic than pugilistic and the rival trainers there, Kevin Rooney and Teddy Atlas, derided him for his ability to make a quiche while they were making fighters. In addition, as a youngster, Bright had hopes of taking the stage, not the ring. This produced many guffaws.

Still, he was a loyal member of the family and observed plenty. When Rooney was finally fired in the King takeover, Bright kept the D'Amato connection going by assisting in Tyson's corner, beginning with the Bruno fight. He worked under Aaron Snowell and Richie Giachetti, and eventually became the lead trainer, a predictably witless bystander in Douglas's destruction of Tyson in Tokyo.

So there was definitely speculation about his position when Tyson returned to boxing in 1992. In fact, Willie Rush was the principal trainer, with Bright being called the cotrainer. But Tyson was not comfortable under Rush, and Bright again became his main man in the corner. Bright could duplicate Cus's prattle, call out the numbers that dictated the punches in the old man's scheme, and just generally provide the fighter a sort of nostalgia. Given Tyson's opponents, and everybody's considerable estimation of his power at that time, not much was thought to be required.

Muzzling him, though, reminded everybody just who was in charge, who was running a significant part of Tyson's career. It was the two boyhood chums, Siegfried and Rory they were called, the men who made Tyson disappear.

Business insiders knew that Horne was not instrumental in the contracts, as he often suggested he was. King called Horne "Candy Slim" and pretended to have much affection for this apprentice, this eager kid learning at his knee. Still, King did the deals. If Horne and Holloway contributed anything, it was atmosphere. It was Horne's comments that set the tone, fight by fight, the contempt dripping from his voice as he spoke for the fighter. It was Horne who established and maintained Team Tyson's paranoia, who managed at least one ugly comment per opponent, who projected hate into the promotions.

His assumption of power was not unique in boxing. Managers routinely adopted the importance and secondhand jeopardy of their fighters, but Horne seemed to enjoy his position way too much, using this new platform for his own grandiose purposes. He was not well liked outside Team Tyson, is one way to put it.

Putting the gag on Bright, who accepted it meekly ("It's only sensible for them to arrange my interviews," he said later), was one more piece of evidence that Tyson was not masterminding this comeback. He was not actively involved, at least, to the extent that he would speak for his camp or otherwise indicate that he was in charge of the team. King was; chums were. People spoke for him, whether it was King or Crocodile or Horne, and Tyson seemed to like it that way just fine.

Tyson stood aside from the fray, looking bored, his face registering nothing. His detachment was phenomenal. His talkers created the comfortable din he seemed to want, and the comeback continued no matter what he felt or didn't feel like contributing. He was merely the instrument of destruction, presented at the last minute when everyone's interest had finally begun to flag.

On fight night, for just such a Tyson unveiling, the MGM Grand underwent its usual international transformation. The casino had always been alert to a kind of ethnic marketing and regularly presented Cinco de Mayo cards featuring Mexican boxers—usually Chavez—that drew tremendous Hispanic crowds. This time, instead of featuring the Spanish-speaking hotshots from Mexico's more prosperous regions, the hotel had the look and sound of a soccer match. That is to say, for all the expense that the trip might have required, the Brits thronging the craps tables looked decidedly unaristocratic. In addition, their obvious commitment to fun and the consumption of beer and other beverages was more predictive of a riot than close attention or constrained cheering Saturday night.

A Savage Business

Outside the ring, they thronged the walk to the Grand Garden before the fight, an unusual assembly even by Las Vegas standards, hoisting Union Jacks, drinking beer, and singing songs that featured Bruno in their impromptu lyrics. It was quite a sight and sound, so many mad dogs and Englishmen cheering their impossible dream. Then again, their loyalty to Bruno had survived defeat before, and it didn't seem that victory was a very important requirement for the night's entertainment.

Bruno himself may have taken the same attitude. The blustering Brit, the man who watched Tyson beat Mathis and then said, "I whip this punk's ass," seemed to suffer a severe loss of nerve on his way to the ring on Saturday night. His promoter, Frankie Warren, said, "He changed. He felt the whole world was against him. As soon as the TV production guy opened the door to the dressing room, it was as if somebody put a pin in him and took the air out." The confidence that he was presumed to have as a freshly coined champion continued to escape with each step he took to the ring. Bruno watchers were aghast at the fighter's sudden interest in religion; between leaving his dressing room and the conclusion of "God Save the Queen," Bruno crossed himself at least a dozen times. (Not everybody's count was the same, but the ringside average was 12. Warren, who was with him on the walk, said, "He must have done it fifty times." Later, back in England, they wrote that he looked like the Pope on speed.)

"Fearless Frank" didn't look so good standing up there next to Tyson, who was ghoulishly outfitted in his black towel, pacing impatiently back and forth, Crocodile's mouth motoring away at his ear, giving him a one-man pep rally. "Big Frank," whose sculpted body ought to have instilled fear in Tyson, instead seemed to be shrinking into some smaller version of himself. Warren said later that he "just froze. I was interested to see what would happen if he could get to five, six rounds, but . . ." "Our Frank" was about to let down an entire country.

It wasn't that he lost, which is what those 10-1 odds suggested would happen anyway. It wasn't that he got knocked out; Bruno always gets knocked out. It was the physical manifestation of fear that was so shocking and, to his countrymen, disappointing. Intimidation was the one weapon that survived intact in Tyson's arsenal, but even so, neither McNeeley nor Mathis had seemed to dissolve so entirely in the face of it.

In his own defense, Bruno later said, "He was on me like a harbor shark," a colorful and accurate enough version of Tyson's attack. If Bruno had meant to take a second in the ring and somehow formulate his bravery, he planned badly because he never had the time. Tyson lashed out with a right hand immediately and Bruno realized that none of his many prayers were going to be answered.

Bruno tried to fight back, his punches whistling over and beyond Tyson's head as the fighter bent at the waist to duck them. Tyson's lead rights bore in on Bruno repeatedly, and one of them may have been responsible for an inch-long gash over the Brit's left eye, which opened toward the end of the first round.

Disaster was unfolding, on schedule. It was like a "scary" police chase or a "deadly" tornado. The outcome was inevitable and now impossible to imagine otherwise. The funnel cloud chewed up the scenery, chewed it up and spit out the pieces, and the audience leaned forward so as not to miss an uprooted barn or a flying tanker truck. A 247-pound man, all muscle, was about to be ripped from his own earthly moorings.

Bruno meanwhile had determined that a reasonable strategy might include clinching and holding and hoping for the best. His long jab had proved useless, so he used his reach to encircle the challenger. In the first round alone he had clinched 15 times, drawing two warnings from the referee, Mills Lane.

Bruno fell into 15 more clinches in the second round and was even penalized a point for one of them. Tyson also registered his disgust, shoving his left elbow into Bruno's throat. But Bruno didn't really have much more to do, his few serious blows landing without any effect on Tyson. Less than a minute into the third round, Tyson ended Bruno's pitiful pantomime with a right to the body that made the champion wince, then a left hook, then 13 power punches, of which nine landed. Bruno slid down the ropes, a pathetic slurry of a boxer, and Lane stopped the fight just 50 seconds into the third.

Just like that, Tyson had regained one of his championships, and it indeed seemed he was immediately preparing for a jubilant life. He knelt head-down on the canvas, walked over to Bruno's corner and hugged him and kissed him twice and laid his own head on Bruno's, where pigeons once formed halos. The moment certainly was a felt one for Tyson, his remote manner now informed with gratitude. He turned to the crowd and threw more kisses and, squaring up his own squat musculature, pointed to the gaudy green belt he now wore and thumped it, his snarl telling his pride.

His performance would be criticized, of course. Bowe told his hometown paper, the New York *Daily News,* that Tyson was in for trouble if that was the best he could do. "The greatest sin in boxing is to leave yourself wide open," he said. In fact, the fight of the evening was thought to be the women's match between Christy Martin, King's house queen, and Deirdre Gogarty, a "special attraction" that provided more action than any other fight on the card. Still, others were impressed with Tyson, somewhat. They thought he had reclaimed some of his old magic. He moved his head, he went to the body, and he was plenty powerful. Buster Douglas spoke for a lot of people: "He looked pretty good to me."

It was true, he looked pretty good against Frank Bruno, whose effort was less valiant than anybody'd hoped. But Tyson had done what he'd set out to do and he'd done it with some style. The finishing flurry was all the drama you could pay for. It was the mobile home sailing over an Oklahoma field, the overturned Buick at the end of the police chase, the cops standing by the sprung doors, their guns drawn. Bruno hadn't been very game, but the jeopardy in which he'd been placed seemed genuine enough.

Tyson seemed pleased, although he was wary, too. He never did go to a press conference afterward, but when Showtime announcer Ferdie Pacheco asked him inside the ring how it felt to be champion, Tyson allowed that he couldn't be sure. In his comparative jubilation, he would be cautious. "Less than a year ago," he said, "I was in a cell under harsh treatment. It's going to take a few days to sink in."

Bruno slunk back to England, where he got off much easier than he had in the States, where he was considered to have disgraced himself. There, he was gently advised to retire. "Do us all a favor, Frank," the *Sun* pleaded in an editorial, "and spare us any more agony. You've been one of our greatest sportsmen and everyone admires you. . . . We don't want to see you on the rope again." Others weren't so accepting of the result. Trainer Emanuel Steward said, "Instead of shorts, he should have been wearing diapers." Tyson's former trainer, Richie Giachetti, said, "That guy is sick. That was the most disgraceful performance I have ever seen."

Later that summer Bruno would announce his retirement because of eye injuries. He would tell his countrymen that his doctor said he could lose the sight in one eye with a blow to the head and that, in all likelihood, he couldn't pass the vision part of the physical if he tried.

"We've all had a big cut of the cake," he said. "I've had my fair share and I don't want to be greedy." His countrymen allowed his retirement gracefully enough and he preserved his fame, no matter what had happened in the ring that night. Afterward he made mouthwash commercials, played the part of a bus driver in a Spice Girls movie, and made frequent cameos on TV shows.

Greed was left to more practiced men than him. Tyson had not left the building in his black utility vehicle before negotiations were beginning for the next financial takedown. King promised that "this is the Tyson era and we will fight all the champions, then we'll fight all the contenders and pretenders." This was reasonable, if you happened to believe that King's champions were the most worthy opponents available. Certainly they were the most desirable for Tyson, considering risk-reward ratios. But nobody else believed that Seldon and Botha were even deserving of title shots. And lawsuits were already chipping away at King's quickly constructed monopoly.

Bruce Seldon, the ceremonial WBA champ, was supposed to be next, but Lennox Lewis was claiming he was next in line. The WBC had earlier said that Lewis was to get the winner of the McCall-Bruno fight. When that didn't happen, Lewis brought suit in New Jersey, where his promoter operates. And Francois Botha, who was taking care of the IBF title for Tyson, was also being challenged in the courts. Botha had been ordered by the IBF to defend against Michael Moorer, as had been previously arranged, but when the drug test from Botha's fight with Axel Schulz showed steroids in the White Buffalo's meat, Schulz's promoters sued for a rematch.

The neat and orderly scenario had started unraveling the day before the Bruno fight, when a New Jersey judge issued an order barring Tyson from signing a contract to fight anyone other than Lewis until the latter's suit against the WBC was resolved. It was ironic, of course, that King might be ensnared by the same political and legal machinery that he had employed to gain his three champions. Worthier fighters than his own were trying to get a cut of the same cake that Bruno had been unable to digest.

King was going to need money and some legal luck to work through these challenges, which he was prepared to do. There was too much money, all of it easy, to let Lennox's dreaded promoters, Main Events and HBO, into the game. Maybe Bowe would have maneuvered himself back into position by then. Maybe Holyfield or Foreman. These fighters were not only dangerous to Tyson, but they were promoted by other men. They were to be avoided at all costs. King sighed at the amount of work that lay before him. "I need a fair Jewishprudence," he said, forecasting a siege of litigation on both sides that, presumably, would be nondenominational.

King would be besieged on other fronts as well. Six days after the Bruno fight, Tyson popped up, telling writers on a teleconference call that he had been getting jobbed at King's cashier cage. "I think I deserve a lot more than thirty million," he said, "and I don't think I've been getting what I'm entitled."

King's own greed was proving contagious. "I have children to take care of," said Tyson on the nationwide hookup, as jaws went slack from coast to coast. "Nobody cares if my children are starving, if my children are on welfare. Nobody's gonna give me no handouts and say, 'You are a great champion, we owe you this.'"

"Mr. Billionaire" was using the athlete's classic appeal—he was doing it for his family. The exploitation—being made to fight for $65 million his first year out of prison—could not be endured on their behalf.

A Savage Business

The source of this outburst, however, was not Tyson's examination of his own bank account, but a small-type item about King's. The week of the Bruno fight, there surfaced a small piece of news concerning King and his deal with the MGM Grand. It seemed that King, after negotiating a $100 million contract for Tyson out of the MGM Grand and Showtime, had gotten himself a bonus for so much good work: According to filings to the Securities and Exchange Commission, the MGM had given King an interest-free loan of $15 million to buy 600,000 shares of the company's stock. The deal included a stock-price guarantee that assured King a profit of at least $15 million by the contract's conclusion.

Tyson might have wondered where his cut was. "Regarding what is a fair share," he continued, "I don't wish to discuss too much of that at this particular time. When it comes right down to it, fuck the bullshit. I'm not being treated fairly. That's what it really comes down to.

"I truly believe," he warned, "that with what I have done in boxing, if I don't get what I want, I might as well say fuck my whole career."

King got one more scare a month later, when a 25-year-old woman said Tyson had sexually assaulted her in a Chicago nightclub. The woman, LaDonna August, was not a beauty queen but did work in a beauty salon in Merrillville, Indiana. She said Tyson bit her on the cheek while kissing and fondling her. However, patrons and the manager of The Clique, a Southside watering hole, wouldn't back up the woman's claim, saying Tyson was surrounded by bodyguards (the club's) and friends, that he never went into a private area, and that he was, for that matter, drinking nothing stronger than water. The case went away quickly enough, provoking more sympathy for Tyson the target than embarrassment for him. However, not a few people wondered what Tyson the family man was doing in The Clique to begin with.

Richard Hoffer

It was growing obvious, if it never had been, that the road to that first billion, whether it be Tyson's or King's, would have to be traveled at some speed. The ride was getting bumpy.

Chapter Seven

"The punches were buzzing my brain"

A heavyweight title fight produces a lot of electricity, mainly because it places in a confined space two men, each weighing more than 200 pounds, each with the ability and desire to deliver shuddering and incapacitating blows to the head. Heavyweights are rarely as artful as their smaller brethren, hardly ever develop the skills and finesse that lighter men depend on. They do not devise and execute complicated strategies, do not rely so much on footwork or other niceties of their game, do not peck, weave, or dance. What they mainly do is position themselves across from their opponent and, as opportunity permits, throw the heavy hand that blanks out an entire nervous system, empties a man's head so completely that no activity is possible beyond shallow breathing and the spasmodic twitching of a leg.

There is nothing like a knockout.

Some fans—purists—guiltily defend their sport by favoring the technicians, the athletes whose hit-and-not-get-hit credo celebrates a more refined idea of self-defense. It can be a sweet science, they tell you, if you are just educated enough in the sport to appreciate a man's feints, his bobs, his overall ring generalship. Perhaps. But in heavyweight boxing, for sure, the attention always falls upon the man who can most regularly short-circuit another, the man who can rattle his opponent's brainpan with devastating consequence.

You hardly need ask why. The finality, the authority, the clear-cut superiority that a knockout demonstrates is sports' greatest conclusion. Even boxing, where might most often makes right, is cluttered by a system of judging so subjective that the individuals within a panel can seldom agree. But a knockout answers the question, beyond a doubt, of who won.

And there is the pure spectacle of it. Nobody wants to see somebody get hurt, not badly, anyway, but everybody enjoys the sight of a man collapsing, sometimes as if in sections, to the floor of the ring. Who knows what this says about human nature, but people who otherwise celebrate life also thrill to certain kinds of destruction: Train wrecks, building demolitions, knockouts—these produce a strange satisfaction, a titillation that might be obscene, in entirely healthy people.

Mike Tyson's growing fortune was made possible by his ability to generate a calamitous event. His career, in fact, was jump-started by a series of videos made by Jimmy Jacobs and Bill Cayton, who had made a decision to film every one of Tyson's fights, even those first ones that weren't televised. Edited down to the fight's climax—say, a man named Robert Colay landing on the seat of his shorts in the first 30 seconds of the bout—these cassettes were distributed one at a time to a list of 35 to 40 boxing writers and other mood makers. Later Jacobs and Cayton stitched them together into a series of 10 convulsions that was mailed to many of the country's sportswriters. The effect of these cassettes was nearly pornographic—money shots, one after the other.

Tyson's 15 knockouts in 1985 made for some pretty vivid footage. After one full year of boxing, he had fought 19 times and he had dematerialized his opponent on each occasion. Heavyweight boxing was in horrible condition at this point, so the tapes of this concussive little monster began exciting interest. Before 1985 was out, his first year as a pro, he had appeared on the *Today* show, on *David Letterman*, and had been profiled in *Sports Illustrated*, all thanks to his punching power.

His was a promising novelty. He was too young, too inexperienced to be a factor in the division, and even through the first half of 1986, when he was fighting William Hosea and Lorenzo Boyd, he was still confined to forgettable competition. But those knockouts made him something better than a champion (though he'd become one before 1986 was over). "It made him a household name," said Cayton. He was a property.

Just two days after Tyson knocked out Steve Zouski in March 1985, HBO recognized the meaning of these violent conclusions and signed him to the first of their contracts, $450,000 a bout, with the idea that Tyson would soon enter its title unification tournament. His showstopping power could no longer be ignored.

Tyson had moved into that special category of fighter, the knockout artist—men of force, pent-up frustration, what have you. He was joining the legendary punchers, like Rocky Marciano, George Foreman, Joe Louis, Sonny Liston, and Jack Dempsey. These were men who not only were reliable when it came to the knockout but were deadly flamboyant as well. Though Tyson never did drive bone into an opponent's brain, as he once said he had tried to do, he probably came close enough many times. Certainly he belonged right there with Jack Johnson, who left the ring after a vicious knockout and discovered two of Stanley Ketchel's teeth in his glove.

Following the Bruno fight, Tyson's knockout percentage went to 84, third best among the heavyweights, behind Marciano and Foreman. Strangely, nobody had ever discovered the trick of kinesiology responsible for this high ratio. His fast hands, delivered from his squat stance, somehow translated his square musculature into a source of horrible impact. Beyond that, nobody could say. There just wasn't much research being done on the subject.

The puncher's ability to concentrate such tremendous force onto a small area—a temple, for example—has never really been analyzed. Archie Moore, who was the all-time leader in knockouts with 145, assumed like everybody else that it was just a physical condition that you either had or did not. When he was working Foreman's corner for the Ali fight in Zaire, a fight that was widely presumed to guarantee Ali's mortal injury, Moore let it be known that Foreman's power was a product of such high and inborn physics that it could not really be laid out for the common man, or ever developed by the ordinary citizen. "Foreman has TNT in his mitts," Moore said, "and nuclearology as well." He had been born that way.

Foreman's career was the best case for boxing's natural-warhead theory. The tonnage was simply there, an act of nature that man could neither build nor destroy. This, of course, was absolutely proved over time. As he aged, Foreman's power remained entirely intact, undisturbed by diet or inactivity or the preacher's temperament. Keep in mind Moore's promise, all those years back in Africa, that even if Big George happened to miss with one of his punches, "the whoosh of air will lower the ninety-degree temperature in Zaire very considerably." Now, consider what Bert Cooper— good old Bert—said after he was konked by a 40-year-old Foreman in the early and most awkward stage of the big man's comeback: "The punches were buzzing my brain."

Later, at the age of 45, Foreman still had the freakish power to reverse a losing effort with a single sweep of his huge right arm. Michael Moorer, who had been relaxed and confident of easy victory in their 1994 title fight, inexplicably circled into the maw of blackness and afterward lay for several seconds on his back, blinking uncontrollably, his brain having been buzzed.

Tyson was not the thudding, detonating puncher that Foreman was and, even with his remarkable percentage, was not usually a one-shot kind of fighter. He had no nuclearology. But his power, which had more to do with his hand speed, was unmistakable, and any combination of unobstructed head shots was sure to still the synapses in his opponent's jellified cerebellum.

More mysterious, however, than a fighter's ability to deliver the doomsday blow was the other fighter's ability to accept it. Some could and some couldn't. Bruno, for all his mass and the thickness of his neck, simply couldn't. This was an unlucky truth for Bruno, who became so wobbly after big exchanges that it was just part of his shtick, a predictable and lamentable flaw, a precondition that his countrymen largely accepted. It was too bad. Some fighters had glass chins, others' were impossible to crack. Bruno's was crystalline. The neurology was unexplainable.

Certainly fighters found the subject beyond their reach. To be knocked out, no matter the strength of the chin, is to be sent into a never-never-land from which no experience is ever returned. To judge from their vague tales, it is a relatively painless journey, the only complication being confusion and a sense of dislocation. Tommy Morrison, who was never knocked cold in his own heavyweight wars but did suffer a memorably savage beating from Ray Mercer, could only recall a sensation of "lost time." Evander Holyfield suffered a hard head punch in an amateur fight and, though he fought on, didn't remember one thing about the bout. Didn't even think he'd had one. "I went home and my mother asked me how I did," he recalled, "and I said that the coach never let me fight. I couldn't understand why he did that. The next day I realized what happened."

To suffer such "lost time," to have a hole in your life like that, is apparently beyond language. I once asked heavyweight contender–bon vivant Tex Cobb what it was like to get hit by Earnie Shavers, a man whose single skill was the projection of force upon his opponent. He had the nuclearology. Cobb—who was indeed hit hard by Shavers but somehow endured, remained upright, and even won the fight—was a man very friendly with the English language. But he was visibly frustrated by the question, his inability to articulate the singular sensation, the shock, the sudden unavailability of motor skills, the overall bewilderment.

Cobb ought to have been able to describe what it was like to take a punch, since that was his chief asset as a boxer, the taking of punches. He had horrified a nation, or at least Howard Cosell, by continually wading into Larry Holmes's fists in a title fight years before, his mug a terrible paste of running flesh before the night was over. He made no apologies for his willing absorption of punishment, especially as he extracted good paydays for it, his best being the one for the Holmes beating. The story from that fight was that he took his $500,000 purse (this was $200,000 less than the contracted amount after King had docked Cobb for failure to publicize the 1982 fight) and disappeared to Australia, coming home broke several weeks later. "He spent it on beer," a friend said, "so it's not like he wasted it." The wages of chin.

But sitting in his living room in Nashville, where he had gone with his wife in the late 1980s to become a country songwriter, he was actually upset that he couldn't properly describe the condition. "Stand up," he said to me, leaving the room to get a telephone book. "Hold this in front of your chest." This was all said with an authority that brooked no question, no "What in God's name is going on." Plus, it was happening very fast.

Happily, I was taping the interview; otherwise I wouldn't

have been able to reconstruct the event, so suddenly did it occur. Listening to it the next day, though, I could restore the fighter's familiar sense of "lost time," re-create a vacant part of my life with secondhand sources.

There was on the tape, first of all, the voice of Cobb's wife saying, "Stand him in front of the couch, honey," as if some old family parlor trick was about to be reenacted. There was, second, a loud whomp that sounded surprisingly hollow, something like a baseball bat being struck against an inner tube. Third, there was a clatter, perhaps of ashtrays or dishes or other ceramic pieces that were on a table behind the couch. There were then several seconds of quiet, all objects coming to a complete rest; spinning ashtrays slowing to a stop, the tape unspooling silently. Finally a thin, tremulous voice could be heard, perhaps coming from behind the couch but who could tell? "Geez, Tex," it said, kind of pitifully. And that was it, except for some booming laughter that was much easier to place.

That, it turned out, was simply a blow to the chest, and probably not one delivered at full strength, though it's true that Cobb was never a cautious man (he might have decided to throw caution to the wind, see what he could do with a sportswriter). It was also important for me to remember, so as not to overly dramatize the incident, that Cobb could not punch. As rugged a guy as he was, he was still one of the weakest hitters in the division. And there was the matter of the phone book, which dampened the blow. It was a pretty thick phone book, too. Nashville.

So a blow to the chin, delivered full-bore by someone with truly mortal mechanics, ought to be fairly traumatic, well beyond my sepsis of surprise. It was now easier for me to guess at the shock someone experiences on the anvil end of the strike, the overwhelming confusion it produces. Without ever having taken one to the kisser, I could now sympathize with, say, Trevor Berbick, who groggily kept trying to regain his feet, falling down again and again, after Tyson landed a left hook—a punch "with bad intentions," he explained later —to the top of his head.

That one knockout, which gained Tyson his first title in 1986, was a clinical example of scattered consciousness: Who can forget Berbick's flailing arms as he tried to disengage himself from the bottom ropes, his repeated attempts to regain even a knee, his drunken and shimmery posture as he tried to reassert himself into daily life? I couldn't say I knew what that felt like, not exactly. But I was newly appreciative of his distress all the same.

The remarkable thing about boxing, when you think about it, was that every fighter had to condition himself for just such a complete humiliation. It was inescapable. At some point in his career, no matter how good he was, he'd probably lose his vertical hold, perform the macarena, or adopt some other foolishness. It would be hard to avoid. Even Tyson, knocked out by Buster Douglas, couldn't get away with his dignity. He had been pounded senseless, of course, driven so far into a survival mode that his only reaction was to grope on his knees for a mouthpiece, as if that was an immediate solution. It was silly and sad to see how a punch could strip layers of intelligence away, to the point where only small, pointless, residual behaviors remained.

(Knockouts have a way of revealing the most primitive nervous activities, offering a window through the skull and into the fighter's core purpose. The most bizarre and chilling knockout ever might have been junior middleweight Vincent Pettway's dispatch of former champion Simon Brown. Brown received a left hook to the side of his face, slammed backward, and lay on the canvas with his lights out, throwing his fists in practiced flurries at the sky.)

That's how it is with knockouts, though, silly and sad and

scary, always entertaining. They were possible to enjoy because, as horrible as they looked, they never seemed to result in anything but what they were, the sudden and brief loss of consciousness. In 20 years of covering heavyweight fighters, I have never seen one of them severely injured in the ring. This was remarkable considering the amplified violence their oversized bodies promised. In that same time I had seen four fighters fatally injured in the ring, but none weighed more than 135 pounds. Men nearly twice their size merely produced an exaggerated goofiness in their opponents.

Of course, they did damage each other, but the toll was revealed in the long run. Muhammad Ali, Jerry Quarry—the progressive thickening of speech among the breed was a terrible consequence of all their "bad intentions." That delayed disintegration was the subtext in every poorly matched fight, every bout with men too old or weathered or too eroded by punches to the head. Those fights produced a queasiness that made them impossible to enjoy.

But the others, with the promise of safely discharged energy, were less the guilty pleasure. And, amazingly, science is somewhat reassuring on this subject: The single most entertaining instant in boxing is also, in a way, its safest.

The doctors who study the brain and the damage done to it generally do not encourage boxing or anything whose premise is blows upon the head. Yet their studies show that the spectacular knockout may be the least of medicine's worries when it comes to the sport.

The actual knockout, they now believe, is caused by a rotational force that is applied to the head with enough oomph to momentarily alter the brain's electrical impulses. They used to think it was the straight-on punch—the classic anterior-posterior blow—that did the work and that it caused everything to stop functioning. They now think that the top of the fighter's brain, the seat of his intelligence, keeps clicking along; it's the brain stem, that extremely protected hunk of matter that governs the basic bodily functions, that actually blinks out, altered amperage causing a brief cessation of power before the circuits can be immediately restored.

Dr. Flip Homansky, a frequent ringside physician at Las Vegas fights, believes the sudden knockout is nature's surest, however surprising, way of protecting the brain. Down the fighter goes, out like a light, suspended for 60 days—the fighter's brain repairs the cellular damage and nobody's the worse for the wear. That's why he thinks a heavyweight knockout in particular is one of the least anxious moments in boxing. One big punch, with TNT in the mitt, and the evening's safely over.

The guys who fight at the lighter weights, on the other hand, do not have the ability to pull the plug on their opponent with a single firecracker blow; rather, they must do the job with repeated punches, which cause subdural concussions and bleeding and, as Homansky observed, "turn their brains to mush." Medevac to area hospital to follow.

Curiously, the big men are unscathed and often unfazed by their knockouts, not just medically but personally. They report no pain or sensation of any kind, or even memory. They do not normally have headaches (which would be a red flag to the physician). You or I would be gulping aspirin if we simply conked ourselves on a low overhang, yet these guys, because of adrenaline or who knows what, have not a single complaint. Or not normal ones: Berbick, who had gone down twice after that one punch from Tyson, did beef about his stoppage. Clear-eyed, but without any noticeable ambulation, he whined that the fight had been called too soon.

The doctors do not kid themselves about the damage from repeated punches. Those who have the gift of an iron chin—Ali comes to mind—are said to have an idiosyncratic response, an individualized reaction to some stimulus. Just as alcohol might affect somebody one way and somebody else another way, people have differing brain structures, differing abilities to take a punch, differing tolerances. Differing character, even. Brain scientists are also investigating a genetic component, a strand of DNA that predisposes some fighters to suffer dementia while others who have taken the same amount of punishment do not.

The consensus, though, is that while it might be okay to take a devastating punch, it's not good to take too many of them, maybe not even more than one. In favor now is the theory of the second-impact syndrome, which says that a subsequent injury to the brain before the cells can repair themselves within a week or two can be the most dangerous of all. Serious catastrophes happen then—massive injuries, tremendous brain swelling, vast cellular destruction, the turning of a brain to mush, death. That would mean that the fighter who is cleanly knocked out—and suspended, per the rules—is better served by his sport than the quarterback whose bell is rung and is put back into the game for the next series of plays.

That would also mean that the fighter with the iron chin is doing his brain no favors by defiantly wading into firestorms of punches. Ali might be doing more rhyming today if his jaw weren't so sturdy. Quarry (whose similarly damaged brothers, fighters all of them, support the idea of a genetic predisposition to long-term injury) could comb his own hair if he weren't so self-righteously rugged.

If that single instant of impact, and the sudden neurological disengagement it produces, really is the more favorable event, then we boxing fans can loathe ourselves a little less for hoping to see it. It's not the destruction of a human being we're paying to see, just some act of decision delivered with a flourish. Millions of us find the idea just thrilling enough that we fund purses of up to $60 million so that somebody else might set this in motion, some kind of ultimate collision, two trains on a single track, steaming into each other.

Strictly speaking, of course, it is barbaric, the lust for such disaster. We shouldn't really speak of it. It's of another, more primitive time. But, produced colorfully enough, the heavyweight fight with its contract for concussion remains hugely popular, and how do you explain that? Are our brains still hard-wired to seek out opportunities to display or appreciate dominance? Maybe it's just one of those ceremonies of finality in an ambivalent culture, a chance to see something decided in a ritualized and explosive way, no compromise, for once in their—and our—lives.

Maybe this is what Tyson pledged every time he entered the ring, sockless and with torn terry-cloth for a robe, to produce a result that was beyond the possibility of debate. Maybe what he offered, in his elemental way, was an abnormal clarity. The struggle for life was now sharply illuminated, freshly seen under the flash lightning. He'd just shake it down upon those poor bastards' heads.

Chapter Eight

"Please don't hate me"

Bruce Seldon seemed as puzzled as the next guy, or rather the next 10,000, even the next million. He lightly rubbed the top of his head with his glove as he looked upward at one of the two huge video screens in a lofty corner of the MGM Grand Garden Arena. The knockout, being replayed over and over, as there was now a sudden lack of programming, didn't make much sense—to him, to anybody. It didn't seem like he'd gotten hit hard enough to cause him to take a face-plant like that. It didn't, to tell the truth, seem like he'd gotten hit at all. But there he was, his supple and muscular body flopping to the canvas twice in just 109 seconds. Seldon rubbed his head and looked confused.

This is how it was, September 7, 1996, as Tyson closed in on his title unification: people booing, wanting their money back, all of them as confused (and just about as roughed up) as Seldon. It was a head-scratcher, all right.

But the confusion was quickly beginning to sour into something far worse. As Seldon rubbed his head, the bewilderment fermented straight into humiliation. The crowd cried, "Fix! Fix! Fix!" A man close to the ring apron speculated that Seldon had somehow been electrocuted; it was all that could explain the half-round extinction. His buddy offered another suggestion: "He might have gotten stung with one of those *Wild Kingdom* animal darts."

Showtime's ring interviewer was likewise skeptical. What exactly had happened in there anyway? Seldon said, "I didn't realize how hard he can hit and how fast he was. They are saying Mike Tyson is a destroyer and I am witness to that." But what about these punches, the ones nobody else ever saw? "The first time," said Seldon, as reasonably as he could, "he grazed me." Maybe, he thought, it was "an elbow that touched a nerve." But, the "second punch, he caught me flush on the chin. He rattled my eyes, and I couldn't see clearly."

This didn't satisfy the interviewer's disbelief, which was still resonating in the angrily departing mob. Nobody else, after all, could describe these punches. Was it possible he, in fact, had tanked the fight? Seldon, a WBA champion for God's sake, was shocked at the suggestion. But with the crowd's disgust washing over him, he was beginning to understand what he had just lost—in all likelihood his reputation as a fighter, maybe even as a man. "I treasure that crown," he said, defiantly. "It wasn't a fixed fight. I didn't train twelve weeks to come in here and take a dive." But it didn't matter what he said; it was enough that he'd been asked the question. The tape played over and over, the phantom punches taking shape not from this angle, not from that one. The real destruction, Seldon was beginning to see, was just beginning.

Whether by the accident of his sport—a touched nerve or a rattled eye—or perhaps by some predisposition to lose, he had defined himself in the worst possible kind of failure, the failure of heart in the heat of battle. And he knew it. This was going to be bad, all right. Seldon turned to his comanager, Rocco DePersia, and said, "Please don't hate me." Then he left the ring, stopped to cry hysterically in his dressing room, and was carried away in a white hotel courtesy van.

Saturday, June 28, 1997. A night of boxing infamy: Evander Holyfield gets an earful from Mike Tyson.

"To the mosque!" Tyson, in his white kufi cap and flanked by his minions, exits the Islamic Center of North America on the day of his release from an Indiana prison.

The ever-eccentric Don King salutes his supporters outside his 1995 trial for wire fraud.

The apple doesn't hit the canvas far from the tree: Tom (right) and Peter McNeeley, father and son, both proud, confident, and woefully overmatched.

Vinnie Vecchione—the man behind Peter McNeeley's $540,000 payday.

Estranged bedfellows. Seth Abraham, president of Time Warner Sports, with the omnipresent Don King and the late Steve Ross in 1990. In the way of all partnerships with King, Abraham is a former ally, current enemy, and future . . . ?

Tyson's fourth comeback fight ended nearly the moment it started. Above, Tyson knocks down WBA champ Bruce Seldon. Below, referee Richard Steele counts Seldon out in the first round after his second fall of the fight.

Mike Tyson with his second wife, Monica Turner, touring the theme park of the MGM Grand—the hotel casino that put up millions of dollars for the exclusive right to host Tyson's comeback.

Only in Las Vegas: Mike Tyson with his pet white tiger, Kenya.

ing's protégés and Tyson's right- and ft-hand men: Rory Holloway (left) d John Horne (right), sitting with ike after a sparring session at olden Gloves gym in Las Vegas.

A very scared and very beaten Frank Bruno being held up by referee Mills Lane. Tyson's victory over Bruno gave him the first leg of his intended championship trifecta.

Former Tyson trainer Teddy Atlas gets a kiss from his heavyweight champ, Michael Moorer. Atlas, the man who had once held a gun to Tyson's head, accurately predicted Tyson's unraveling in Holyfield II.

Tyson-Holyfield I: Holyfield roughed up both Tyson and the Las Vegas casinos by delivering his eleventh-round TKO on November 9, 1996.

Before the rematch between Tyson and Holyfield: As usual, only Don King is smiling.

A frustrated Tyson shoves Holyfield during their infamous rematch seconds after feasting on Holyfield's right ear.

Chaos in the ring after referee Mills Lane signaled Mike Tyson's disqualification. Finally, with a ring full of people, Tyson gets aggressive: Tommy Brooks, Holyfield's assistant trainer, labeled it a "typical bully move."

A defeated and apologetic Tyson begs for his professional life at a press conference after the second Holyfield bout.

A Savage Business

He was never seen again, not in a ring, not in a gym, not anywhere in the public eye.

This was a cruel entertainment, if it was one at all. A systematic dismantling, the chipping away of someone's resolve until there is nothing left, is one thing. A man who is overmatched in skill or character can be made to finish on bent knees, be made to slide across ropes as if on a rail, be made to stare vacantly into a million homes, the drool forming at the corner of his mouth. Be made to do any number of foolish things, really. That is fair. It is, in fact, by the sport's very prescription, fun.

But this seemed neither fair nor very much fun. Watching a man lose his heart was a sickening experience because the shame, in this case, had to be shared. The clamor that urges a man forward, or causes him to be put into this spot, does not usually require any responsibility. But allowances had been made for this fight, corners cut, and anybody who knew anything about boxing was a partner in the disgrace. Why was Seldon in there anyway? There was a public complicity that could not be denied.

Seldon's appearance, after all, represented pageantry more than pugilism, and the public had accepted this going in. He was just another portable champion, a guy of such transparent purpose that it was hard to even get a bet down on him. Come September 1996, when this fight took place (after another Tyson postponement in July—bronchitis this time), nobody seriously thought he'd win; his chin was even more disastrously vulnerable to rotational force than Bruno's. But, as he'd served King with occasional distinction in the past, he was at least expected to provide a flourish here and there before he handed over his title. The champion's determination might even offer some cushion to that brain stem, his new pride becoming the bumper to bounce off insult.

But Seldon neglected to provide the flourish, or even give

Tyson a chance to provide one on his own, and the title passing was accomplished without any of the usual ceremony —say, an exchange of blows—that sometimes makes the mismatch palatable. The whole thing could have been done just as safely and without a Don King press conference at the offices of some notary public. To see the stripped-down version of the Bruno fight, stripped so far down that the public part of the event was merely a formality, was to be confronted with the baldness of King's plan. Everybody—King, Seldon, and even the fighter's cigar-smoking proxies at ringside—was part of the embarrassment.

It happened quickly, at least. Seldon, a reformed armed robber who had woven some sweet and convincing themes in his rehabilitation, had brought to the fight a lot of athletics and a lot of happiness. His enjoyment of the cheap little title was so genuine that you had to wince at his pleasure. He was more promising than most, in other words. But to everybody's horror, he was virtually liquefied in Tyson's solvent of street-corner terror, right at the bell. Having pledged a blistering jab ("He's never eaten leather like this," he had said), Seldon watched it get compacted right into his shoulder. Tyson, in a flurry of activity, collapsed the distance between them within seconds, causing red alerts to begin flashing in Seldon's head. *There was nothing to be done* was the response from the bridge. *All hands man the lifeboats.*

Who can say if he acted dishonorably? Given what he, or any heavyweight fighter, was asked to do, who can really say that he hadn't acted sensibly? Maybe he did exactly what anybody else would have done—should have done—in that situation. In the weird seconds that followed, Seldon quickly went down from a . . . what? A short left hook, most thought. "A right hand on top of the head," guessed Tyson. Who could say?

The punch was so mysterious that referee Richard Steele couldn't believe that Seldon, who pitched face-forward, had

A Savage Business

actually been hit. He thought it must have been a slip. "I was attempting to wave it off," he said. "But he seemed hurt, so I picked up the count. I've seen a lot worse, but then I can't tell how hard Mike Tyson punches."

Tyson then threw a left hook that most people did in fact see. Seldon again went face first, bouncing up in a neutral corner, where he displayed the assured and upright stance of a Slinky. Steele pinned him against the ropes and that was that.

It would have been absurd to discount Tyson's power—"I myself am punching pretty hard these days," he said afterward—but the lack of discernible contact would forever pin Seldon, fairly or unfairly, with the label of quitter. "Seldon had a nervous breakdown," said his trainer, Emanuel Steward. "The man was scared to death." A couple of days later, George Foreman weighed in with his dismay. "If you're afraid," he said, "don't get in the ring. I can't believe he falls down after he gets brushed by an elbow and then he shows up the next day and picks up his check."

Such was the tenor of criticism that drove Seldon into hiding. But his fight was not much worse than Bruno's, which had also been conducted (for a little while longer, it was true) in an atmosphere of faux fright and intimidation. Maybe there was something rotten about the whole campaign, something so criminally cynical that there was cause for consumer complaint. Again. Tyson had provided some return on investment in the Bruno fight, where he had at least physically consumed his victim. But where was the value here? The crowd at the MGM, an even million homes around the world at $39.95 a pop—what did they get for their money this time? A little flurry of punches, a ghost knockout? It was one thing to see Tyson crush weak competition with the residue of his talent. It was another to see him do it with the residue of his personality.

In a way, of course, the fight *had* been fixed. They'd all

163

been fixed. And everybody knew it. The rankings had been tweaked and the champions advanced and appointed so that Tyson's course might seem logical, admirable even. He's going to unify the title, how brave is that. But even the casual fan knew that the comeback was supported by a matchmaking that was, at best, mischievous. Not one of the four fighters Tyson had met so far had been intended to generate anything more than publicity, and of course a tremendous flow of cash. Seldon, poor Bruce Seldon, was simply the lever used to raise some dough.

To this point, Team Tyson had raked in roughly $80 million—$15 million for frightening Seldon into submission—or about $10 million per round in his comeback. The lack of willing competition didn't seem fatal to Team Tyson's business plan. It's true that the MGM couldn't fill all its seats, and it's true that Showtime's figure of one million buys for the Seldon fight was down nearly 30 percent from the Bruno show six months earlier. But for Showtime it was still the sixth-best pay-per-view fight of all time. The numbers said one thing, basically: People just wanted to see Tyson perform, do something, enact some strange fantasy of brutal domination.

The result was a dishonesty that not only crucified the loser unfairly but also robbed the winner of appreciable achievement. When Tyson, having won the WBA title, looked up into the arena's polluted atmosphere and said, "Cus, you got two down and one to go," well, you almost felt as sorry for Tyson as for Seldon. The emotion that belonged with this victory was totally absent. Tyson had to manufacture it in the middle of the ring, pretend there was meaning where there obviously was none. Even he had been cheated.

Anybody who tried to fill these events, this one in particular, with importance came across as a goof. The Reverend Jesse Jackson, who had baptized Tyson a religion ago, showed up for the fight and got a little more carried away than usual. Admitting that Tyson did not have "the penchant for social awareness that Muhammad Ali had," the Reverend Jackson was nonetheless impressed with the forum that Tyson was building. "Mike can defeat anyone," he said. "That is an awesome statement among four billion people." Tyson had a chance, he thought, to use this image of power "to engender a feeling of conquest and heroism."

Well, nobody had seen anything heroic, and it wasn't much of a conquest. There was a suspicion, too, that out of four billion people, there might be one who'd put up a better fight than Seldon.

Seldon, it must be noted, was not pigeonholed as a coward coming into this fight. He had done some fairly impressive things in his career, though nothing to suggest he ought to be making $5 million in a real championship fight. In 1991 he lost to both Oliver McCall and Riddick Bowe, the Bowe fight a one-round knockout in Seldon's own hometown of Atlantic City. That was not promising.

On the other hand, he had weathered a few rocky innings with warhorse Tony Tucker to win the WBA title in 1995, and though wobbled by Joe Hipp later that year he managed to defend it easily enough. There was no question that his eyes could get rattled on occasion, but Seldon was still determined enough, most times, to withstand the punishment.

DePersia, his comanager, had gone so far as to offer a profile in courage before the Tyson fight. And unless DePersia, a New Jersey lawyer, was perjuring himself, the fighter was indeed a man of iron will. "I bristle when people question Bruce's courage," DePersia said.

Before the McCall fight, Seldon's mother had called De-Persia to say her son was sick and the fight should be canceled. Yet when he visited the gym he found Seldon holding his own. He learned later that Seldon had told his sparring partner to make him look good so DePersia wouldn't pull him out.

DePersia said Seldon fought David Bey with hands so bruised and swollen they couldn't get the tape off them after the fight. And Seldon knocked out a fighter named Hassan Shabazz in the fifth round of their fight, three rounds after he had broken his hand. As for the title victory, Seldon had somehow absorbed a perfect right from Tucker, his ears actually flipping forward from the force, without taking a knee.

Seldon, moreover, was a man you wanted to believe in. His tremendously muscled body, however irrelevant that usually is in boxing, was the veneer of a great natural athlete. DePersia liked to tell people how his man could run a 50-second quarter mile, jump 40 inches off the ground (from the floor to the top of the ring), stand under a basket and dunk, walk on his hands the length of a gym, and, for that matter, swim and dive.

Tyson was the first to question the importance of these feats. "What's he going to do when he gets in the ring?" he wondered. "Is he going to pole-vault? Is he going to run the hurdles?" Still, it didn't seem that natural athletic ability would be a drawback, all other things being equal.

And maybe some things were equal. What could Tyson know that Seldon didn't? Seldon had done more time in institutions, for more crimes, and had come back lots further than Tyson ever had. While Tyson was enjoying the clear air of the Catskills at the D'Amato estate, Seldon was going away to prison in Annandale, New York, having pulled off the capper of his small-time career, attempting an armed robbery of a liquor store at age 15. He was no celebrity prisoner, either, with rappers and promoters visiting him. He was just another guy in the system. He spent most of his time—four and a half years—in lockdown.

Seldon, out of respect for his mother, Joan Graham, sought

out his own rehabilitation there, finding boxing, joining the team, and merging with the rest of the prison population. Even getting his high school diploma in prison. "My mother was, has been, and still is everything in my life," he said before the fight. "I knew that me being in prison was devastating to her and I knew I couldn't go on the way I was. I owed it to my mother to change."

And he did change. Out of prison, he embarked on a short amateur career under the training of Carmen Graziano and quickly moved up to the pros, where he unreeled 18 quick victories. But the fight with McCall, where he quit in exhaustion, and then the three-knockdown KO by Bowe in the first round later that same year, nearly drove him into retirement by the age of 25. And then it got worse when Graziano, who'd become a father figure to him, died of a heart attack in 1992. And worse still when his mother died of a heart attack the following year.

Seldon did persist, though, and through the miracle of the modern system of rankings found himself in contention for the vacant WBA title. DePersia had gotten Seldon to No. 8 in the rankings on his own, but found it slow going from there on. However, in 1993 DePersia signed a contract to fight for King, beginning with a Greg Page bout, and things started happening. After knocking out Page, a rated fighter, all Seldon had to do was beat Nathaniel Fitch, Tui Toia, and Bill Corrigan to make it to No. 1.

But from there he did stop the 35-year-old Tucker to win the championship. And in his first defense, which was on the undercard of Tyson's McNeeley fight, he did outlast Joe Hipp. (Not too many heavyweights had ever been asked to defend their titles on undercards, but Seldon didn't mind a bit. "I'd rather be second on a card everybody sees, than first on a card nobody sees," he said, understanding perfectly his drawing power.) It might not have been the most distinguished record in boxing history, but it was impressive considering the springboard he'd gotten; he was no Olympic sweetheart, just some guy fighting for $200, getting his name misspelled on the programs, trying to live down an armed robbery. He'd come a long way.

But if Seldon wasn't the worthiest champion the WBA ever had, or the best credentialed, he was at least one of its best ambassadors. One of boxing's most agreeable, for sure. He turned down approximately zero requests for his time, gladly doing interviews ("To know me is to love me" was his personal mantra), appearances, and benefits. He went to every juvenile detention center in south New Jersey, giving his comeback-from-hell lecture. He went to jails, he ran charity races, chugging down the straightaway alongside a wheelchair, holding some kid's hand. He was, by any measure but chin, a good champ.

He was also, considering the mania surrounding Tyson's comeback, almost completely overlooked, but he was cheerfully available nonetheless. In the days before his title defense against Hipp he had trolled through the press room, childishly happy when some reporter flagged him down for a quote, not a bit upset when he was ignored.

Moreover, his confidence sounded terrific. There was nothing to make the long money snap him up at odds like 22-1, but his talk, however cheap, was encouraging. While properly respectful, calling Tyson "the man who's considered the greatest fighter of all time," he was also full of a proper bravado. "The last three guys Tyson fought stood like statues," he said. "They went in with good intentions, but it's going to be a factor that I can actually move around." Seldon continued, saying, "The key to beating Mike Tyson—standing up to him. Letting him know I'm not afraid of him."

In addition, Seldon was reminding his fans that he was still in his win-one-for-mother mode of fighting. Before the

Tucker fight he'd played a tape of her singing with a church choir; after he won, he took his championship belt home and spread it across her grave. Also, he had schooled himself on tapes of Douglas's upset of Tyson, that he had a cement jab —on and on.

"Everybody kills me with their mouth," Tyson said, wearily.

Still, Seldon did attract one convert. Retired daredevil Evel Knievel, who was lingering in town to bet football (to bet anything, actually), watched the underdog work out the week of the fight and was impressed enough to ask the fighter and his crew to dinner. Two nights before the fight, Seldon was charming Knievel with the story of his mother, how he's a devout Christian, how he's the best athlete in the game. Knievel, who once soared over the fountains at Caesars Palace down the street (his landing was problematic), tends always to identify with Las Vegas risk takers. He offered to come by Seldon's dressing room the night of the fight and deliver a pep talk. Seldon declined that, but Knievel was undaunted. After dinner he rushed to put $6,700 down on his new friend to win.

But that was about it for Seldon's bandwagon.

Come the week of the fight, as routinely happened for these events, Tyson got all the attention. But for the first time in his comeback, he responded to it. He still wasn't what you'd call available, but he was beginning to pop up here and there, always appearing cranky about it, but talking just the same.

In fact, ever since the Bruno fight he'd been conducting a regular open house at his Las Vegas estate, welcoming *Esquire, Ring* magazine, and even CNN, which emerged with some rather strange footage of Tyson chasing a tiger around his fenced tennis court. Don King was on hand for that and was rather agitated after seeing Tyson and the tiger tussle.

"Oh, my God," he said, "did you see that? The tiger done tried to box him. He threw a right-hand paw, then a left-hand paw—my heart's coming right out of my cardiovascular region." King revealed the source of his arrhythmia: "I'm thinking, there goes a hundred million down the river, in a basket."

Tyson, for all the pleasure he took in his animals, was taking great pains to convince his visitors he wasn't one of them. He was embarking on a suburban life, or a version of it, anyway, and he wanted to prove he belonged in the neighborhood, that he was a true citizen. Bitterness remained, though: Asked a serious question, he barked back at *Esquire*'s Mark Kram, "Don't you know? I'm not supposed to have a mind. I'm a monster."

To prove that he wasn't, which was the point of these interviews, Tyson trotted out some booktalk. He had done a few jailhouse interviews and he discovered that booktalk in particular tended to get swallowed whole by his more literate guests. In fact, he had done much reading, but perhaps less than his interviewers implied; once, given a copy of *David Copperfield*, Tyson said he was surprised to learn the Las Vegas magician had authored a book. Still, talking about books was a reliable ploy. So in the course of this interview, which ranged from serial humiliations ("in my first marriage . . . by girls who said I grabbed their butts") to his prison stoicism, when his defiance landed him in the hole ("I could have done the whole trick there"), he found the opportunity to drop this into the reporters' notebooks: "You like Tolstoy?"

Tyson was doing more than asserting his humanity in these interviews. He was also shaping a legend, as if from scratch. It was as if he were just now deciding who he wanted to be, or, rather, who he wanted to be like. He was trying on personalities, seeing how each one played. This was hard for him because his past gave him no footing. So now he would be struck by the dignity of his neighbor, Wayne Newton, who was said to be bankrupt yet was calm enough to dispense life advice over the backyard fence like Wilson on *Home Improvement*. He'd want to be like him. Or he'd develop a fascination with Bugsy Siegel. Or Dickens. Or John Gotti.

Perhaps this groping for personality wasn't new. Years ago, after he'd lost to Douglas but before he'd been convicted of rape, I'd traveled with him on a corporate jet, Caesars Palace's actually, from Las Vegas to a press outing in Los Angeles. I was struck then, watching the verbal horseplay between him and Holloway in particular, that he believed he was heir to nothing, a social orphan who was still in search of his ancestors, so that he might know who he'd grow up to be. During the ride, the talk turned to the possibility of previous lives, an idea Tyson seized with gusto. He believed he must have lived as an African warrior—perhaps of the Zulu tribe—many generations ago. He was very sure of it.

The one thing these reporters' visits proved was that Tyson was still searching, ransacking history for his pedigree, as if he too found D'Amato's creation incomplete. His walled Las Vegas compound, littered with luxury cars and misted by trickling fountains, was peopled by statues of the great conquerors—Genghis Khan (actually cooling his bronze heels in Tyson's spa), Toussaint-L'Ouverture, Hannibal, and Alexander the Great. Perhaps he believed now that he had lived as Genghis Khan in a previous incarnation. Or maybe was just descended from him. That would explain a lot.

Tyson was treating the past like a buffet, tasting a bit of this, a little more of that, circling the steam table until he figured out who he really wanted to be. A session with reporters just four days before the fight revealed how poorly grounded he was in the reality of his making. He didn't know if he wanted to be like Muhammad Ali or John Gotti (or, of course, Wayne Newton).

Richard Hoffer

That interview in particular was an astonishing reverie, a stream of consciousness played out before 14 writers at Don King's Las Vegas town home. The writers listened slack-jawed at first, then a little irritated when they realized what kind of trouble they were going to have making sense of their transcripts. What was the lead here? "John Gotti was a serious individual," Tyson said at one point. "He helped people, he fed people. They were ignorant of the reasons why they were helped or fed. The fact is that they were helped."

Was that any odder than the fact that in prison Tyson had kept in touch with Stan Lee, creator of the Marvel Comics superheroes? Could something be made out of that? Or that he thought members of Alcoholics Anonymous were weak because they wanted to associate with people like themselves?

Did I say his talk was wide-ranging?

If there was any thread to his speech (the next day's sports editions didn't reveal one), it was that he considered himself an outsider still. He was proud of that—likening his own rebellious spirit to that of Jack Johnson—but he was also self-pitying. Stand-up guys like Gotti and Jack Johnson alienate society and always get punished in the end. A tough guy, even a guy as tough as himself, would end up getting crushed, even if just a little.

He had told Mark Schwartz in an ESPN interview earlier that the young Mike Tyson, who was the superior model, just never had a chance in this society. "I like that guy that I was before I went to prison," he said. "I was a good guy, I was just foolish. I was a helluva guy, okay? But that guy who went to prison in '92 couldn't survive in this world."

Moreover, he said, the effects of confinement, no matter how he resisted them, had dulled his talent. "I'm a better fighter than I was back then," he said. "But I couldn't beat that guy back then." So he had paid some price.

The greater toll was his new confusion. He said he might give up all his possessions—"sell most of my property"—and go to Mecca and "make homage." Or, once his travel restrictions were lifted, he might "go to Europe and explore different situations." He'd like to see the Louvre. Then he'd be happy? "I've never been happy," he said.

Then again, he had to admit, "I am living the American way, I am out of prison, I am making thirty million a pop."

Which he was going to give away.

The interview session dragged on for an hour, with Tyson himself showing no inclination to draw it to a close. It was at times the old Tyson, who, his guard down, had rough charm and humor. "Somebody wrote a story that I had sex with twenty girls in one night," he said. "I'd like to take credit for that."

But it was also the new Tyson, wary and needy, not unlike the caged tiger he loved so much. His devotion to that tiger was strange, really. Here he was, jailer, the man who would domesticate a wild beast. Did he ever find irony in his civilizing role with the tiger? He did not. Yet, discussing Kenya, his $250,000 white tiger, Tyson constructed an unwitting metaphor: "Now she is too big to play with," he said, with some regret. "She's still a kid, still has a childish mentality. Circus handlers deal with them with force. I deal with them with love. They are like us. They want affection."

The reporters all wrote that down. Maybe, much later, they'd remember what he'd said, make sense of it, think of Mike Tyson as somebody who was interesting, a little threatening, safely caged up until his next opportunity to do something that might be rewarded with affection. Think of him as, say, a pet tiger.

In any event, the last thing on his mind was Bruce Seldon.

•

Tyson's séance proved to be a calm in the storm—or, as King might have put it, the oasis in the desert—that week. The press conference held the next day was the usual Don King vanity production, largely a marshaling of vocabulary on his part, the large attendance being proof that a lot of people had time on their hands. Crocodile was there, a sort of warm-up act, shouting "Hand-to-hand combat!" and "Mystique is a powerful force." Again, the fact that he failed to make any sense was not considered a handicap to the promotion.

Then Seldon's party entered the room, and the best you could say of their effort was that they got into the spirit of things. Four of them produced simulated train whistles and began tooting away, apropos of nothing beyond the wooden whistles' availability. They might have rung cowbells if they'd spotted them on a store shelf first. "We tried to bring this down to an even lower level," said DePersia, happily. Done and done. The effect, all in all, was to make sensible people want to throw themselves on the simulated tracks.

King, who can also work on the even lower level when he has to, introduced Tyson by saying, "The best that ever lived and history will dictate that, if we can keep both of us out of jail." That floated over Tyson's bowed head, but barrister DePersia perked up and handed King his business card. It all went pretty much like that.

When it came Tyson's turn to speak, he was at turns cryptic and apologetic. After two hours of King and anybody else who could wrestle the podium from him, Tyson had reason to be unfocused and vague. First he said, "I went through some ordeals and am still dealing with some situation and may go back."

Huh? "Nothing that concerns you," he said, "just something I expressed." What about the fight, then? "I am pious and humble but I am in a hurting business and this is what I do." Then, as appropriate to the proceedings as a wooden train whistle was, he said, out of the blue, "Wouldn't a lot of people like to be me?" It was no more or less bizarre than any other of King's press conferences, and about as informative as usual, too.

All the really intriguing stuff was happening behind closed doors, where King was fighting to preserve the title unification series of his own devising. There were problems, the main one taking the form of Lennox Lewis, the WBC's top-ranked contender. After he'd lost his title to McCall, Lewis had petitioned the WBC for a rematch, saying he'd be willing to fight the leading available contender (who was Lionel Butler) just to get back to the head of the line. The match was okayed, and having won that fight, Lewis was under the impression he'd fight for the title again, against the winner of the Bruno-McCall fight.

That hadn't happened because Tyson, just out of jail, had been confirmed as the top contender at the WBC's 1995 convention. Lewis would get the next mandatory.

When it became obvious that that wasn't going to happen, either—Tyson plowed ahead with the Seldon fight—Lewis sued the WBC in a New Jersey court. The WBC, hoping for a settlement, said Lewis would fight Tyson for the WBC title and that the crown, moreover, would not be at stake in the Tyson-Seldon fight.

This was made all the more agreeable to Lewis when King stepped forward with $4 million in step-aside money and the promise of $12 million more for a Tyson fight in June 1997. This was easy money.

But Lewis, though he kept the $4 million, said no, however reluctantly, to the part about fighting Tyson in June. What it boiled down to was that Tyson was a Showtime fighter and Lewis was an HBO fighter. This gave King the opportunity to portray himself as the victim in a feud that nobody could remember starting. King's scenario had him looking out for the public good, only to be thwarted by Lewis and the dreaded HBO.

"We want Lennox Lewis," King said the week of the Seldon fight, "but he's yellow as a yellow ribbon, afraid he'll get his ass kicked again. He's a pimp, just wants money for nothing." Worse, according to King, he was stupid. "Ray Charles could see this. If he loses, he gets sixteen million." King was correct in the seeming obviousness of the plan: Lewis could not conduct his career in any other way and make as much money. A title fight with McCall might not be worth even $2 million to Lewis. "I'm throwing money around like it was peanuts," King said.

King insisted that he negotiated fiercely to make the fight, but that Lewis's manager, Panos Eliades, kept coming back at him requiring yet one more contractual concession to HBO. King said he made them all, until, finally, Eliades came back with a refusal. According to King, Eliades said, "Seth [Abraham] won't let me do it. He's obsessed with you."

Abraham said, "Having Don blame me for the Lewis situation is like Custer blaming the weather for Little Big Horn." Abraham said he was never a principal in the negotiations.

That was probably naïve. John Davimos, Michael Moorer's manager, was of the opinion that Abraham was bungling the whole thing. HBO, he claimed, could have signed up Moorer, who became the IBF champion. And, for that matter, should Tyson be stripped of his WBC title, HBO could reasonably expect Lewis to beat McCall to win it; HBO would have two champions. And if HBO were to allow Lewis an out in its exclusive contract, it might regain the WBC crown from Tyson in the ring, with money and glory for everyone.

At the heart of the matter, according to HBO, was Showtime's exclusivity clause with Tyson. Showtime had poured too much money into Tyson up-front to watch HBO get the biggest fight of his comeback. HBO, meanwhile, wasn't about to let Lewis slip from its grasp. As much as King lobbied in the press, even printing up a little manifesto called "If the Truth Be Known," the differences between the two were basically irreconcilable.

But King got a lot of mileage from the issue in the meantime, characterizing it as a feud he'd clearly won. "Time Warner," he said of HBO's parent company, "I whipped their ass. Beat them handily." Of the presumably defeated Abraham he was almost sympathetic. "The man is frustrated," he said. "And I can't blame him, having a motherfucker like me on his ass. I taught him all he knows, just not all I know."

Of course, Tyson was going to have to give up the WBC crown as a result of Lewis's court settlement, and HBO was going to get its heavyweight entrée anyway. Lewis would probably have to give McCall a rematch, this time with trainer Emanuel Steward in Lewis's corner, not McCall's. The miracle of that first fight, which King never tired of repeating ("Look at the tape," King would say, "Oliver hit him with his eyes closed!"), would not likely be repeated. Steward, everyone realized, had been more instrumental in that upset than King's patriotic crooning.

Since King couldn't really have expected to land Lewis for Tyson, he was already negotiating with the thoroughly faded Evander Holyfield for a November 9 fight. After losing to Bowe a year earlier, Holyfield had fought just once, beating Bobby Czyz in May. That fight, which had been predicted as a blowout, proved to be somewhat difficult for Holyfield. The selection of Holyfield as a Tyson opponent was likely to cause fresh howling from the medical community, if not the boxing commission.

But if it was going to be a bad fight, there would at least be lots of angles to exploit for the promotion, and King was trying them out even before Tyson had the chance to dispatch

Seldon. "Holyfield," said King, "has been a problem for Tyson for eight years. He can't wait for Holyfield. And Holyfield, he wants to beat Tyson like God hates sin." If ever a fight had the makings of a morality play, this one did, with the Bible-thumping Holyfield and the ex-rapist Tyson.

Unfortunately, the Seldon fight didn't have the good-vs.-evil format that King favored. In fact, by the time Seldon entered the ring on fight night, with King strutting around the canvas and Tyson pacing back and forth, there were so many former felons in one place the fight was a virtual parole violation. It wasn't a record number of felons for a boxing ring, probably, but it was a lot all the same.

Unfortunately, at the moment the fight was to start, not all of the principals seemed to have been sufficiently hardened by the experience. The only inspiration Seldon had brought into the ring, it turned out, was a framed photograph of his mother. Not quite enough. DePersia has reflected on that moment of truth. "I know he has courage," he said, "but I also know he's an emotional individual. Maybe, thinking back on it, we should have had Evel Knievel come by."

DePersia said everything had been fine in the dressing room, "but once we got into the ring, I thought we were in some jeopardy. He wasn't himself. There's nothing quite like it, though, and it's hard to explain to people who've never been in your shoes. But all of a sudden a lot of things are conspiring against you, all those interviews where people ask if you really think you have a chance, the famous people in the audience. The feeling in that room is quite different. It tightens any human being."

DePersia knew, however, that it was not tightening Tyson. "Mike has been in that situation," DePersia continued, "and I don't think Mike was feeling what Bruce was. Plus, now Mike knows your guy is tight and he has the physical speed to get to your guy, flying over there, throwing punches at odd angles." DePersia had hoped that Seldon would be able to weather an early barrage and calm down. But he couldn't, and he didn't.

DePersia thought a left hook in the first 10 seconds—"a rocket ship"—had knocked his fighter goofy from the get-go, and that the rest, grazed nerves or whatever, was just the finishing touch. "It's just too bad," he said, "but he was tight as a drum."

What happened afterward, DePersia believes, was of his own doing. Seldon didn't want to talk to any announcer, saying he was too embarrassed. But the manager told him he had to be a man, speak up win or lose. When Seldon did speak, his dispassionate delivery contributed to the idea that he was very happy to be out of there and not a bit upset.

He was upset, all right. He dropped out of the game, took his $5 million purse, grew his hair in long braids, and lay low. A year later, though buff as ever, he had still not gone into a boxing gym. DePersia hoped he would, noting that there was always the possibility of redemption in boxing. "Maybe," he thought, "we could get out from under this mark. It's painful to measure him by that one night. A bum he's not."

Perhaps he's not. He bought a house about an hour west of Atlantic City, a home that included an apartment for his father, a man he'd grown up without. It's a common theme among many fighters, the need to repair fractured relationships, to use their money and influence to build families they never had. Fighters are both horribly and wonderfully unpredictable. You never know what a guy will do come crunch time, is what you find out.

Tyson's future was more immediately assured. While Seldon was still weeping in his dressing room, King was unspooling a little video trumpeting the Holyfield fight. FINALLY read the banner strung up above the dais, a reference to a fight that had been scheduled five years before. It had all been arranged in advance; Holyfield appeared, wearing a T-shirt and vest, then Tyson, in a black suit and pumpkin-colored vest. There was no mention of Seldon whatsoever, and the "impromptu" show for the press revealed how dispensable he'd been. A fight had actually been the preamble to a press conference, not the other way around. Seldon hadn't mattered a bit; this, behind closed doors, was the main event.

The perversity of this night, where a fight had been held for the express purpose of supplying King with a forum to advance his next moneymaker, where a fighter had been humiliated beyond repair, was being enacted elsewhere in the city, too. It was as if the unsatisfying result, and the cynical premise that produced it, had released a poison that was drifting through the halls of the MGM, through all of Las Vegas.

Beyond the arena, as King was bringing together Tyson and Holyfield, a high-profile rapper and his entourage were stomping some poor Crip, a gang member who had gotten in Tupac Shakur's face earlier in the evening. Shakur, both a rapper and actor, and the huge Suge Knight, chief of Death Row Records, lashed into the guy pretty good; it was all caught on hotel surveillance cameras. Shakur and Knight and the entourage—the whole bunch of them members of the self-styled MOB crew (Members of the Blood)—left the scene in high spirits on their way to Knight's Club 662, around the corner on Flamingo Road. (On a telephone keypad, the numbers convert nicely to MOB.)

For Tyson fights, the streets of Las Vegas had increasingly assumed more of an urban feel than is generally suggested in the travel ads. The families park their strollers early, withdraw sensibly from the hubbub to their rooms, and check out what's on the Disney Channel. Outside, the white Benzes, the black Lexuses—windows tinted out—roll up and down the strip, their hood for the night. The music's loud, the gold jewelry heavy, the valet line now a scene from every black movie of the nineties as it disgorges all manner of gilded gangsters and dark-glassed wannabes. This, in the Tyson era, was the place to be for upwardly mobile hoodlums.

So it wasn't surprising at all that two factions might do battle in a hallway across from a casino food court. Anybody with sense could have expected that. A little surprising, though, that less than an hour later, Shakur would be shot fatally at the corner of Flamingo and Koval, when a man in a white Cadillac (windows tinted out) got out of his car and blasted through the window of Knight's black BMW.

Police never did solve the killing, not even deciding for sure that Shakur was the target. The rap war, East vs. West, would claim other industry lives from that shadowy world, and in this case it was hard to guess who had the more dedicated enemy, Shakur or the ruthless mogul, Knight. The police were satisfied, though, that the killing had nothing to do with the fracas outside the Grand Garden. That was unrelated. And, of course, it didn't have anything to do with the Tyson fight. The fact that the bout had somehow convened this hatred and then failed to vent it was, officially anyway, entirely irrelevant to the case.

Chapter Nine

"He made a misstep in the alcohol division"

It was nineteenth-century science that allowed people to be categorized by the shape of their skull. A bump here or there might indicate certain character traits, intelligence levels, even destiny. For a while there, it was a promising means of identifying personality—the diagnostic tools were cheap, at least—but it proved not to be a very reliable form of classification in the long run. Phrenology was soon passé, becoming more of a parlor game than a means of medical research, and hardly any such simplifications concerning size and shape exist today. We live in a more informed and politically correct age; nobody shall be pegged by color, feature, or the knobs on his head.

One physical bias persists, though. In boxing, as a fighter breaches the 200-pound level, his mental makeup becomes suspect. The evidence is entirely anecdotal—this is not something the journals have any literature on—but it's strong enough to make this prejudice almost reasonable. Heavyweight fighters, for all the excitement they bring to the sport, are the most unreliable performers in the game. They suffer amazing breakdowns under pressure, react unpredictably in time of crisis, and require unorthodox and sometimes hysterical motivation just to endure, let alone achieve. They're all head cases.

A Savage Business

Mike Tyson, out of the ring, was a kind of head case himself, of course, but the one thing that made him both popular and profitable was that, inside the ring, he was competent and even keeled. He seemed alone among the heavyweights of his era in this regard. While he could somehow cause psychic disorders to develop in his partners, he suffered none himself. You could count on him to do the work at hand.

The rest of them, besides being head cases outside the ring, were so prone to spectacular disintegrations of spirit inside that a fight ticket was equivalent to a day pass to the psychiatric ward. The whole division, if it hadn't always been crazy, was during Tyson's comeback shot through with instability and all manner of erratic behavior. The matchmaking that had been going on was mean-spirited, certainly. But there was always the nagging belief that maybe nobody was left to provide sane competition anyway.

One theory: It was a basic and irreversible problem with heavyweights, with men who grew up big. Emanuel Steward, who got his start training lionhearted welterweights in the 110-degree heat of the Kronk Gym in Detroit, had always thought heavyweights were troublesome commodities, otherwise likable lugs who'd usually disappoint you. They were too faint of spirit, for one thing. This was a sweeping statement that caught up some genuine warriors—Steward wouldn't have minded working Muhammad Ali's corner. But there was something about the kid who was always the biggest on his block, who because of his size grew up the class bully, that caused Steward to say never mind.

This theory may be pseudo-science, too, but there is a logic to it. Just as basketball mandates that everybody who is seven-foot must play, regardless of ability or desire, so does boxing advance the bigger and stronger kid, regardless of temperament. The game is always on the lookout for a heavyweight—the moneymaker. A lot of character flaws can be stuffed behind a left hook.

The fellows at the lower weights, on the other hand, have to survive on determination, have to make up for their lack of size with an overachieving mentality. They grow up the underdog and become accustomed to overcompensating. In the ring, their hearts having been tested from day one, they rarely surprise you with a failure of nerve. They don't suffer much self-doubt.

Steward found he could rely on those smaller men to a much greater degree than heavyweights. A kid like Tommy Hearns, whom Steward tutored toward multiple-title prominence, had to pass a gut check every day he went to the gym. "There was something about that gym," Steward said, remembering the oppressive heat and overbearing testosterone level, "that made it impossible to stay if you didn't have balls."

Heavyweights were different. Although Hearns did help make Steward a millionaire, it was far more likely that a heavyweight would become a trainer's lottery ticket. So it was that Steward patiently stuck with Michael Moorer, a heavyweight-to-be who was obviously talented but as mentally fragile and high-strung as an opera diva. He was such a reluctant fighter that if he got hit on the arm during sparring, he might just call off his workout. And in a real fight he might just coast along, as if there were a tacit agreement that if he didn't fight, neither would his opponent. He required a lot of maintenance.

Tyson flourished among these men because he seemed to need nothing beyond that old towel he used for a cape, his black trunks, and some gloves. Nor did he need anybody at his side or in his corner. His very loneliness was cause for just enough righteous rage to ensure proper battles. He wouldn't fall apart. He never had, anyway.

But the rest of them . . . their fights always represented some kind of risk. They might perform well enough on the way up, but there always seemed to be some threshold of danger that they just couldn't step over. Bruce Seldon, for example, was brave, but only up to a point. No promoter could sensibly expect a genuinely thrilling performance from a heavyweight when the stakes were high; some kind of breakdown was more the norm.

Here's the backdrop against which Tyson was lucky enough to wage his comeback: Nearly every heavyweight contender besides him was certifiable, or would become so. Not a one of them could be trusted to repeat a difficult triumph or defend a title. The fact that there'd been 10 different champions while Tyson was gone hinted at their inconstancy of desire. They'd quit, they'd hug, they'd cry. They'd quit the game and apply for jobs as crossing guards, $10.49 an hour. They were, all of them, pretty much nuts.

Going back to Moorer: He and Steward, the trainer whom he had once called Pops, drifted apart, and the fighter came under the sway of the even more volatile Teddy Atlas. Moorer was no less reluctant under Tyson's onetime trainer but in this era was too precious a commodity to be allowed to follow what he felt was his true calling—police work, of all things. So Atlas preached, cajoled, threatened, and humiliated Moorer into exercising his ability. In Moorer's fight for Holyfield's title in 1994, Atlas grew so disgusted that he once refused to let Moorer sit on the stool between rounds. Atlas suggested they change places; he'd fight Holyfield. Provoked, Moorer went on for the upset; ever afterward, Atlas was actually more famous for the win than Moorer.

This was the new WBA-IBF heavyweight champion, and yet he commanded so little respect that George Foreman, then 45 and notoriously picky about his fights, nearly broke his neck to get to him. Foreman, it turned out, had scouted Moorer a long time ago, watching him work with Steward. "He don't like to fight, does he?" Foreman asked Steward. "I believe that if there's any kind of pressure, where he has to dig down, he'll give."

When there was finally something for Moorer to give, Foreman begged promoter Bob Arum to get Moorer for him. Then he had to sue the WBA to sanction it. Clearly Foreman saw Moorer as the opportunity of a lifetime, something he couldn't afford to miss.

In the fight, held in November 1994, Foreman looked terrible, Moorer beating him to every punch, blocking everything the big man threw. Steward watched the fight at home, convinced as ever that the unrelenting Foreman would crack through Moorer's thin facade of confidence. Just the act of blocking Foreman's punches, instead of slipping them, resulted in an unwitting erosion of will for Moorer. Steward knew that. Foreman plodded ahead, and finally, Moorer circled into his big right hand and was floored. The films show Moorer opening his eyes and starting to raise his head and then lying right back down, as if strangely relieved. Moorer had done fine—up to a point.

In a far sadder display, Oliver McCall, who had become rechemicalized since winning and losing his WBC title, suffered what seemed to be a nervous breakdown right in the ring. It was among the most horrifying events in sports, far worse than the garden-variety lapses of intention that the heavyweights seemed so prone to. This was a public unraveling, a bona fide coming apart, a man so helpless he could do nothing but stand and cry, with the whole world looking on.

McCall had never been a sure bet, anyway; dogged by drugs since the age of 13, his life seemed always to be in the worst kind of jeopardy. But there was an undeniable talent there, a strong chin and a determination that spotted his career with marks of distinction. The knockout of Lewis had been chief among them, but there was a growing belief that the accomplishment there belonged to Steward. Steward had given him a game plan for that fight, but more than that, he had given him attention. Steward, who fashions himself a full-service trainer, cooked for McCall, talked endlessly with him, even bought him the tuxedo he wore to sing in Steward's Detroit restaurant (keeping him out of his usual haunts). Clean and sober, McCall had never enjoyed such calm as he did in preparation for that Lewis fight.

But that relationship broke apart when King's men began to realize McCall had a chance. They moved in on the fighter and widened a chasm between him and his trainer. By the time McCall was champion, Steward was on his way, actually switching sides to train Lewis.

For their rematch two and a half years later, McCall was a different man. Steward knew, first of all, that McCall would revert to his straight-ahead style and once more be vulnerable to Lewis's right hand. "That man who counterpunched you," Steward told Lewis, "he don't exist anymore."

But more than that, McCall had failed to stay away from the drugs. Since beating Lewis for the title and losing it back to Frank Bruno, McCall had twice been arrested for possession of drugs and twice been entered into a drug rehabilitation program. Bizarre circumstances attended his life, whether it was getting million-dollar checks (hidden in his sock) stolen in St. Louis or driving down pedestrian malls. He was advanced as an opponent nonetheless, for a fight that had less to do with his future than that of some media giants. The winner would determine whether HBO, Lewis's contract holder, or Showtime, King's network of choice, would control a heavyweight title.

This fight was, then, extremely important to heavyweight boxing, as it would determine Tyson's ability to blaze through the division and unify the title. If Lewis won, that would be more difficult; a marriage between HBO and Showtime would have to be performed and everybody had seen how difficult (or expensive) that would be. However, if McCall won, the 4-1 underdog would restore the title to King's family, as he had once before, and Tyson would have smooth sailing.

The fighters, as ever, were just pawns in this brokering of power. The fact that the bout went ahead in February after McCall tore through a Nashville hotel lobby in December, upending a Christmas tree and generally behaving like a madman, suggested the degree to which these men were fodder in corporate wars. Their lives were considered totally insignificant in the greater grab for the promoters' own economic opportunity.

HBO, which was broadcasting the fight, has since tried to distance itself from the event. Seth Abraham said he knew McCall was troubled—who didn't?—when King wouldn't offer him for interviews. "He was wrapped in a cocoon," Abraham said. "King knew he couldn't fight, we all knew." Abraham said he offered King a number of compromises to keep McCall off the fight. He said he promised McCall the next fight, no matter who won, if King would just find a substitute for him. But King, refusing, was ever sanguine. "He made a misstep in the alcohol division" was how he explained McCall's minirampage.

King noted that McCall, having entered his third rehab program in less than a year, was clean again, had been supervised within an inch of his life, and was going to drug counseling sessions, right up to fight night. "He's as clean as a chitlin," said his trainer, George Benton.

And McCall, who stood to make $3.1 million, was doing his part to reassure the public, too. "I'm very spiritually motivated now," he said. "I'm deep off into Jesus." He was wearing a gold cross on a chain and telling the writers he'd had a magnificent epiphany recently. "Man comes out of darkness, sees the light, continues to walk toward the light, to grasp the light, which is righteousness and the Word of the Lord," he said. "That's where I'm at now. I'm in the light."

Since he had so recently been entangled in actual Christmas tree lights, this commitment to spirituality was obviously not surefire. Still, he was talking the talk, and in boxing that's as good as walking the walk. Maybe this, and his decision to enter the ministry, was comforting to the doubters. In any event, the fight went forward in Las Vegas with the usual heavyweight hoopla, and everybody got pretty much what they deserved.

McCall, visibly frustrated by Lewis in the early going, simply stopped fighting. Come the fifth round, after he had refused to throw one punch in the previous four minutes, he was weeping openly. Lewis, confused by McCall's zombie state, didn't punch much himself. Referee Mills Lane exhorted McCall to fight; McCall, through his tears, promised he would. But McCall just stood there with his hands at his sides, Lewis's punches bouncing off his confused head, and Lane finally stopped the fight.

"I think the young man should talk to someone in the mental health field," said Lane. Even McCall's trainer was shaking his head. "When I looked at him, I knew what the deal was," Benton said. "All that talk about reading the Bible was bullshit. Something was loose."

By July, McCall was ready to admit that he should have postponed the fight, as he was going through a "stressful situation." He was hoping for another chance, though, and soon.

There were all sorts of crack-ups in the division, McCall's just being the strangest. Tommy Morrison was always an exciting prospect, a big hitter who happened to be white. He had marquee value, too, having appeared as a Sylvester Stallone foil in *Rocky V.* And he'd beaten George Foreman. Of course, he had this . . . lifestyle. People remember that for his Michael Bentt fight in 1993—a tune-up for his scheduled $7.5 million fight with Lewis—Morrison had posted a map of Tulsa dividing the city into quadrants, marking the locations of the four girlfriends he was importing for prefight preparations. Bentt wasn't going to be a problem; the geography of his various romances might.

He lost that fight. And, when he was finally matched with Lewis in October 1995 (for $5 million less than he'd have gotten before), he lost that one, too. His manager, Bill Cayton, had earned Morrison a lot of money, made him quite famous, but the lack of discipline was wearing Cayton down. He cut him loose one last time after that fight.

But there is always a promotional use for a white heavyweight who can punch. King signed him to fight Arthur Weathers in February 1996, a bout that would begin his resurrection as a contender. Weathers was the kind of stepping stone anybody would like to mount. "I bleed when I watch fights on TV," Weathers had admitted. Morrison would fight twice more for King and then, it was understood, become an opponent for Tyson. Done right, this would net Morrison more money than he could ever spend back in little Jay, Oklahoma.

But, for reasons that weren't immediately clear, Morrison was pulled from that fight. He had somehow failed the physical. It was very mysterious. Then came a report that he had tested positive for HIV.

Less than a week later he held a press conference back in Tulsa and, in a surprisingly eloquent address, admitted that his unchecked desires had led him to this place. His hopelessly juvenile attitude toward women—a limo loaded with girls, he and his buddies taking turns with them—had wasted not only him but perhaps entire communities of women, for all he knew. "I have never been so wrong in my life," he said.

Morrison, at the time he was saying this, had actually been

settled down for a while with a fiancée, whom he later married, and had adopted a workmanlike attitude. But, except for a final fight he took in Japan later that year on a George Foreman card, his career was over. He retired for good, telling people how wonderful it was never to have to get into a ring again. Movie scripts continued to come in, but he couldn't shake boxing altogether. This wild womanizer was last seen working the corner of an all-female bout in Biloxi, Mississippi. It didn't strike him as the least bit unusual.

Riddick Bowe was on the way out, too, one more good fighter Mike Tyson would never face. He'd survived poverty a lot better than his Brownsville buddy; he just couldn't handle success. He never was the most disciplined guy, but after the first Holyfield fight, his crowning achievement, he became increasingly difficult to round into shape. As he grew older, it showed. He should never have had trouble with Holyfield the third time around, and he certainly should have done better against Andrew Golota in their two fights in 1996.

His eventual retirement, actually done at the suggestion of his manager, Rock Newman, occasioned a sigh of relief among his followers, who in any case were becoming fewer and fewer. Legendary trainer Eddie Futch, Papa Smurf to the cartoonish Bowe, had left the camp in disgust after the first Golota fight, the one where the Polish fighter's low blows caused his disqualification and a riot in Madison Square Garden. Bowe had finally become too lackadaisical even for his own crew.

The rematch, when Golota was again outscoring Bowe (who had ballooned to 252 pounds) before losing it on low blows, convinced everybody else that the party was over.

Bowe, with his height and enormous skills, would have been an intriguing opponent for Tyson but, between Tyson's prison sentence and the usual warfare between media conglomerates, was also an unlikely one. Instead, his legacy was the Holyfield trilogy and a lot of excellent capers, not all of them of his doing.

Things just seemed to happen when Bowe was around. Newman, of course, attracted a lot of chaos, but even he couldn't be held responsible for the Fan Man dropping into the Holyfield rematch. For other milestones in Bowe's strange career Newman and Bowe could certainly share the blame. Once at a press conference, when opponent Larry Donald wouldn't shut up as asked, Bowe gave him two pretty good shots. Then, before his fight with his hated rival Jorge Luis Gonzalez, Bowe responded to Gonzalez's insults by throwing a glass of water at him. Las Vegas later passed the Bowe rule, stating that fighters would not appear together at such functions.

In the ring he could be just as careless of regulations as he was out. Buster Mathis, Jr., went down on one knee after a Bowe barrage, and the man they called Big Daddy stooped to deliver a right hook. Knocked him clean off his knees. Bowe got off very easy with a no-contest decision.

It was a testament to his disposition that Bowe could behave this recklessly and still maintain the public's affection. There had been nothing uglier than Golota I, when a Bowe henchman stormed across the ring and conked Golota in the head with a cell phone, kicking off one of the great riots in boxing history. The sight of Golota's trainer, the notoriously unhealthy Lou Duva, being carried out of the ring on a stretcher (he was okay) was just one more news clip that suggested boxing was still not the kind of thing to take the whole family to. Yet none of it ever seemed to sully Bowe, good ol' Bowe.

The man who once barnstormed Europe, meeting the Pope and performing other ambassador duties of his own imagining, decided after Golota II to take a break and join the marines. This required some rule bending by the corps (Bowe was 29, with a growing family)—but the decision lasted just 10 days. It had been an amazing and utterly doomed decision, but again there was nobody standing up to criticize him. He was just acting out another of his childhood fantasies, not unlike the estate he dreamed up, the one with a kitchen in the bedroom.

When he retired for good, beyond the possibility of Golota III, he still managed to make the news—or the monologues, anyway. A story appeared in the spring of 1997 that Bowe was applying for a crossing-guard position near his home in Maryland. A lot of people thought this was pretty funny, that Bowe possibly had a fixation with uniforms that went well past his preoccupation with public safety. If he got the job, he'd get to wear a sash.

But all Bowe had wanted to do was work with kids, possibly as a peer mediation instructor, in a district where some of his nephews and nieces attended school. To a lot of people—some people, anyway—the man who was called Ridiculous Bowe early in his career didn't seem so ridiculous for wanting to fold some kids under his right hook. This was the same guy who had walked his mother to work all those midnights ago, and now he just wanted to keep some kids off the curb. Ex-champions could do worse.

With Bowe gone, the pool of heavyweight talent was drying to a puddle, drained by tragedy, poor management, and the usual eccentricities of the fighters themselves. It was no wonder that Team Tyson, hoping to invigorate their campaign, sought out Evander Holyfield for their next event. Holyfield, unlike his brethren, was a bighearted performer. It helped, probably, that he hadn't grown up a heavyweight but had become one artificially, adding those slabs of muscle in his work with bodybuilders. He wasn't one of them, the bully who'd meet the one kid who'd stand up to him and fold himself up in fear. Holyfield wouldn't do that. He wouldn't win, that much Team Tyson knew, but he wouldn't cooperate in his own defeat, at least. He'd give a show, wouldn't fall when somebody wafted a right hand at him. He'd restore some credibility to the comeback.

Considering what was out there, or even what had been out there, Holyfield was perfect.

Chapter Ten

"Champ? Champ? You there?"

Evander Holyfield was such damaged goods going into his first fight against Mike Tyson that anybody with the slightest responsibility for the match was scrambling for distance. Nobody wanted to figure any more prominently in his ring death than was absolutely necessary. So there was the usual battery of physical exams ordered by the Nevada commissioners, but there was also a second workup from the Mayo Clinic, and even medical visits to his training camp. The idea behind all this reassurance, beyond the satisfaction of Holyfield's health, seemed to be that the officials in charge would have just enough plausible deniability to erect a legal defense in the highly likely event of a tragedy. Morally, of course, they were committing first-degree murder. There was no question about that.

Holyfield, after all, was no longer just a spent bullet. He was actually a bomb waiting to go off, and he might take out everybody associated with him, including the Nevada State Athletic Commission. The NSAC had always been among the most respected in the industry. It had credibility and integrity and, even though it's the spigot through which enormous sums of money flow, had never been overtly influenced by the power of promoters or casinos. It really had conducted itself admirably in balancing the health of the business with that of the fighters. With Holyfield risking his life under their watch, even for $11 million, it might have looked as if the scales had tipped too far in favor of commerce.

The commission was understandably spooked. It had long been haunted by the ghost of Muhammad Ali, who fought an entirely purposeless fight in 1980 against Larry Holmes. Nobody ever blamed the commission outright for the mismatch, a bout that would never have been made except for the remaining drawing power of Ali's name (and Don King's persuasion). To behold the trembling husk that Ali is today is to find fault with anybody who contributed to his condition, and all those involved with that hopeless venture certainly figure in his awful shaking.

Holyfield was never the national treasure Ali was, but neither was he the kind of personality that could endure a similar neglect unnoticed. If he was going to be marched into the ring for some ritual sacrifice, bases would have to be covered.

Besides the exams at the Mayo Clinic, the second such required visit for Holyfield in two years, the commissioners also insisted on making two separate trips to Holyfield's training camp in Houston to watch him work out. As it turned out, everything came up aces, with Holyfield passing a full neurological test, an assessment of his cardio and pulmonary fitness, and also a look at his left shoulder. The commission couldn't very well withhold his boxing license—if there's one thing Holyfield seems to be, it's a perfect physical specimen—and it eventually voted to give him the go-ahead. But one of the commissioners who wasn't able to vote had been a longtime skeptic when it came to Holyfield. And a doctor on the medical advisory board, who also didn't vote, was on record as asking Holyfield to retire. There was a belief, in other words, that they were sending Holyfield to his doom.

A Savage Business

This belief was reasonable. The very inconsistencies of health and performance that had made Holyfield popular with Team Tyson were exactly what was causing such queasiness in the boxing community. He'd won just two of his last four fights—including the loss to Michael Moorer that was initially blamed on a heart condition—and even in victory he was suspect. It had been three years, when he had beaten Riddick Bowe, since he'd looked right.

The fight with Bobby Czyz was perhaps even more disturbing to the medicos than Holyfield's sudden fatigue in the final Bowe fight. With Czyz, in a fight held May 10, 1996, Holyfield appeared strangely lethargic. Czyz was a credible enough opponent, but he was on the downward trajectory of his career, heading into the announcer's booth where his alleged Mensa qualifications could be put to better use. Like Holyfield, he had built himself into a heavyweight, but had had to come much further; he had started as a middleweight.

Holyfield had his way with Czyz, but as obviously determined as he was to whack Czyz out, he could not floor him. Czyz finally took a standing eight count in the fifth round, complaining of a burning in his eyes, and the fight was stopped well short of anything encouraging to Holyfield's prospects in a Tyson fight. Win or not, it was his worst showing. And if it wasn't immediately remarked upon in the Tyson camp, it was certainly noticed elsewhere: Except for Czyz, Holyfield hadn't beaten anyone inside the distance in five years, and hadn't actually knocked anybody down for a full count in six.

Of course, Holyfield had his reasons, he always did. Holyfield is beyond compare in many ways, but he does share with his more pedestrian colleagues the ability to find excuse for failure. The noncompliant left ventricle, or stiff heart (or hole in the heart, as he later described it), was the source of defeat in the Michael Moorer fight. That excuse was not of his making, of course, but rather a seemingly quick-and-dirty diagnosis of a fighter who was exhausted and dehydrated (who may or may not have been healed by televangelist Benny Hinn). Later, his heart having been cleared, Holyfield said the real reason was a shoulder injury.

After the third Bowe fight, when he failed to capitalize on the knockdown, he said he had been sick with a virus earlier in his training and never should have gone through with it. As for Czyz, he said he got overexcited and fought like an amateur.

Others weren't buying it. More likely he had become just another of boxing's shell casings, spent and harmless, maybe even a disaster waiting to happen.

Certainly it was a long time since he'd been truly dangerous to anyone but himself. Teddy Atlas had seen a physical decline in Holyfield's abilities beginning in 1988, when he moved to heavyweight from cruiserweight. Atlas claimed he had put together a tape showing the deterioration to fire up Moorer, and had even urged his fighter forward when, during the fight, he saw how impaired Holyfield actually was. Against Czyz, Atlas was aghast at Holyfield's performance: "I hate to say this, but he looked almost talentless. I have a lot of wonderment about what I didn't see in that fight."

Emanuel Steward, who still believes his greatest feat as a trainer was in helping Holyfield overcome Bowe in their second fight, was similarly skeptical of Holyfield's return to the heavyweight elite. In his mind, the victory over Bowe had been a trick, an artificial result. "I mean, Bowe was bigger, he was better, what could Evander do?" Steward said. "The only thing I could think of was that Evander was a pretty good dancer. We worked on his rhythm that whole camp, and that's how he won." Steward, who left Holyfield in a money dispute after that fight, noted that Holyfield seldom sparred anymore—he did just 38 rounds for Bowe III—and preferred to indulge himself in a body-building camp, where he'd come out looking huge and buffed but otherwise unprepared for the bump-and-grind of a tough fight.

Even all the old Holyfield people had been gradually withdrawing support. Shelly Finkel, the mild-mannered rock and roll promoter, had quit as Holyfield's manager when the fighter refused to retire after the Moorer bout. And Main Events, which had promoted Holyfield through the lean times, though it maintained a business interest in his bouts, likewise was discouraging him from pursuing his career.

And that was even before Don King brought up the idea of a Tyson fight. At one time the match had made so much sense that it couldn't have possibly been made. A meeting had been scheduled in 1990, but Tyson got knocked off by Buster Douglas, leaving a subsequently fattened Buster for Holyfield. Then, in 1991, their bout was postponed because of a Tyson rib injury, then canceled when he was convicted of rape.

Now the only sense it made was economic. In bouts with Douglas, George Foreman, and Bowe, Holyfield had acquired many millions and a high recognition factor. The fights were generally more valuable for the opponent than for Holyfield himself, but the effect was that Holyfield, having survived them, was the third most famous heavyweight in the world, behind Tyson and Foreman. And maybe the richest: He'd made $120 million for himself. He would make you money, too.

And even at this stage in his career, he would deliver some action. Though he was an excellent boxer, he almost always allowed himself to get drawn into wars. Sometimes, he admitted, the fighting "bored" him. He had to mix it up. This suggested he'd be a partner in his own demise, probably hastening it by digging in against Tyson. He had too big a heart to go easy. That might offer a corrective to the sport, where boxers seemed to be going too easy, but it wasn't promising for Holyfield's continued health.

But, except for the commission and some of Holyfield's old

friends, who really cared? All the promoter knew, all the fans knew, was that here was a guy who wouldn't have to be coaxed into battle, who might fight back, who would provide out of what was left of his old holey heart a chance to see a grisly spectacle.

Disapproval of the Seldon swoon had proved one thing for sure: that Tyson needed a willing accomplice in these fights. If a fighter had to be prodded out of his cell on death row and strapped, screaming, into the electric chair, well, that wasn't going to work in the long run. People might pay gladly to see a fighter commit suicide; they just didn't want to be witness to an execution, no more than the commission did. That made everybody uncomfortable.

There was also a feeling that, as long as it was going to be a mismatch, it would have to be somewhat protracted. Holyfield could probably help in that regard, but just in case he couldn't, one of the pay-per-view distributors offered a pay-per-round gimmick. Cablevision Systems Corporation, with 2.8 million customers in the Cleveland area and on Long Island, came up with the idea of charging $9.95 per round, up to a maximum of $49.95. If Holyfield did decide, against all his history, to take a splash in, say, 109 seconds, the viewer would be out just ten bucks.

This seemed like a fine idea at first, somebody looking out for the consumer for once, until the conspiracy theorists convened on the subject—and that didn't take long. The possibility of Tyson carrying Holyfield beyond five rounds, then smacking him out at his convenience, suddenly occurred to someone, and before you knew it the over-and-under proposition had been removed in Las Vegas sports books. That was just one scenario. In fact, the length of the bout wouldn't matter financially to anybody but Cablevision; the performers themselves were not on the clock (Tyson would get his $30 million, Holyfield his $11 million, no matter what). But

—in Las Vegas, in boxing—the opportunity to modify a result for personal gain is too rich to be ignored. "It's a perception we don't like," said Marc Ratner, executive director of the commission. "It puts extra pressure on the fighters, ringside doctors, and referees."

These were the concerns, then: Could Holyfield survive a Tyson beating without provoking a congressional investigation into the sport's brutality, and could he survive one for at least five rounds so as to provide the glimmer of competition Tyson's comeback had so far lacked? There wasn't much worry about him winning; odds against him opened at 25-1 and drifted upward as the fight neared and the small-time gamblers leapt on the long money. Nobody worried very much about the short money.

That was one thing that was safe, the short money. The big boys knew their position and stuck to it. The sports books were entirely unfazed by the late bets, taking all the Holyfield money the fools wanted to pour in, not worrying about covering it. Among real bettors, Tyson was like a certificate of deposit: He didn't pay a lot to win, but the money was guaranteed. Lee Samuels, a fight publicist who worked in the Hilton sports book when the Tyson comeback was beginning, remembered the sense of certainty that ruled the town during this comeback. He showed up at work one night the week of the Peter McNeeley fight and discovered the operation was over a million dollars in jeopardy: The sports book had not bothered to cover the McNeeley money. He called his boss in a panic and wondered what he should do. "Take more McNeeley money," he was told. Take all he could get. Fifteen months later, the rule still applied. *Take the Holyfield money. All of it.*

Truth be told—and it never is until too late—Holyfield's training was not going all that great coming into the fight. If anybody knew what Holyfield knew in the early weeks of his workouts, the odds would have soared up to Buster Douglas territory. Every morning, after the entourage assembled in the House of Pain, a nondescript building in an industrial section of Houston, at 6 A.M. and had its circle of prayer, a sparring partner named Gary Bell would begin teeing off on Holyfield. Bell, who was Tyson's doppelgänger in the ring (and out, too), was starting to get scared. "When is this guy going to catch me on my doggone chin?" he wondered. Well, he might never, was how it was starting to look. Holyfield, who is not a man ordinarily given to doubt, was beginning to panic.

But Holyfield, over the course of his 34 years, had found time to drill several wells in his life, sumps he could return to in times of need and withdraw the required inspiration. Religion was one of them, of course. The religiosity factor of a Holyfield fight was generally quite high; interviews tended to take on all the important aspects of a tent revival. God was always "dropping" things to him by way of visions and epiphanies. And he found strength, fairly or not, in the assumption that because of his strong beliefs he was the chosen one in any given fight.

"I will beat Mike Tyson," he said before the fight. "There is no way I cannot, if I just trust in God. God is that good."

This was irksome and sounded arrogant to lots of folks, particularly his opponents who held their beliefs more privately and didn't understand why Holyfield deserved all the miracles. To everyone else, whose trust in God had long since been scattered at the pari-mutuel window or the blackjack table, this talk was just foolish. When it came to cashing big tickets, God didn't really care.

Still, if it provided the fighter some calm in his life, good for him. Including the few seconds he'd have in the eye of the storm come November 9, he could use all the calm he could get.

For this fight Holyfield had developed an additional resource, far more unlikely than religion: He'd gotten married. This was a major surprise. If he had simply gotten engaged, as he usually did before a big bout, it wouldn't have even made anyone's fight notes. An engagement for Holyfield was just another way of saying, "I must have a fight coming up." Afterward he'd conduct his business in Las Vegas or Atlantic City, go home to Atlanta, and call it off.

Before Bowe III, a year earlier, he had shown up in Las Vegas with the usual wedding announcement. He'd told friends that he cried whenever he thought about moving into his 5,200-square-foot home alone, and he was going to wed a 24-year-old student at Clayton State College. That never happened, which was no big news, either.

He was always getting engaged, he was always breaking up. This, despite a vow he'd never wed until he retired. He'd decided that in 1991, after a six-year marriage had dissolved. Maybe he could settle down afterward. Of course, he had bought an engagement ring in 1992, but only because he'd gotten a deal. Holyfield, a flagrant spender on the one hand, could be notoriously careful on the other. The ring, no matter its availability, was for later.

Yet that same availability was a temptation he couldn't resist, and he'd trotted out the ring on three occasions between 1992 and 1995, before thinking better of the idea each time. He always got that ring back, though. "I spent too much money on it for them to keep it," he said.

But this time he'd actually done it. He showed up in Las Vegas with Dr. Janice Itson, a 34-year-old internist from Chicago whom he'd seen in person no more than three or four times. They'd gotten married one week after he returned from his Houston training camp, celebrated the nuptials at a Shoney's restaurant, and back to camp he'd gone. As it had been an unconventional courtship, the actual wedding couldn't have been any surprise.

It had begun at a Benny Hinn revival and had been conducted over the phone, as the two principals quoted scripture back and forth. Even though Hinn, at the same meeting in Philadelphia in which he "cured" Holyfield with a laying on of hands, had announced that Holyfield's future wife was in the house, as Itson was, Holyfield had out-and-out dismissed that possibility; Itson was a nice enough girl who did not fit the feisty profile of his usual candidates.

He did call her in Chicago afterward, though, and was surprised that, during a 10-hour conversation, he managed just 10 minutes on his end. This was interesting, he thought. So he asked her to come to Atlanta to visit him and his children (he had six with three different women); more conversation but no romance. Holyfield recognized that, on paper, she was a perfect match. But in person she was a fizzle. He hoped to kindle something by taking her on a Hinn-led tour of the Holy Land in 1994, but again nothing happened and he gave up on the idea. He told her they'd just be friends.

And for two years, they remained that, phone buddies, burning up the wires with scripture talk, family talk, you name it. They got along so well . . . over the phone. He had another brainstorm. She should come to Atlanta and watch his kids. Biggest fight of his life, he told her. Really laid it on. "He sounded like he was going to cry," she said later. So she came down, with just two suitcases, leaving her work at a Chicago HMO to do some baby-sitting.

On his visits back to Atlanta, he continued to be impressed with her, in a practical way. "She knew things I didn't," he said. She was extremely savvy about business, good with the kids. Too bad, Holyfield thought, "she wasn't my type."

Holyfield was hoping to have it both ways, though, telling Itson that no matter what happened, they'd always be together. Itson remembered him saying they'd "always be together, even if I got married to somebody else." It was a bizarre take on their relationship, yet everybody around Holyfield noticed how preoccupied he was with her. The woman he was dating at the time wondered why he kept talking about his kids' nanny.

Then, on one trip back to Atlanta, he noticed she was kind of pretty. How had that escaped him? He returned to training confused. Then, during one of his early-morning workouts a month before the fight, God "dropped it to" him that he should marry Itson. He called her that night and, in a kind of sweet talk a lot of other women might have been able to deflect, said he wanted to get married but would have to do it Friday because of his schedule. Otherwise it was off.

Back in Atlanta Thursday night, he failed to mention it any further, and Itson, knowing his record with engagements, didn't press it. Then at midnight he suddenly whisked her off to a hospital emergency room for a blood test. The next day, again, nothing was said. Then, while they were together in a church meeting at four o'clock, Holyfield wondered, "When does this marriage office close?" They got there before it did —at 4:30—and Holyfield, in his T-shirt and jeans, produced a certain five-carat ring of some unspoken mileage and they were married. From there it was off to Shoney's for pie and then to Houston for his training. Itson sort of shrugged the whole thing off: "God does foolish things," she decided, "just so he can confound the wise."

If Holyfield had often been a fool, at least he was not a romantic fool. This was a marriage that had started more as a partnership than anything else (although Itson was soon enough pregnant). Itson, besides becoming a hands-on-mother to the three children at their house, was installed as the keeper of his various enterprises, a job she took to with surprising gusto (firing deadwood, examining suspicious charges on bills). But her first, and perhaps most important, contribution was to get the fighter squared away in his sparring.

He had been calling home, complaining of his inability to put punches together, worrying about how much pain he was going to undergo in the Tyson fight. After one such call, at 5:30 in the morning, Itson decided this was a man putting too much pressure on himself. The solution, she was sure, was in a hymn she knew—she told him to go find his song-book and report back. He returned to the phone with "Be Magnified," a hymn that puts man in proper perspective with his Lord. "Sing along," she told him over the phone.

That day he bloodied a sparring partner, and a recording of "Be Magnified" was put in the gospel-music rotation that was the soundtrack to his comeback. The whole camp was singing it; they could hardly not, it was so constant. Gary Bell, who said he had been pushing Holyfield around the ring, was now taking a whipping. Dr. Janice Itson, it should be noted here, had never to this point seen a boxing match.

Holyfield, as if his marriage wasn't telling enough, did not operate according to the laws of boxing—or anything, really. He was an odd duck, full of inconsistencies, contradictions, and outright foolishness.

Take money. He can tell you, to the penny, what he earned per hour pumping gas at Atlanta's DeKalb-Peachtree Airport as a teenager ($2.10), how he paid cash for everything up-front because "it's worse to have something and have it taken back, than to never have it at all." Yet, for all these conser-vative instincts, he couldn't prevent a 54,000-square-foot mansion (that 5,200-square-footer was a starter kit) from sprawling well beyond its budget into the $15 million range.

Then again: After his upset of Bowe, he refused to pay Emanuel Steward $300,000 to help him train for Bowe III (they split up over $100,000) and decided to save $25,000 on a cut man (yes, he was cut in his next fight). But: According

A Savage Business

to a story well circulated in boxing, he didn't flinch at dropping a million bucks at blackjack in Atlantic City.

Sportswriters in Atlanta would chuckle among themselves when, covering a Falcons game, they'd see Holyfield, the richest man in Atlanta who didn't actually own Coca-Cola or CNN, pop into the press box at halftime. There was no doubt in their minds that the attraction was the free hot dogs.

Money is inevitably a complicated issue for somebody who grew up poor, somebody like Holyfield who thought all the big houses he saw were make-believe houses, "TV houses." Fighters will often admit to confusion in this area. Holyfield was probably no different than most.

But Holyfield was unusual among fighters in one way, at least. He'd admit to spasms of fear, feelings of dread. This just wasn't done in boxing, and it was doubly surprising to hear it from Holyfield, whose reputation was 100 percent bravado. Yet, as talk of Tyson invariably brought the subject up, he spoke easily of how he controlled these uncertain emotions.

He made it plain he wasn't afraid of Tyson, but he had been afraid of other fighters. In fact, as a young amateur he was afraid of them all. "I was scared of everything I did," he said before the Tyson fight, "but especially boxing." As a youngster he was doing well and the kids were so well protected with pads and gear that even Holyfield knew, afraid as he was, that he wasn't in real jeopardy. "As much torment as I was living in, I assumed I would quit before I got to, say, eighteen." That, from his studies on the subject, was when boys became men and began to come home with broken noses.

This terror was unrelieved until he was seventeen, when he was matched in a 147-pound bout and was knocked silly by a left hook. He understands now that he suffered a concussion; all he knew about the fight was secondhand. Apparently

Richard Hoffer

he got up off the floor, spit out his mouthpiece, and bit his opponent on the neck. He went home, certain he'd been denied the chance to fight at all ("Coach wouldn't let me box," he told his mother), and went into a sound sleep.

The bout came back to him, most of it, the next day, and he had an important realization: That was the worst they could do to him? He hadn't felt a thing. Didn't remember much, but certainly had no memory of pain or discomfort. "I was never afraid again," he said.

This was all curious stuff—he bit a guy?—but none of it would have affected the betting line, no matter how much of it was known. The fact that he wasn't prone to fear in the ring was encouraging to Cablevision Systems, who hoped to collect the full $49.95, but was otherwise irrelevant. His beating would simply be sustained over many rounds, instead of just the introduction.

However, what most people didn't know was how excited Holyfield became in the face of bullies. Perhaps because he felt he'd been victimized as a kid—bullied in boxing all those young years—he was especially anxious to topple that big, mean kid, the one who'd made him afraid for so long.

People first noticed this when Holyfield was trying out for the 1984 Olympic team. Because of his age and origin, he was an outsider, called "Country" by the younger guys and mostly shunned. This was fine with Holyfield, who preferred to mind his own business anyway. But there was this one boxer, Ricky Womack, who really had it in for Holyfield. They were rivals for the same spot but it was more than that. Womack was the team bully, and was good at it.

Womack intimidated everybody, but his principal target was Holyfield, which he demonstrated at their weigh-in once. While "Country" was just standing there, Womack walked up to him and stomped hard on Holyfield's instep. This, however, was a dangerous position to take with Holyfield. He

208

beat Womack twice in the box-offs to get an Olympic berth. Holyfield went to Los Angeles, won a bronze metal in the 178-pound division, got a pretty good send-off into the pros, and ended up with a big house. Womack, ever the bully, picked on an old woman in an armed robbery. He's in a big house, too.

Similarly secret was Holyfield's relationship with Tyson, another outcast at that Olympic camp. Tyson, just 17, was trying for the heavyweight spot, so the two weren't rivals. Rather, they formed a bond, mostly based on Holyfield's sympathy for the young, hardworking fighter with the slight lisp. Holyfield saw that the other members of the team were cruel to Tyson. But Holyfield also saw a kid "that worked harder than anybody else," was lonely, and "just wanted to talk to somebody."

"He was just a big kid," Holyfield said, "but he always listened to what I said."

One mini-legend concerns a sparring session in the camp at Colorado Springs when the two knockout artists were put together for a little work. Tyson promised to use one hand, to neutralize their weight difference, but he quickly dropped that concession and the two were going full-bore until a coach stopped them before they'd even gone two rounds.

But there is an even lesser-known story that came out of that camp, one that might have swayed the betting line, if only a little. In a rec room one afternoon Tyson was taking his turn on the pool table. He scratched and, refusing to sit down and wait another turn, started to rack them up. Holyfield jumped up and said he was next. The two squared off for a second, maybe no longer, and Tyson ran off to his room. Holyfield racked 'em up.

Still, Holyfield always maintained an affection and respect for Tyson, even going so far as to say that Tyson inspired him to move up to heavyweight. He figured if Tyson, short and squat as he was, could compete there, perhaps he could, too. But he always recognized the bully in Tyson, and he knew he had another Ricky Womack in his sights.

Emanuel Steward remembered Holyfield talking about a Tyson fight, wistfully more than anything. "Tyson's just a little bully," Holyfield would tell Steward. "Just a little kid." Steward, though he felt Holyfield had done him wrong, nevertheless was one of the few people in boxing to give him a chance against Tyson. "Evander's just got an obsession with bullies," he said. "It's part of his mental makeup."

Holyfield was also ridiculously competitive. Ron Borges of the *Boston Globe* once visited Holyfield at his original Atlanta compound and got a tour of the various athletic facilities built on the property. There's the pool, he'd tell Borges, then pause and remind him he could beat him swimming. There's the basketball court. Could beat you at hoops. Bowling alley. Beat you there. On and on—exasperating at first, then just comical.

Dino Duva remembered Holyfield camps where everybody would have to go bowling with him. They'd play along until Holyfield pulled a frame or two ahead, then they could all go home. "He's an okay bowler," said Duva, "not great, but okay. He'd just play until he beat you." Everybody was glad when that happened sooner rather than later, because otherwise a long night lay ahead.

For Holyfield, success in the ring meant the ability to proselytize outside it. He wasn't obnoxious about it, but, as you might expect of him, he was unrelenting. An unguided conversation with him could quickly swerve into religious territory, from which there was no return. It was possible to see how his faith reassured him; the parable of David and Goliath was very much in his mind this particular November ("No Philistine was gonna whip him," he'd say of David). And it was possible to glimpse what he was fighting for, the chance to move his pulpit into a bigger church. "I know," he said of this huge event, "that it put a lot of eyes on me." And how could it not be inspirational to those borderline converts? "A lot of them, they say 'I don't think he can win.' If I win, 'There is a God!'"

Well, perhaps. On the other hand, the basis of his message was that this fight would go to the godliest and that, obviously, was him. Holyfield played this self-righteousness in a minor key, but it could still be heard by all. For sure, Tyson heard it. And although it had been profitable for him to be pictured as the Antichrist (though it was not an effective defense in his rape case, where attorneys tried to argue he was a well-known devil—all beauty contestants beware), he was stung by it all the same.

He, or perhaps just his camp, seemed particularly upset by a comment Holyfield had supposedly made five years before. According to John Horne, Holyfield had said he "would never fight a rapist. [Tyson] wasn't even tried then. You don't do that to a guy in your field."

Holyfield insisted he'd never said any such thing, but Team Tyson was determined to make much hay of it. At a New York press conference in October, with all parties present, Horne managed to make an issue of it, trying for some reason to turn an attractive matchup into some hellish grudge match. "Mike Tyson has never raped anybody in his life," he said, "and the only rape is going to be committed on November 9. That's when he's going to rape somebody."

Holyfield sat silently through this as Tyson cronies began shouting, "Get out the stretcher," and "He's got to pay." Even Tyson, uninvolved at first, responded. "I read the papers," he said. "He knows what he said. If he's not man enough to say it, that's on him."

Thus, with the promise of a rape in the ring, did another breath of fresh air waft through boxing. The two former teammates, once united in their stand against narrow-minded boxers and coaches, were now in each other's face over matters that had largely been invented by John Horne. Tyson to Holyfield: "You're out of your league." Holyfield got within his mustache of Tyson's face and appeared to be trembling—some thought in fear, others in anger.

Behind them all, Don King stood with his arms raised, yelling out from his pulpit, preaching his own special gospel of chaos. "We've got a violent situation here," he yelled, happily. Praise the Lord.

How much of this was spontaneous—Horne ranting about the disrespect Holyfield had paid "my man" and how he personally hoped Tyson would "inflict the pain"—and how much was planned was impossible to know. In any event, that single exchange was enough to plunge the promotion into Team Tyson ugliness. A fight that might have been organized with dignity, like a Bowe-Holyfield bout where mutual respect was the overriding theme (the fighters' mutual exasperation became comic in that context), was now characterized by hate.

Holyfield could be irritating, there's no question. Anybody who wears a scripture passage into the ring (Phil. 4:13) is bound to come off as a little too high-minded for his own good. And, in fact, Holyfield had said something back then about Tyson's upcoming rape conviction. *Flash,* a boxing newsletter, quoted Holyfield in its February 29, 1992, issue as saying, "It would be wrong for me to be fighting somebody convicted of such a crime as rape. I'm very disappointed, and it's sad in a way, but the punishment fits the crime."

Still, had it been necessary for Team Tyson to make the rape of one boxer by another the fight's central metaphor? Is that what sold tickets? "If Tyson's people are doing this for the hype," Holyfield said, "they are dead wrong."

Something about this bout was making the boys edgy, that

was for sure. Tyson, in his dealings with the press at least, was not in a much better mood than Horne. He'd already complained that, as a result of his press coverage, he'd been "dehumanized and abused too long. I wipe my ass with the papers I get." In a conference call with members of the media a week before the fight, Tyson abruptly left the interview, bored, upset, who knew? Reporters hung on the line for 10 more minutes—"Champ? Champ? You there?"—before the fact of his departure dawned on them.

Maybe it was Holyfield's equanimity. He was guaranteeing victory, which, in the face of his certain destruction, almost seemed unsportsmanlike. Admit your defeat, for godsakes! Visitors to his Houston camp got the same treatment, though, a surreal show of confidence. They'd watch him work at the downtown gym, follow him to the training house in a gated Houston community off one of the main drags, watch him eat his biscuits and gravy and eggs, listen to him prattle on about the edge he had in psychology and, of course, his faith. They'd even take notes from the framed print hanging on a wall, *The Reasons I'm a Winner—Evander Holyfield*, which listed no fewer than 21 instruments of victory (number seven: "I have overcome many adversities, and as a result I am smarter and closer to God").

As the fight drew nearer, he maintained this confidence. And even though he might not be the right man to listen to when it came to gambling (if those Atlantic City stories were true), he was nevertheless advising people to jump on those long odds, make some money alongside him. "People who need to get the rent paid," he said, "can get it paid now."

At some point, most everybody agreed, Holyfield had stepped beyond the contender's traditional whistling-in-the-graveyard. This was no longer just the mindless kind of chatter that bolsters a man as he awaits his own demise. He was now delusional. Shelly Finkel, who held out little hope for

Holyfield, said, "He has a great ability to rationalize." Holyfield, of course, had already demonstrated a talent for that. "No offense to anyone's beliefs," said Teddy Atlas, referring to Holyfield's cure at the hands of a televangelist, "but that does say something about the guy's ability to deal with reality." So, many believed, did his supreme confidence going into a Tyson fight.

Tyson, for his part, had gotten over his initial anger at Holyfield and had come to think of him as just one more piece of work as the fight approached. He was coaxed out of his routine seclusion the week of the fight and met some writers in King's town house again, with a computerized baby grand tinkling Mozart in the background (and King grinding coffee beans in the kitchen). There he revealed himself to be decidedly less agitated than he'd seemed before. He downplayed his and Holyfield's friendship from the amateurs—"Nobody counseled me, we just hung out one night"—and also dismissed the idea that he was going to repay Holyfield for his lack of support. "I don't hate anyone," he insisted. The fight was only business. "I'm just here to render my services."

It was, again, a struggle to find a theme in his 75-minute discourse, a ramble that rivaled the pre-Seldon monologue for its stream-of-consciousness. But one thread that stitched everybody's notes together was his new and dispassionate approach to boxing. He was a young businessman with surprisingly conservative politics, just a guy who wanted to make a few bucks for his family and not see it get eaten up by some welfare policy.

As for boxing, he admitted he still liked the part about getting into the ring. But to hear him talk, the bells he really liked hearing were those from the cash register. "Boxing's pretty interesting," he said. "Thirty million a whop. Not too bad. I've been beaten half to death for nothing." He was punching in, punching out. "All I know is that Saturday I'll pick up thirty million, and then Monday I'll sign up for another thirty million."

He didn't seem to feel much pride in his achievements or much concern for his legacy. He felt professional and dignified, though, a good worker who wouldn't disappoint. Others, he pointed out, could not say as much. Roberto Duran, for example, his hero, had actually quit in the *"No más"* fight with Sugar Ray Leonard. Tyson had cried at the result. The one thing he'd never do, he promised that night, was quit. "I didn't feel too proud after the Douglas fight," he admitted, "but I never quit a day in my life. Take a beating, what the hell. It's not too bad. Only thing left is dignity, and some people have different concepts of dignity. To not take a beating is immoral."

He knew that some of his recent opponents had failed to take their beating, had "taken the money and run," yet he also understood that they had been forced into uncharted territory—by his intimidation or his punches, he didn't know —and responded in a human fashion. Holyfield, for that matter, might quit. "Stranger things have happened to stranger people," he said.

In another room the Yamaha kept cranking out the Mozart, and Tyson, the savage beast, was soothed. He began talking about his children—three daughters—and how his career was now devoted entirely to their well-being. It was for them he was making the $30 million a whop. "My life is over," he said, "but my children's life is just beginning. Now I've got to do something I've never been equipped to do. I've got to set an example."

He knew that his past would haunt him, that "the crappy deals in my life are no secret." But he hoped he could somehow set the record straight. "Now, I can't hang out with the guys as much because I've got to tell them what I used to do was bad. I've got to explain to them I did it because I wasn't a smart guy back then. I'm not really looking forward to it, but it's something that has to be done."

His kids would have advantages he never had, that was for sure. And it was a source of much pride that his children would be "the first generation of the Tyson family not on welfare," which he had now decided was a "bad crutch," and a reform for which he'd vote, if only he still had a vote.

Maybe, he wondered, it would have been different for him if he'd grown up with the same privileges. Maybe not. "I would like to think I was that way because of financial reasons or my environmental status," he said. "But I don't think that was the reason, really."

Tyson, perhaps by design, was now presenting himself as a grown-up, a man who would take his beatings, who would accept responsibility for his past, who could earn a good living for his family and was devoted enough to his children that he might change a diaper—"I'm capable of doing it," he said. It was possible to sense, at these little talks of his, his idealized version of a man. It wasn't that he was giving you what you wanted to hear—parole board talk; rather, you glimpsed him reassembling himself into what he thought a decent enough citizen must be. It was almost as if he'd been studying different models of popular domestication, taking something from this one, something from that. He even sounded like Bill Cosby at one point. Talking about the day when he'd meet his daughter's first date, Tyson became suddenly pleased with the idea of fatherhood. He imagined himself in this future, patting a seat on the couch next to him. "Sit down right here, buddy," he said to this future date. Everybody laughed—a little nervously, of course.

The talk zigged this way and that and, like a Holyfield discourse, became less and less useful. Soon everybody got up to leave. But a few remained to hear Tyson—again, almost reluctant to see his audience depart—tell of a visit he'd gotten at the Indiana Youth Center. Tupac Shakur had come by, and —in a turnabout that his sentencing judge might have enjoyed—Tyson was giving the rapper advice, telling him to get out of his gangster life. Shakur went into a racial rant, rapping against "whitey" and "the system," and Tyson was stunned by the familiarity of what he was hearing. "Was I like that?" he asked his friends afterward. Maybe, they said. In telling the story, Tyson covered his face, laughing, and said, "Oh, no."

Afterward, here's what you thought: Tyson was making a grab for normalcy. The thug from Brownsville was reaching out for all those American conventions, the suburban life where the only person he'd have to intimidate would be Rayna's date. He felt he could afford to be a good townsperson now. He was making $30 million a whop.

This portrait of a young Republican was not the sort of thing that encouraged anybody to think Tyson's heart was still in the game. Still, given the competition that had been arranged, it wasn't a game he had to be that into to win. And besides, he had always shown the ability to slough off the thin mantle of civilization once he got inside the ring to reveal the fighter's true pathology. He was reliable in that way; bones would be driven into brain, synapses splintered, flesh skinned to the skull. If the opponent would just stand for it (and Holyfield would) there'd be a colorful palette of gore for everyone to enjoy, no matter Tyson's growing concern over his tax bite.

The prospect of fully realized violence was driving sales to record levels. Two days before this event, Cablevision, to name one, was reporting a buy rate of three times that for the Peter McNeeley fight. The promotion was steamrolling ahead to its typically awful conclusion.

In his hotel room the night of the fight, it was finally occurring to Holyfield just what he had gotten himself into.

There are not many fighters willing to acknowledge their

doubt, but Holyfield was suddenly coming to the realization that he might be in trouble. He wondered how much pain he'd have to suffer, how much work he'd have to do, whether he'd be embarrassed. It may be true that there are no atheists in foxholes, but Holyfield also knew there were rarely faith healers in Las Vegas dressing rooms. He was a little tight.

"Lord, you look nervous," said his new bride. Uh, yeah, he tried to explain. He was about to get into the ring with a killing machine. Dr. Janice Itson, who was definitely not the fight doc, decided on a prescription of dance. That's what her husband needed to do: dance. Holyfield's formidable jaw, you can be sure, dropped to the industrial-strength carpet. Did she have any understanding whatsoever of his task, of his jeopardy, of his opportunity for failure on so grand a scale? She put on the gospel song "Mighty Man of War," and they danced away. Later, when it was all over, she would say, "Boy, is he an excellent dancer."

The fight unfolded like a dream—Holyfield's, presumably. Holyfield ambled in under the notes of a soft ballad; he was singing along on the ring walk. Tyson entered at a run, Crocodile articulating the carnage his man was about to produce. It was enough to send you running to the sports book to add more money to your Tyson plunge.

But then it went off so contrary to expectations that it was difficult at first to understand what was happening. It dawned on ringsiders rather quickly that one thing that was not happening was Tyson destroying Holyfield. He might not even have been in the same fight with him. Furthermore, the impression grew, round by round, that Tyson was now in a fight he could never win. Looking at a tape of the fight, it is possible to see how Holyfield asserted his dominance from the get-go. But watching it happen in front of your eyes, there was the natural inclination not to believe them at first. In an upset like this, there is always lag time between a comfortable preconceived notion and reality.

A Savage Business

Tyson's comeback had been so assured, so carefully scheduled, the destination so obvious and well marked that the recurring metaphor had been of a train steaming across a desert landscape, the diesels chugging implacably, driving, driving, driving. Train Tyson, having left the station in Indiana a year and a half ago, now had a momentum that prohibited the very idea of an unscheduled stop. It could derail, everybody knew that, but it couldn't be stopped, or even slowed very much.

If you favored such a metaphor, what you soon heard was train cars clanking in the night air, piling into one another as the familiar machinery of menace was wrenched to a standstill. Evander Holyfield was bringing it to a grinding, screeching halt.

Holyfield, who had led his own team in a revival-style rendition of "Be Magnified" in the dressing room (it was so rousing that even the commission inspectors were singing along), was truly inspired. He did what no other heavyweight had done in Tyson's comeback: he fought back, countering with his own right hand, a maneuver that seemed to stop Tyson in his tracks.

Holyfield was all over Tyson—who had weighed in at a career-high 222 pounds—actually pushing him around. You would not have suspected that Tyson had a seven-pound advantage in weight as Holyfield backed him into the ropes. Tyson would lead, Holyfield would counter, they'd clinch, and Holyfield would muscle him around a bit.

It was amazing to behold. Tyson demonstrated his awesome firepower in the fifth round with a right to Holyfield's body that he doubled up into an uppercut. It was a devastating combo, but Holyfield only backed up a little and then rushed in to clinch. He did not fall or even look like he had thought much about it.

The fight was inexorably spinning beyond Tyson's control. In the sixth round, Holyfield head-butted Tyson, opening a cut at the corner of his left eye that caused referee Mitch Halpern to call time and ask for a ruling from Dr. Flip Homansky, the ringside physician. Homansky motioned for the fight to continue, but it was an injury that clearly nagged at Tyson. And then, perhaps a minute later, with the crowd crying "Holy-field! Holy-field!" the challenger countered with a left hook and an uppercut that sent Tyson to the floor. It was only the second knockdown of Tyson's career, and the first time he got back up.

The bout lasted five more rounds because, in the reptilian portion of Tyson's brain, some prehistoric wiring kept pushing him forward. He was lost, not really conscious, but somehow determined to take his beating like a man. In the seventh round, their two heads met, hard enough that Tyson nearly dropped from the clash. He gasped in pain, stood upright, and complained once more to Halpern about Holyfield's head butts. It was the surprise of the bully who had always assumed his own advantages were fair and deserved. In the 10th it got worse, as Holyfield connected with 23 power punches. Holyfield finally connected with a right that drove Tyson across the ring and would have driven him into defeat right then and there, but for the bell. Many months later Tyson would remember that he didn't feel those punches, but rather heard them—"whoosh, whoosh, whoosh."

The tilt of the battle was such that Tyson's corner, an admittedly confused group, could justifiably have kept him on his stool before the 11th. Their advice to that point had not been very useful, consisting of such counsel as "Go out and hit him, kill him." They were of no more service here, and so Tyson marched out to gather his obvious destiny. Holyfield, keeping out of grabbing range now, unleashed a volley, uncorked jab after jab, combinations, slamming him into the ropes again, and Halpern stepped in to stop the fight.

It was a strange sight then to see Tyson, off in some ether,

A Savage Business

the physical part of him supported by his corner, men in homburgs marching him out of the ring, perhaps out of boxing history. It was all over. It had been over for several rounds, actually.

The shock of this outcome couldn't be fully absorbed at one sitting. It was too strange an idea to make immediate sense. Holyfield had beaten Tyson? Knocked him out? The only possible reaction was a mindless commotion, a roar rolling through the arena. It was not a partisan noise—cheers for Holyfield, boos for Tyson—but just a well-voiced confusion. It was a mass articulation of surprise, a powerful sound.

There was no explaining the turnaround. It could not be explained away by strategy, although many tried. Holyfield claimed he had known for years that "when he dips and throws a left hook, either you get hit or you hit him first with a right hand." It's true, and others had observed it, that by hitting Tyson first you could frazzle the circuitry of his reflexes a little bit. You could forestall his advance for a nanosecond. But that didn't really explain the completeness of Holyfield's mastery.

Tyson was no help afterward, either. He said he "got caught in something strange," perhaps in the third round, and had "blacked out." "I don't remember the round," he said. "I don't even remember the fight."

He understood that he had lost and to whom, though. Dressed, his forehead bruised purple, he spotted Holyfield on the press conference dais and strode over to offer his hand. "It's been so long," he said. "I jut want to touch you."

It was odd, yet not at all awkward. The two of them understood something they couldn't possibly share with anyone else. They alone knew what a terrible, awful, and beautiful thing it is that they do. They had that between them.

But that moment, sweet for boxing, was soon lost. Around them the engineers were twisting knobs, shoveling coal, resetting dials, trying to get this damn train going again. John Horne was assuring people that this was "nothing he's not mentally prepared to handle. This is just a job to us." Don King said they would "reconnoiter the area, deploy our forces, alter the game plan." And Rory Holloway was saying, "This is just a minor step in the life and times of Mike Tyson. Not even in the Top Ten list of tragic things."

Holyfield was barely coy at the suggestion that he could retire now. "I guess I could," he said, "now that I have a wife." But he seemed to be saying, with his lopsided, gargoylelike smirk, that of course there'd be a rematch.

Everybody grows large in the safety of the postfight scene, but Tyson alone remained shrunken in his defeat. He had been made mortal again, and stripped of his invincibility he was much smaller, beyond the possibility of inflation by Team Tyson. It occurred to you, perhaps for the first time, how short he actually was compared to Holyfield. The bleatings of his "staff" sounded all around him, but he refused to grow back into his old self. Instead he was sad, proud, dignified— human, for once. Not King's wind-up monster—not in this moment—just another guy, somebody like you or me, who'd had a bad day at the office. He had been made ordinary.

Asked if he'd come back from this defeat to fight again, he spread his hands and said he had no choice. In this hubbub, with Train Tyson promising only a short stop for repairs, it was not an answer so much as it was a complaint. It was as if, at last, he understood his role in these proceedings and he wasn't so sure he liked it. "I make so much money to fight," he said, "how can I not come back?"

Thirty million a whop.

Chapter Eleven

"They didn't like me. I knew that. I felt that. They never liked me."

Defeat is sometimes the ultimate personality corrective. What doesn't destroy you, as the old philosopher liked to say, might make you wear sunglasses and a fake goatee. Floyd Patterson, another of Cus D'Amato's prodigies, was engulfed in enough shame after Sonny Liston knocked him out that he put a makeup man from Poughkeepsie in his employ. He told the writer George Plimpton that he had disguises sufficient to keep him undetected in any of his normal daily activities. His favorite was a sort of Charlie Chaplin outfit, cane too, that he once wore to a fight in Madison Square Garden. He hobbled up and down the aisles in great arthritic distress. But he also had a variety of paste-on beards and sideburns, even wigs, to confound those who would spot him at the grocery store and recognize Floyd Patterson, loser.

George Foreman was even more profoundly affected after Muhammad Ali tricked him in Zaire. Costuming wouldn't cloak his disgrace. The big man had wasted himself on Ali, who had simply stood against the ropes with his elbows up, then clobbered Foreman so mightily that his entire corner was scattered. Suddenly he was nothing, and he had nobody.

Foreman might have been a good case study for Mike Tyson, so similar were they in personality and circumstance.

Like Tyson, Foreman had been, to the point of his defeat, a sullen intimidator whose dubious idol was Sonny Liston. Like Tyson, he had been a lifelong bully who began with a misspent youth (Foreman grew up in Houston's Fifth Ward, terrorizing everybody with his bulk and boorishness) and was used to having his way. Like Tyson, he was a remorseless oppressor. The former Oakland Raider Lester Hayes, who grew up under the rule of Foreman's Hester House gang, has the following memory of Foreman:

"First time I met George Foreman I was in the seventh grade, hanging around a neighborhood store. Up walks George Foreman and he asks me to loan him a nickel. I was eating a greasy-spoon hamburger, too, so he asks me for a bite of that. He took the entire burger. The next time I saw George, the idea of a nickel was null and void. I loaned him a quarter. It seemed to me huge inflation was taking place. Of course, I would have gone home and found a quarter for him if I didn't have one on me. He was a very, very big kid and had a reputation for savage butt kickings. That was his forte. So by the age of twelve, I had met George Foreman twice and I found both occasions extremely taxing."

That pretty much characterized everybody's experience with Foreman. He was infatuated with the idea of violence to others and was so taken with the notion of being a highly dangerous criminal that his vision of an attractive personal appearance was a long scar down his face. Much, much later the idea seemed sad to him. "Can you imagine, my goal was to have a scar on my cheek?" he once said. "I tell you, I wore a Band-Aid across my cheek until the day I could get a real one."

But for a long time the image wasn't a bit sad to him. He and his handlers flourished as his reputation for bullying others—Lester Hayes, Joe Frazier—grew. There is always a place in the heavyweight division for just such a character. There's even a compound word for them: moneymakers.

A Savage Business

Then that fight in Zaire. Ali, besides uncovering the big bully, stripped away Foreman's appetite for victimization and totally ruined him as a profitable draw. Afterward, Foreman was virtually unemployable. His glowering shtick was no longer an act that would sell, not with the memory of him folding almost in two in Zaire. He was a loser.

That defeat, every bit as shocking as Tyson's, changed Foreman himself in ways small and large. Throughout the long campaign in Africa, he had been utterly disdainful of his support troops. He had a PR man named Bill Caplan who was not even allowed to speak to him. Caplan would pass him notes trying to set up interviews, and Foreman would crumple them unread. Their only interaction was Ping-Pong, which was the big pastime in Foreman's camp; Caplan, who had been humiliated by his boss in every public outing, beat the big man with a vengeance. Archie Moore, Foreman's chief strategist, begged Caplan to let Foreman win. "No way," Caplan told him. It was the small revenge of the bullied.

After the fight, after Foreman had been revealed for what he was, his corner, with the exception of Caplan, disappeared in disgust. Their moneymaker was down for the count and their natural impulse was to get out of the country. Alone in the dressing room, if you can be alone with 200 newsmen crowded around you, Foreman broke a long and uncomfortable silence with these amazing words: "I have a statement to make. I just want to say that tonight"—long pause—"I found a true friend in Bill Caplan."

It took Foreman a long time to take himself apart and put anything back together again. It was two years before he could really admit to defeat. "Man," he told a reporter, "he whipped me fair and square. He'd probably whip me again." It was the first time he could say anything like it, and the effect was amazing. The weight of the loss finally slid off him.

By then Foreman had been beaten again, in a strange fight with Jimmy Young, and had once more been plunged into

225

the fighter's purgatory, a lifeless limbo between his previous importance and the resurrection that would soon be necessary. Nobody before or since has ever articulated the actual feeling of defeat better than Foreman, recalling how he felt in Puerto Rico after the Young fight.

He was "in a deep, dark nothing, like out in a sea, with nothing over your head or under your feet. Just nothing. Nothing but nothing. A big dark lump of it. And a horrible smell came with it, a smell I haven't forgotten. A smell of sorrow. You multiply every sad thought you ever had, it wouldn't come close to this. And then I looked around and I was dead. That was it. I thought of everything I worked for. I hadn't said good-bye to my mother, my children. All the money I hid in safe-deposit boxes! You know how paper burns and when you touch it, it just crumbles? That was my life. I looked back and saw it crumble, like I'd fallen for a big joke."

Foreman, out of this abyss, found God, retired from boxing, became a curbside evangelist, and later had his own church in Houston. It would be nearly two decades before he came back to boxing, so thoroughly transformed that he was unrecognizable—his disguise being incredible girth and a cuddly and comic persona that made him the most beloved fighter of this era. He had become the Anti-Foreman.

As the inevitable rematch approached, Tyson did not appear to have undergone a similar metamorphosis. Fighters have been more resilient in defeat than either Patterson or Foreman (Ali suffered no such crisis in defeat), but you still expected some evidence that Tyson had smelled the sorrow, had felt a nothingness beneath his feet, had felt the victim of a big joke. In almost everybody's mind, the Douglas fight had been an aberration, the upset a consequence of his training (jetting from Tokyo to New York's China Club!), his celebrity, his cockiness. But the Holyfield fight was much harder to explain away. A bully had been exposed. Surely Tyson, whose life had so neatly paralleled Foreman's, had the chance to look back and see burned paper crinkling at the slightest touch.

But no, he wasn't admitting to any such despair. The difference may have been that, while Foreman's men had jumped ship. Tyson's stayed at his shoulder, murmuring into his ears. *You took him cheap, Mike. You overlooked him, champ. Big paydays coming.* John Horne and Rory Holloway constructed comforting realities for their fighter. That was the true function of Team Tyson, to filter and shape experience to the maximum benefit of the promotion. Ali had his Bundini Brown, too, a professional shouter, but that was more Ali's indulgence of a slightly ridiculous friend. To have a man like Crocodile on the payroll, as Tyson did, suggested how important it was to keep Tyson's head filled with gibberish, to keep everything else out of it.

As a result, Tyson did not deal with defeat, except perhaps at night when the din of Team Tyson subsided. Perhaps then he imagined himself as a dark lump of nothing. By day, though, it was a brave front all around. More dignified than before, a little magnanimous even as he refused to be addressed as Champ by his cronies. But otherwise he pretended to be unchanged.

Holyfield was jetting around the country in the weeks after the upset, appearing in parades and filling TV screens with his huge mug, enjoying his victory, his life. From Las Vegas he had flown to Los Angeles to appear on ESPN's *Up Close* and *The Tonight Show* with Jay Leno. Then it was off to New York to do *Good Morning, America*, Regis and Kathie Lee, a spot on *Saturday Night Live*, and over to Chicago for Oprah.

Tyson, who would have been longer odds to make that circuit than to be beaten in the first place, simply retired into his staff's explanations, quietly awaiting his vindication. Horne explained that, while Holyfield was indeed beating his fighter's "butt," there had been other factors involved in the result. "Mike was not in his best condition at all," he said. After the Seldon fight in September, Tyson had been forced to spend more than three weeks dealing with a civil suit brought by Kevin Rooney, who was seeking a portion of Tyson's earnings. Then, because of his probation, he had to return to Ohio for a specified period before he could begin training in Las Vegas, just a month before the fight.

At the time, nobody thought Tyson would need more. "Mike Tyson has whipped a lot of butt," Horne said. "When you become that dominant and you're fighting a guy who was knocked out by Bowe and couldn't knock out Czyz, you tend to take him lightly."

Tyson himself was not so prone to alibi. Then again, he had little memory of the fight itself (immediately afterward, still in the ring, he asked one of his cornermen what round he had knocked Holyfield out in). This may have been helpful to his ego. After a passage of time, when the rematch was announced for May 3, Tyson did allow, "I never dreamed he could fight that well." Still, the defeat had not produced any doubt in his mind, caused him to reconsider his talent or reappraise his chances. He said he was "going to fight him like I knocked him out the first time. I'm going to win the title for the third time and be in the books with him." Later he said, "I had a bad night, but I am the best fighter in the world."

So nothing had changed, except that the defeat had drained some of the hubris from Team Tyson. Horne wasn't making a peep about Tyson raping Holyfield this time, at least. The reason that had come up to begin with, according to one insider, was that Holyfield had supposedly "dissed" Horne at a basketball game they'd both attended. When Holyfield was asked about that, he was clueless. However, Horne felt strongly enough about whatever happened to feed Tyson the "rape" angle, and went so far as to say, rather improbably, that he'd "slap" Holyfield himself. Having seen his man get halted against the ropes in November, Horne apparently felt less dissed than he had before.

There was one more concession to the November failure, though, and that was to replace Jay Bright with Richie Giachetti as lead trainer. Bright's corner talk had not been very inspiring or instructive. Giachetti, a tough and growly customer who had just the sort of scar down his cheek that Foreman once coveted, had been Tyson's trainer following the Buster Douglas fight and had presided over four victories before Tyson went off to jail. After that, Giachetti took sides against Don King in some testimony and was, or so Tyson believed, unavailable to him. Giachetti did have championship experience, although he never felt that he was properly credited for Larry Holmes's reign. But he certainly wasn't from the Catskill camp. Returning to Giachetti suggested that Tyson's old-time resources were no longer thought sound.

As for firing Bright, that was not much of a problem for Tyson. "That was an easy decision," he said, laughing. "He's family, and family's the first to go."

But, really, that was about all Tyson did in the way of acknowledging defeat. Holyfield had battered him post to post and yet he maintained a confidence in public that was reassuring and, as far as the rematch went, necessary. Besides, the recent history of these duels was that they developed into trilogies. Ali had to fight Frazier three times to settle his hash. Holyfield extended Bowe to three fights, as far as that goes. The truth is that Floyd Patterson had been the only fighter in heavyweight history to avenge a knockout loss when he came back 12 months later to defeat Ingemar Johansson in 1960. But the perception, built on these recent bouts, was that as a series grinds on, the fights may tend to become less and less glorious but they do become more and more profitable. It seemed that a business plan was being applied to these two men, a plan that assumed Tyson would redouble his resolve and take back what was rightfully his.

In other words, Tyson had not been wearing wigs in Albany or shuffling through Southington, Ohio, on aluminum braces. He did not hand his soul over to any power higher than Don King. He wasn't ready—and everybody assured him this was so—to slink away into the night. Train Tyson, which had puffed to a halt in November, would pick up steam again.

There was one loser from the November fight that might have wished to slink away somewhere, anywhere, and that was the Nevada gaming industry, which according to one insider had been hit for as much as $5 million, a record loss for any single event. The sports book may not have had a Foreman-like crisis of confidence after that, but they were very badly shaken. There is nothing quite like the feeling—water under your feet might be an approximation—of watching that much money disappear in front of your eyes. But that's exactly what happened, in one of the more important, but less reported, elements of the upset.

As a rule, sports books have trouble imagining an upset—not to be pedestrian, but this is why they're upsets—and for Tyson-Holyfield they very confidently opened the betting with odds as high as 25-1. Now, if they'd opened the betting at 10-1, that still would have meant that Holyfield had absolutely no possibility of winning. Twenty-five to one, which is where the MGM line opened, meant the contest was more comical than competitive; at 25-1, they were just having a little fun with numbers. Beyond a certain point, lines are irrelevant, more a matter of publicity, really, than gaming.

Art Manteris, who runs the sports book at the Las Vegas

A Savage Business

Hilton, said there was at least a small business purpose to these particular numbers beyond the declaration of Tyson's magnificence. The arrogance of the Tyson comeback had been contagious, and even the plungers had come to recognize what poor sport it was to bet the fighter. "Tyson fights in general are not big betting events," Manteris said. Nobody would bet the underdog, and so the favorite's price was very low; a gambler could make as much with his money by keeping it in a Christmas club account as by betting Tyson. The only way it might be fun was if the underdog paid lottery-type money. That's why the little players always jumped on the sucker bets. And to entertain them, at least, the sports books offered sucker bets.

What was different about this fight, though, was how many people began taking the sucker bets. In this case, the line makers didn't underestimate Holyfield's chances so much as they did his popularity. Holyfield money began coming in by the wheelbarrow—the big hitters, too. Who didn't like Holyfield? At 25-1, who didn't love him?

The sports books kept dropping the odds, getting as low as 5-1, but their position had been made precarious by the opening number. It was not possible, no matter how they shifted the line, to cover the late Holyfield money. Nobody wanted Tyson at those odds. At the end, Holyfield bettors were wagering not against other Tyson bettors (there were hardly any) but against the casino.

Normally this is a good place for the casino to be. Normally. If the betting is strictly balanced, as most people assume it to be, the casinos' profit is merely the spread in the two positions. This, as any gambler knows, assures a comfortable income. But Las Vegas is not able to subsidize those cheap buffets on just the vigorish; the casinos are players, too. To them, the Holyfield money represented pure profit. It wasn't a position they needed to insure or otherwise worry

231

about. Anyway, as the fight nears, it's always the short money that pours in. The big bettors climb aboard to make their small but certain profit. In the meantime, take the McNeeley money, take the Bruno money, take the Holyfield money. Take all of it.

Their confidence is well earned, of course; they are not often wrong, and in any case, they have huge advantages of psychology. A gambler might win, but if he does, he will most certainly come back. Generally the casinos are still standing when he does. "I've met a lot of great players," one casino worker said. "And I beat them all."

But the players won this one, and they won it big, and the only consolation for the casinos was that everybody would be back. They just hoped they'd still be standing. This one had been an unqualified disaster. The Tyson money, no matter how the odds closed, never did materialize, just more and more Holyfield backers. Dino Duva bragged afterward that he assured college educations for everyone in his family, reaping $230,000 in the names of nieces, nephews, and other assorted Duvas. (The late Dan Duva, interestingly, had made a similar pile years before betting on the Buster Douglas fight; he didn't particularly believe in Douglas, he just thought the odds of more than 40-1 were ridiculous for a boxing match.) Donald Trump even got into the act, so he said, winning $20 million on Holyfield. (Of course, no book in the state could confirm that, and Trump's claim sounded more like a desperate attempt to make a Liz Smith column; he had also boasted after the 1987 stock slide that he bought into the market at the drop and made a killing on the next day's rebound.) But if Trump didn't hold a Holyfield ticket, a lot of genuine players did. However dappled with blood the canvas might have been that night, the casino floors were awash in it.

There were some repercussions, to be sure. Maybe in the old days, when financial affairs were conducted with a greater sense of adventure in Las Vegas, some people would have disappeared. But these days the big corporations that run the casinos have human development staffs, so the carnage is carried out with considerably less flair. And besides, the money lost that night, record loss or not, was still not enough to topple an ITT or a Hilton or a Kirk Kerkorian; the betting done on boxing, though high profile, is just a blip on the casinos' sports screen. "It doesn't compare with any other sport," Manteris said. The largest amount bet on a boxing match in Las Vegas was the $25 million wagered on both the Marvelous Marvin Hagler–Sugar Ray Leonard and Oscar De La Hoya–Julio Cesar Chavez fights. The state record set by the 1997 Super Bowl is $71 million. The casinos could get it back, easy, probably on a big football game (the bigger the game is, the casinos usually reckon, the more wrong the public will be). Still, casinos don't like to be in the gamblers' perennial position of having to get it back; they are not in the business of trying to break even. So, naturally, jobs were lost. "There were, uh, ramifications," said Manteris, laughing. The MGM, for one, soon had a new sports book director. And the guys who were left would be a little more cautious the next time Holyfield came to town. Or when Tyson did, anyway.

The upshot seemed to be that the town was hurt more badly by Tyson's defeat than Tyson was. Team Tyson, which after all hadn't lost any money on the promotion, was very comfortable as the rematch approached. There were even rumors that Tyson was being nonchalant in his preparation, not quite jetting off for drinks at the China Club, but partying more heartily than is generally considered good for training. Giachetti fiercely denied these rumors as they were reported, but the idea that Tyson was less spartan than usual made people think—best case—that he had some enormous confidence at hand.

Then, when Tyson suffered a head butt in training and the

fight was postponed to June 28, Tyson followers were even more encouraged. So Tyson had been a slow starter in camp; now he would have all this additional time to knuckle under. "Now," said Giachetti, "we're working on other better things. We're going back to some of the things he learned working with the great Cus D'Amato. I am bringing Mike back to what he had when he had the title. . . . You're going to see the real Mike Tyson, the one who won the title ten years ago."

Others, of course, put a different spin on these events and concluded he had no confidence whatsoever. His camp was a shambles, went the new thesis, another loss was in the making, and the "head butt" (the quotation marks indicating conspiracy theory) was a desperate attempt by Team Tyson to restore the fighter's required persona.

Tyson often lent himself to such contrary psychiatry. Teddy Atlas, Tyson's long-estranged trainer, had emerged as the comeback's unofficial Freud, a man who spoke of Tyson's tortured psyche with authority and a surprising elegance. Atlas was a story in his own right, as any doctor's son with a huge scar down his cheek from a knife fight ought to be. But throughout Tyson's career, and the comeback in particular, Atlas had become more famous as a source for Tyson anti-mythology, a consistent and constant debunker of the man as fighter and human being, than as a trainer. Whether he was any more or less gaseous than D'Amato, who'd created the original Tyson mythology, hardly mattered. He was, when you got right down to it, the only person who had actually held a gun to Tyson's head, and that bought him some credibility.

In fact, it was the rippling repercussions of that single act back in 1982 that formed the basis of Atlas's principal psychoanalysis. He had always found it interesting that, after he pulled the gun on Tyson to warn him away from an adolescent sister-in-law Tyson had fondled, D'Amato fired him and let Tyson slide. Atlas suddenly understood that even an ascetic philosopher like D'Amato could be reduced to a babbling and hypocritical fool simply because he now had a kid "that could punch like a sonuvabitch." When it came to the handling of Tyson, all bets were off. Atlas adjusted his predictions for the fighter accordingly.

His call for this fight was . . . strange. He was telling people not that Tyson would win or lose, but that he was going to quit. Kevin Rooney, a dedicated Tyson enemy after his lawsuit (he was awarded $4.4 million for a "lifetime" contract; the decision was overturned), had already told some writers that Tyson looked scared of Holyfield in that first fight. After Holyfield took Tyson's best shot, according to Rooney, Tyson hosted an interior debate between "the hero and the coward. But the hero won out, so at least he stayed in there and took a beating." As fantastic as that interpretation was, Atlas (who had become a Rooney enemy too in some forgotten tribal feud) was now saying Tyson might just quit on his stool, or "spit the bit." Atlas had certainly one-upped Rooney.

"It was a no-brainer," Atlas said later.

Atlas, by the way, was the working proof, fight week, that boxing had a sense of humor. HBO, which was turning Jack Newfield's book *Only in America* into a movie, had hired Atlas to play the role of Giachetti, possibly because they both had facial scars (otherwise they were about 150 pounds apart). This caused no end of fuming on both sides, as the rival trainers now could insult each other on matters of theater and appearance as well as technique. About his own performance as Giachetti, Atlas said, "Sometimes they'd cut and say I wasn't mispronouncing words enough." Giachetti answered, "Maybe he should be an actor, because he can't train for damn sure."

Holyfield, meanwhile, was going about his business as usual. A visitor to his Houston camp got the same exact treatment as before: an early wake-up call to see Holyfield's small team gather for their 6 A.M. circle of prayer, a chance to see a light workout against a backdrop of gospel music (including, yes, "Be Magnified"), a return to Holyfield's house to watch him eat his eggs and biscuits and listen to his thoughts on faith, pressure, and love. Holyfield is a pleasant enough conversationalist, not given to athletic platitudes (religious platitudes are another story), and often refreshing in his candor. Yet these interviews, as always, were pointless to anyone trying to confirm his battle plan. His mantra for the rematch seemed to involve the idea of a mental breakdown on Tyson's part, pushing him into unknown territory where he would have to consider his chances for the first time in his life. "Pressure burst pipes," Holyfield said. Beyond that, he wasn't much help to any of his visitors.

Yet almost every reporter who visited him found a place in his advance story for a small training-camp aside, a throwaway line that must have been a recurring joke, coming every morning after that predawn prayer. "I wonder where Tyson is right now," somebody would say. "He better be training," somebody else would answer.

This would be sufficient to remind the cynics, the folks who'd begun to tune out Holyfield and his heavenly chatter, that the fighter was not leaving the result up to God, not entirely.

On fight week, as the reporters mobbed the MGM and haunted his open workouts (Tyson's, typically, were closed), he was relaxed and confident. Perhaps it was his $30 million payday, the equal of Tyson's this time. But here he was, accessible almost to a fault. It seemed, to media people now accustomed to more furtive fighters, that there was too much Holyfield. It was getting to be a pain to be on hand for every little quote, to attend every workout, to report every passage of scripture. Wasn't this guy experiencing any tension at all? Didn't he feel the need to withdraw to his suite? Dance?

And the poor reporter who hoped to escape the madding notebooked crowd (and, perhaps, Holyfield) by strolling the air-conditioned atrium of the nearby Fashion Show Mall might still stumble upon the fighter, signing his new line of athletic wear at a pushcart: Holyfield Warrior T-shirts, tank tops, and running suits. This, amazingly, was happening two days before the fight. Tyson was invisible and Holyfield was omnipresent.

Actually, Tyson did materialize. He was not quite as available as he had been before the first Holyfield fight, when he invited Roseanne on a rather otherworldly house tour for the syndicated show *Inside Edition*. That visit produced a keeper of a transcript as the two celebrities discussed the world's cruelty and their need to be buffered. "I made this," Tyson told Roseanne, "this is like a little—what do you call it?—a moat?" Roseanne decided she needed a moat as well. "You've got a lot of symbols of protection around here," Roseanne said, eyeing statues of Hannibal and Genghis Khan. "Moats and stuff."

In the background, King could be heard saying, "The queen of TV with the king of boxing! Yes! A sparkling event! We must get a trinket, something for Roseanne!"

There was nothing like that this time. However, King had persuaded—begged, according to Tyson—the fighter to return to his house for the by-now ritual Monday-night round-table. These interviews had become a much-anticipated source of material for the writers, who would seed their daily stories with these rare and increasingly strange Tyson quotes. Beyond that, many of the writers looked forward to these visits much as a medical researcher might enjoy checking in on a favorite patient with a particularly curious condition, to update his charts. And it was always great fun afterward to evaluate Tyson's state of mind.

As before, this one began with the usual complaints of duress and hardship. He had been made to come and he wasn't happy about it. In the kitchen, King was presiding over a spread from Popeyes and was considering the possibility of record revenues for this fight. The last had grossed about $100 million. This might do twice that. "After all," he said, reasonably, "we got three billion people in Red China alone." In short, he was happier than his fighter.

Tyson sat at his familiar position, at the end of King's billiard room, with Horne standing at his shoulder. The writers put their tape recorders on the pool table and awaited the familiar prologue, the spillage of bile that seemed to kick-start these affairs. It was an old theme, his portrayal in the press, but this time it was interesting because you could see exactly who was generating the suspicion.

"Nobody's on our side," said Tyson, Horne right behind him, nodding. "The courts are against us, the corporations are against us, the news reporters are against us, the papers —your bosses—are against us. We have nobody on our side, and we're still fighting and we're still doing well."

Many of the writers in attendance had once been fast friends of Tyson. Some of them still wanted to be, finding out Tyson's secret acts of charity, his concern for, say, Scott LeDoux, a fighter he had put on his payroll just because he'd heard the boxer had been struggling. He was, they all would have agreed, likable. Interesting, anyway. Yet lines had somehow been drawn. It became a game to watch Tyson speak and try to catch Horne's lips moving.

King, meanwhile, was conducting a parallel conversation with Mike Katz of the New York *Daily News,* complaining of Newfield's book: "All lies. Everything in there is a lie! So a guy who's a good writer knows how to speculize and drama-tize those lies! You know what I mean?"

A Savage Business

And now Horne was jumping in—his lips moving—as if to ramp up the frenzy. "They hope it leads to you being incarcerated," he offered.

And now Tyson: "And this guy [King], knowing you guys ain't gonna give him no justice, he still, stupidly, has you guys in his house talking to you. They're gonna write some madman tales, how he robbed this guy and killed this other guy. I don't know, I wasn't there, but, shit, if a guy got killed he was probably doing something he wasn't supposed to be doing. Very few people get killed for no reason, from where I come from."

King warmed visibly at this unsolicited character reference. Nobody had ever defended him this eloquently and he squirmed in his delight, like a puppy. "I'm still crazy enough to love America!" he shouted.

The exchange, though bewildering, had not yet exhausted Team Tyson's sense of injury at their continual depiction as monsters. "Ah, fuck you all," Tyson said. "I don't have to suck your dick to justify me being a good guy. Listen, man, I'm a man. I don't go begging someone to love me."

The writers, some of them, got up off their seats to check their tape recorders. This was entertaining enough, but a little too single-tracked for their purposes. It had the makings of one story, not material for five.

Horne, unasked, was chiming in again. "When the intention is to destroy you from the beginning, you can't get no level playing field to set the record straight. You guys go into back rooms, you conference about everything, you help each other out, to destroy somebody who is the only reason you all are out here. No other fighter takes you out of the country. No other fighter makes your jobs so interesting."

Horne's heat was rising, and suddenly, just like that, Tyson was amused. "Whoa," he said. "Wait a minute." He silenced Horne and King, laughing a bit at their outrage. Enough was enough. He had allowed himself to get involved, but his capacity for anger had been met well before Horne's ever would.

The truth of the matter, he said, was simply that "I'm a nice guy and the hell with that." Moreover, "Nobody knows me."

The writers relaxed, sensing that Tyson was once more about to begin a rambling discourse in which he would—in front of their eyes and before their tape recorders—try yet another new definition for himself. They were back on familiar ground.

And he returned to some familiar themes, the upgrading of the Tyson name, his new responsibilities as a parent, his financial legacy. Again, this sounded like nothing so much as a man who hoped to integrate himself into a society he had mostly learned about from TV. He was the breadwinner, the answer man, in the stable and nuclear unit most prized by prime time. He was the dad. His children would want for nothing—"Every time I get into the ring, it helps out their future"—and could always count on a "fighter who's rich" to take care of them.

This, he pointed out, was a serious step beyond his own childhood, when he grew up with "an alcoholic and a pimp for parents." His own children, he said, would "have a great life." His pride was unmistakable.

Yet, for a TV dad, even the kind (as he blurted out) who hates Barney, he had a few odd ideas. His wife—he had confirmed his marriage to Monica Turner only the week before—apparently was not going to be the typical helpmate. Asked if she talked about her day as a physician at dinner, Tyson seemed surprised. "Her job is to love me and my children," he said. "We don't talk about anything. If she wants to volunteer some information, that's fine." That sounded a little cold. "She's just my wife. I love her and she loves me. She has no influence in my life as far as me dealing with anything."

A Savage Business

In any case, as he pointed out, wives were disposable. Or rather, husbands seemed to be. "Wives are known to run off with other people," he said, "because they're human." Unnecessary conversation, in that case, could well become a losing investment.

When it came to child rearing, he had some ideas that definitely did not come from Dr. Spock. Corporal punishment was something he took for granted, and he assured his listeners he would soon be delivering it. "They're too young for that now," he said. One writer sensed the opportunity to lay a trap and asked him when would be a good age for a child to begin taking his whacks. Tyson stepped into it. "I don't know. Ten years old? There's no particular age. I've been beaten all my life." But 10 years sounded right to him.

He left no doubt that growing up with Mike Tyson would be privileged in some respects but strangely disciplined in others. His wife, he let it be known, was capable of more sophistication than he, and his rough edges had yet to be smoothed in both marriage and fatherhood. When his seven-year-old daughter began complaining of a boy named Malcolm who had been pinching her and otherwise shunning her, his heart went out to her. "If they don't want to play with you," he told the little girl, "fuck 'em."

This, he made most plain, was his favored course of social interaction, anyway. He expected people not to love him, dared them to pinch him. It was okay. "I been by myself all my life," he said, leading himself into a rant of self-pity. "I've been taken advantage of all my life. I've been abused. I've been dehumanized. I've been humiliated. I've been betrayed. I'm kind of bitter and angry at people about it. You can't progress [unless you let it go]. It keeps you sharp and witty to be revengeful, but it also keeps you broke."

His expectations of friendship and loyalty were likewise low. Even with Horne and King standing there, he insisted that nobody could be trusted. He said that when he got out

241

of prison he cut off all his old friends, anybody without a purpose. Yet he had few hopes for his new friends. "If I'm gonna get screwed, I'm not gonna get screwed over by people who screwed me before. I'm gonna get screwed by new people." King and Horne assumed blank stares and seemed to hope nobody would notice them for a few seconds. Tyson, who admitted he didn't read much anymore, remembered something from the Communist literature he devoured in prison, a line of Trotsky's: "The leader is always by himself in a time of doom."

There was, in other words, no possibility of joy in his life beyond his redemption as some kind of all-American father. He couldn't take pleasure in his excesses—and he admitted he'd had a few—or even in normal activities. A lavish party for his thirtieth birthday, during which he handed out the presents (six BMWs and Range Rovers), left him bored. He had few hopes for the thirty-first version, scheduled the week after his fight at a New York night spot, $25,000 in ice sculptures or no (at his direction, the ice was to be made of Canadian spring water).

Had anybody failed to get his meaning? That he was essentially alone? That he was unworthy of loyalty and friendship? For the few dunderheads who couldn't tease this out of their tape recorders later, Tyson laid it home: The fighter he most identified with was Sonny Liston.

Whew! A heavyweight who was twice poleaxed by Ali (once so mysteriously that even Ali was begging him to get up, if just for the sake of decorum), who died of a drug overdose in suspicious circumstances, who was so unloved that after he won the championship there was absolutely nobody to meet him when he returned home to Philadelphia. This was who Tyson now aligned himself with?

"That may sound morbid and grim," Tyson admitted, "but I pretty much identify with that life. He just wanted people to love and respect him and it never happened. The easiest way in the world to fail is to try to please everyone. But you can't make people love and respect you. You just have to be who you are." But Sonny Liston? "He had a wife," Tyson said. "I'm sure she didn't think he was garbage."

When it came to self-esteem, Tyson had a reverse ambition: He wanted you to think worse and worse of him; he deserved it. He then told a story on himself that seemed to satisfy a requirement of his self-loathing, how he'd contributed money to a mosque in Las Vegas and, in his view, had been taken off. "I wanted to do a good thing," he said, "to help these guys out. So I invested two hundred fifty thousand dollars. Well, do you think that mosque is getting built? But you know what? I deserved to get beat. I was trying to buy my way in and I deserved to get beat." He laughed. "I made them con me! 'Take this! We're gonna do it for Allah!' I should have known, 'cause they didn't like me anyway. I knew that. I felt that. They never liked me."

The writers gathered up their tape recorders. Tyson might have talked longer; he had long since crossed the threshold of suspicion and was speaking comfortably of things closest to his heart. He liked doing it, you could tell. But what writer needed more than this? They agreed to visit him again soon, check his progress against this melancholy, find out who won out between Ward Cleaver and Sonny Liston. But it was time to go. Not a few of them took pieces of fried chicken out to the waiting vans.

At no time, it was remembered later, did Tyson indicate any keenness for battle. Fight by fight, now that you thought about it, he had become more and more matter-of-fact about the actual boxing. It was something he did to make money, to preserve his entourage, to keep himself out of civilian life, where he was most confused. Boxing gave him a certain life, a zone he could operate in comfortably; he didn't seem to like those closest to him or even trust them, but their familiarity was reassuring. As for the fight, by all accounts he had trained diligently. Yet he didn't seem especially driven by the prospect of winning his title back. In his roundtable, he had mentioned that only once. Perhaps it was just a matter of where the writers' questions had led him. Or maybe he wasn't so consumed by the sport or competition anymore.

If it was just business that Tyson was doing, well, there was going to be plenty of it. Showtime said the fight was retailing for an average of $50, up from the $40-to-$45 range of the first Tyson-Holyfield fight. Whether or not China dialed in, Showtime was expecting a record buy rate. It was spending $25 million just on promotion. The network was particularly enthusiastic because their surveys from November showed that fully 30 percent of the audience were people who had never bought a boxing show before. And this time around, the fans had reason to expect a competitive event.

The MGM was already doing well. It sold out its 16,000 tickets the first day, at prices ranging from $200 to $1,500. Everybody was sure this would be the first $100 million bout —perhaps $130 million—the richest event in sports history.

For their part the sports books were more cautious this time, though they still installed Tyson as the favorite. At 5-2 odds, the casinos were predicting a return to their previous and rightful profitability.

As the odds suggested, there was a sense that Tyson would restore some kind of order by regaining his form and his place in boxing. Among the public, anyway, there was a belief that lightning had struck last November. It wasn't likely to do so again. Holyfield was an overachiever who'd simply had his greatest night. Tyson was still . . . Tyson.

Fight people were not so certain. Big-name trainers like Eddie Futch and Emanuel Steward both thought Holyfield would repeat. A survey of 23 boxing writers published in

A Savage Business

USA Today showed 17 of them picking Holyfield. Only one of them, Ron Borges of the *Boston Globe*, had picked Holyfield in the first fight. Perhaps after "conferencing" in "back rooms," as Horne suspected, they had formed another and different consensus for this fight. In fact, the writers tended to "conference" with people like Futch and Steward more often than with each other.

How could you not be influenced by Holyfield's calm, though? Or by his previous game plan? Or even his corner? Holyfield's trainer, Don Turner, was never thought to be a genius, but his assessment of Tyson the Terror was too accurate to ignore. "He was the best-moved [best-manipulated] fighter of the heavyweight division, better even than Rocky Marciano," he said. "It got so he'd take your guts away and you don't fight back." But the people who did fight back, who saw how easy it was to neutralize him with a jab, both knocked him out.

Holyfield was aware that Tyson might fight him with more urgency this time. "I do know his pressure will be greater," he said. "I don't know if I can make him quit. I don't know what he can do. I just have to weather the storm." But he was likewise certain that he had Tyson's number. When asked how long the fight might go, Holyfield said, "It's a question of how much he wants to take."

Holyfield's presence of mind contrasted sharply with Tyson's; he'd gotten derailed over the issue of referee Mitch Halpern, the man who'd overseen his defeat in November. Halpern, who had not worked many big fights and so was an unusual choice for that first meeting, had acted flawlessly, but Team Tyson was suddenly threatening to walk if he wasn't removed. Just three days before the fight, Horne was calling for Halpern's removal.

"Three days ago we went directly to the commission and said, ain't no way in hell is Mike gonna fight with this guy in the ring," Horne said. "Absolutely not. It's not fair. We didn't have confidence in him the first fight and we don't have confidence in him that he can handle these two big guys again."

Horne was especially angry about Halpern's appointment because he had just learned that Holyfield's camp had earlier asked the commission to exclude referees Joe Cortez and Richard Steele from the pool. In any case, he thought Halpern had been too lenient in allowing head butts and holding.

Ironically, it was Holyfield who had worried about Halpern the first time around, believing him to be of too cautious a nature. He was afraid Halpern might end up being more impressed than he over some Tyson bomb and would stop the fight too early.

The issue this time around simply amused Holyfield. "When your confidence is not great," he said, "everything irritates you."

It was obviously ridiculous, but the commission agreed to meet and vote on whether to remove Halpern on the Thursday before the fight. At the meeting, Horne was his diplomatic self, telling the five members, "If it wasn't for Mike Tyson, you wouldn't be here." That was his closing argument. They voted 4–1 to keep Halpern and they did it pretty quickly.

But Halpern, after agreeing with the decision, got to thinking how he was becoming a bigger story than a referee should be and, while working out later that night, called the commission to tell executive director Marc Ratner that he didn't want to be the focus of the fight. The commission quickly and without controversy assigned Mills Lane to the job. Lane, a judge from Reno, had become the most familiar, most respected, and best-known referee in the sport. His prefight growl, "Let's get it on," was only slightly less famous than ring announcer Mike Buffer's call of "Let's get ready to rumble." The appointment of Lane left the Holyfield camp doubled over in laughter; it was their impression that Lane was a strong Holyfield fan, had even cried after one of the Bowe-Holyfield fights.

Like the official name for this promotion, "The Sound and the Fury," this little hullabaloo signified nothing for either side. The idea that one ref or another would control this match was the smallest of stories. What could it possibly matter? Yet the very idea that Tyson was seeking some tiny or even imagined edge over Holyfield was shocking. Even as Crocodile was wandering the premises in his fatigues, shouting "Mystique is a powerful force!" it was becoming clear that there was no mystique, not any longer. The school-yard bully was going to the teacher for protection, to make sure the other kids played fair.

"When I heard that," said Teddy Atlas, "I thought, what is his qualm? Then it struck me. Tyson's a completely unsure person. And here he was, giving himself an alibi. Tyson knew he was in with somebody who would not be intimidated or physically overwhelmed, he knew he wasn't in with somebody who'd make a silent contract to submit like all the others had. He'd already been tested against Holyfield, and he failed. Miserably. So now, with this ref thing, he was committing a move, making a maneuver where he was going to disappear. He had to set it up all the right ways, go on the record that he was worried about fair treatment, and then, if he found himself in the same position as before, he would have a way to get out, to avoid getting undressed, humiliated. And then he would still survive."

This was a very strange prediction but, coming from Atlas, was not to be dismissed out of hand. Atlas was a firm believer that Tyson was a hollow man, a "fractured kid" who'd surrounded himself with people who would "perpetuate the image of him as a fearless monster." On his own he was one scared man. "Keep in mind," Atlas pointed out, "this is the same guy who used to hide inside the walls of abandoned buildings so he wouldn't get beat up. He's empty."

More than 16,000 people—among them enough celebrities that director John Singleton called the gathering "the Oscars with blood"—paid to see just what was in his tank. The crowd was the usual riot of iridescence in which the patrons mock the blue-collar focus of their attention with the most singular dress available. (Most of these clothes, by the way, are so specific to the event that they can only be purchased on-site. When somebody wandered into Bernini's in the MGM shopping arcade early in the week and asked who was going to buy any of the yellow Italian blazers that were being retailed for $1,495, the clerk airily dismissed him. "These will sell by Saturday.")

The spectators still included the pinkie-ringed plumbing contractors, with blondes of such silicone augmentation that Dow-Corning might as well be a fight sponsor. But in the time of Tyson, the typical fan was more likely to steal from the rap experience—the uptown version of it. This fan was of neon plumage, strangled in so much gold jewelry he resembled a kid's idea of a treasure chest. As for treasure chests, the fight-night woman remained spectacular irrespective of era; cleavage is powerful come fight night.

On fight night the private jets land, the casino limos make the rounds, and all the $500-a-day rent-a-Ferraris are at play. And at the MGM the mortals, Kodaks in hand, form a gauntlet leading to the Grand Arena, hoping to spot the strange figure of royalty that bobs down to a fight, a hat on his head, a $200 bottle of Dom Perignon in his mitt. Though the mortals are cordoned off, they still seem to close in on the ticketed elite—to see so much gold-nugget jewelry, to see women whose fabric requirements don't amount to a napkin. The artery narrows as clots of citizens form to see this odd branch of celebrity, not really minding that the gangsters and

A Savage Business

Westside dentists—who look exactly alike this evening—are just like them, but with less taste and no capacity for self-consciousness. The real celebrities, the one-name people like Demi, Shaq, Mel, Madonna, and Whitney, are saved from this perverse Easter Parade; even a two-name person like John-John has private access to and from the Showtime party.

It is a spectacle, no question, but the importance of the Eddies and Kevins and Roseannes pales as the time of the fight draws near. By 8:30 the seats were filled, the celebrities announced and forgotten, and the rubbernecking was properly reserved for the two principals. These fighters, men who dared great things, were the real kings of society, not actors, pretenders, dabblers in make-believe. Bone and gristle would be ground on the cutting board before these fake people. Attention would be paid.

The tension of a big fight is the most peculiar sensation in sports. This is the one arena where winning and losing is not entirely the point. There are factors of physical damage, the opportunity for true heroism, even of cowardice. Two big men between ropes, and anything—everything—can happen.

Tyson balked on his ring walk, complaining he could hear gospel music from nearby ("Be Magnified"?), but he eventually emerged from a corner of the building in his same spartan rig. Gangsta rap was his soundtrack of anticipation. The place roared as he resolutely made his way to the ring, along with Horne, Giachetti, and even Crocodile, in his fatigues and wraparound shades.

Then came Holyfield, singing along again to the Bible music, as calm as Tyson was fierce. There it was, suddenly, the attraction of this event, the very theatrical idea of good vs. evil, the notion that some higher power would identify his favorite and make sense of our lives, too. The roar assumed a constancy now, as it does for any great fight, turbines of blood lust running at military power. You wondered when they breathed. Crocodile turned to Holyfield and with his finger made a slashing movement across his throat.

Mills Lane, the kind of character who performs marriages at his bench and then advises the bride and groom to "get it on," cleared the ring and assembled Tyson and Holyfield in its center, assured them that rules would be followed, advised them, too, to "get it on," and thumbed his nose—his other prefight ritual. They touched gloves, bounced, returned to their corners, and left 16,000 people—no millions—wondering just what it was like to be like them at that moment. If you imagined it, you could feel the roil in your own stomach; it was better to participate with less, rather than more, imagination.

The fight began with Tyson emerging as a controlled boxer determined to move his head, to play defense, to forgo the one-punch KO that had marked his recent career. This looked promising, to the extent that it looked different. Then, in perhaps 30 seconds, he returned to his single-punch attack, throwing looping hooks as Holyfield ducked, dove inside, clinched, and muscled the shorter man aside.

This was familiar. Emanuel Steward, who had donned a tuxedo to sit with CNN's Nick Charles and comment on the action, did notice something, and he mentioned it to Charles. Holyfield, 6'2", would wait until Tyson punched—which he always did by raising his head straight up—and then burrow in. Head contact would be made, no question.

Other than that, the action was so similar to the first occasion—Holyfield's manhandling of Tyson less a surprise this time—that there seemed little to hope for except a repeat.

The second round confirmed Tyson's doom. There wasn't anything he could do to break from Holyfield's dominance. As usual, he resorted to his winging punches, one of which had once disassembled Frank Bruno but which now on a fearless professional were having no effect. Holyfield took them or ducked them. He didn't seem too concerned. Then, in that second round, Holyfield dove in again and his skull cracked sharply against Tyson's brow, opening a wide gash above his right eye. Tyson was visibly insulted, as if he had been readying himself for just such an injury and had his reaction at the ready. "He butted me," he said to Lane, looking away from Holyfield and into the ref's eyes. Lane agreed but decided it was not intentional. Fight on.

But Tyson was undone at that moment. He had the memory of their ramlike collision from the first fight, an event that had caused him to stiffen in pain—to actually stop and gasp—but that had not caused his opponent to falter. And now he was bleeding, from a huge wound, he imagined, and his vision would be clouded by his own blood and his opponent would measure him again and again for a systematic blinding. His desperation was evident, an urgency that would not confine itself to the rules that he felt Holyfield had so clearly abandoned. So it's anything goes, is it? Tyson threw his big punches, and then in a clinch toward the end of the round he forcibly ground his elbow into Holyfield's throat. In the corner afterward, somebody was administering to Tyson's cut, a pretty bad one. A few people were stunned, though, when Tyson winced and said "Ow!" It was a moment that would be lost in others to come, but wasn't it strange to hear this proud warrior say "Ow!"?

Much more was made of the third round, when Tyson returned to the center of the ring without his mouthpiece. Holyfield was the one who noticed, motioning to his own mouthpiece, and Lane sent Tyson back to his corner where Giachetti was now waving it. It was probably just Giachetti forgetting it, though. Nothing more. Tyson, in any case, had the best flurries of the night. He had lost the first two rounds on everybody's cards, but here he was, more fiercely controlled than before, throwing combinations, even. There was no question, through two minutes of the round, that he was winning it.

What happened next becomes the best evidence that higher powers were, for this evening, directing fate, interfering with normal human behavior to produce an entertainment for their own gothic needs. Tyson, with no more than 40 seconds left in the round, rested his head on Holyfield's right shoulder and, like a lover nuzzling his mate, sought out Holyfield's ear. It is best seen in slow motion, Tyson seeking it blindly, his chin sliding up Holyfield's neck, until he tastes cartilage. He bit mightily, a crunching, eyes-closed chomp.

There was only a small lapse before Holyfield realized what had happened. Tyson spit out the chunk, a half-inch piece, along with his mouthpiece—and then pointed down to it, as if to tell Lane he'd need it back if the referee was going to be particular about such things. Holyfield, ever the dancer, sprang straight up into the air. It was a Jordanesque leap, the hang time augmented in style by his complete rotation. At that instant, nobody seeing it live could possibly understand what had happened. But they knew it was kind of strange.

Holyfield, seeking relief, turned and went to his corner. And Tyson sprang at him from behind, pushing him two-handed. His insanity was evidently one hundred percent.

In the confusion, after Lane first thought about halting the fight (Marc Ratner, the commission's top man, looked dubious when Lane told him that at ringside), Dr. Flip Homansky was called in. Well, there is no good reason a fighter can't continue without part of his ear. There might be a question of whether he should have to, but physically, Holyfield was fine. Lane decided to let the men continue, but went to Tyson's corner to explain the two-point deduction he had ordered. Giachetti was mystified, so Lane told him it was because Tyson had bit Holyfield on the ear. "No, I didn't," said Tyson. Lane, who is 5'7", stood up to Tyson and said, "Bullshit."

A Savage Business

Two minutes passed before order could be restored and the action continued. What could possibly be achieved at this point is a tough guess. There was a lot of money at stake, a history of unsatisfactory conclusions, and a need to get something resolved. So they fought into another clinch and then, perhaps within 20 seconds, Tyson nuzzled Holyfield's other shoulder and bit the left ear. He had now sampled the whole set.

Thus was set into motion one of the great debacles of twentieth-century sports, a crazy and foolish event that set the bar forever for frustration and failure. This would become a milestone in defeat against which all future unhingings could be measured. A man, in his worst hour of need, had simply tapped out, been empty, come up with nothing, gone crazy.

The chaos was immediate and profound, even for boxing. Tyson went back to his corner, and replays show him awaiting his return to the ring as if this were a timeout. His handlers were so discombobulated that when Lane came over to tell him "You're done," they actually thought he had said "You won," as if their man had defeated Holyfield by disqualification. Had made him quit. There was even a moment of celebration.

But then reality set in, as Tyson sensed *he* had lost his manhood this time, and provided a street fury where an athletic one had been insufficient. He charged at Holyfield's corner and, as the ring filled with cops and cornermen, he pawed pathetically at whoever stood in front of him.

Holyfield's handlers were later smug over this raging frustration. "A typical bully move," said Holyfield assistant Tommy Brooks. "He had him all to himself in the ring, but now with fifteen people behind him, he suddenly wants to fight. A coward."

The ring was calmed and Tyson was coaxed out of it, and this was pathetic, too. He later complained, in righteous anger, that he'd had no choice. Pointing to the opening above his eye, he said, "What am I to do? This is my career. I have children to raise. I have to retaliate. Look at me. My kids will be scared of me." He did not stick around to discuss what Holyfield's many children would think of their dad, who now bore a frightening resemblance to the other famous Spock. Tyson wasn't a bit sympathetic that, at the moment he was worrying about his own brow, a ring worker was bringing a piece of cartilage wrapped in a towel to Holyfield's dressing room.

On his own way out, the once-proud warrior was showered with empty cups. Police were made busy dragging people out of the stands as Tyson left the arena. This was how it was all going to end? Later Tyson was seen being driven away from the MGM in a cobalt Range Rover, kid manager John Horne at the wheel. The car was briefly blocked by a limo in a driveway that entered the strip, and a fan leaned over to call him a chump. So this would be his definition at last. Tyson struggled with the door handle. "You pussy motherfucker," he screamed. "I'll kill you!" A nearby policeman pushed the door shut and the car sped away into the desert night. South, somebody thought.

There is no way to know what was in Tyson's head in this moment of defeat. Did he feel nothing beneath his feet? Smell sorrow? Or did it simply occur to him that there were going to be a lot of desert nights left for him, stretching forever, and that they'd pass very slowly.

Chapter Twelve

"I didn't have the luxury of people to help me"

The comeback, which had begun at an Indiana dawn two years before, was over. The cornfields Tyson had stepped out into, the water towers whose shadow he rode under—they might have meant a sense of possibility, of simplicity, of innocence recovered upon his release. On that day Mike Tyson had what almost every man finds himself wanting in his middle years: a fresh start.

Yet all he did was circle back to the same ugliness, maybe finding one that was actually worse. As he was to discover—as all of Team Tyson would—he had passed beyond redemption. Certainly he and his gang didn't suspect it at the time. At first Tyson sputtered self-righteously about Holyfield's head butting and how he'd like to fight him right this instant. John Horne reacted predictably, saying Holyfield had danced around "like a little bitch." Don King, who's a little better at reading the wind, produced some initial bluster about a man's need to defend himself, then became curiously silent.

Except for King, none of them knew how bad it was going to be. The whole comeback had been based on Tyson's ability to deliver fright; surely this was within bounds. So he bit a guy. Bit him twice, okay. It was a promotional fillip, look at it that way—a little more bang for your buck. He couldn't fight anymore, or at least well enough to sustain this caper, so now he was providing little filigrees of violence, small acts of desperation that might keep this monster thing going for another fight or two. What was the big deal?

Tyson, over the course of this comeback, had come to understand his purpose. It had been discouraging to him and accounted for his waning enthusiasm for the sport, as well as his retreat into what he imagined was a family life, but he bought into it all the same—$30 million a whop—and consented to act the freak in King's circus. It was a sordid act, delivering these cheap thrills for the townspeople, and it was clear that Tyson did not always enjoy being prodded through it. But—$30 million a whop—what was a guy to do? Of course, as it turned out, he'd do almost anything.

He did too much, though. The reaction was swift, profound, and enduring. And maybe surprising. Jay Larkin, the Showtime executive who headed all of Tyson's programming, thought it odd that he would be vilified as a serial ear biter when he had been, mostly, accepted as a convicted rapist. "Don't you think that's strange?" he wondered. Yet Tyson had not betrayed his personal code of honor in raping a beauty queen; he had merely taken what was available to him, lawfully or not. Here he had undertaken a far more grievous compromise of honor; he had sold out the warrior ethic he'd been so proud of, become in his defeat a cheat and a scoundrel. He was not so tough. He was a man who bit opponents he could not beat. He was a man who took your $30 million and then didn't deliver much of a whop. He was a man who said "Ow!"

"There'd been a lot of lies in Tyson's career," said Teddy Atlas later. "They came from a lot of different sources. But there's a purity about boxing, I like to think, that no matter how you lie and lie, you are eventually forced into a situation that makes you come clean."

A Savage Business

Tyson had come clean and it wasn't pretty. The townspeople, the ticket buyers King had coaxed into the tent with his rhyming carny bark, couldn't very well sanction this. It was one thing for King to have constructed some kind of cleverly staged diorama of prehistoric time, with this amoral vessel of violence battering a Peter McNeeley senseless. The townspeople could imagine themselves in a whole other epoch and that was kind of fun. But to present this—ear biting as family entertainment—was asking too much of the townspeople. That plunged them further back in evolution than is comfortable for anybody.

The disgust was enormous. And it took those most American of forms, ridicule and legislation, with some Op-Ed pieces on the side. It was a certainty, and you sensed this within minutes of ring announcer Jimmy Lennon, Jr.'s once-in-a-lifetime declaration ("Referee Mills Lane has disqualified Mike Tyson for biting Evander Holyfield on both his ears"), that Tyson had just entered that Hall of Shame where disgrace is measured in monologues. The jokes were forming immediately, as they must in a country that so easily and profitably converts ruin into laughs. He had just been nominated for Sportsman of the Ear. It hadn't been a bad fight, not for pay-per-chew. And so on, to exhaustion. Two months later Jay Leno and David Letterman were still falling back on Tyson jokes for reliable punchlines (No. 4 on Letterman's Top 10 "Mike Tyson Excuses": Ears is tasty). Tyson, somebody said, was being matched with Hannibal "The Cannibal" Lecter in a winner-taste-all fight.

But it was clear that Tyson's social and legal limbo wasn't going to be resolved in a comedy club. With horror this large, something official would have to be done. The Nevada State Athletic Commission announced immediately after the fight —the blood on Holyfield's ears hadn't clotted yet—that it was withholding Tyson's purse and was calling for a hearing

Richard Hoffer

10 days hence to decide future action. There was a real possibility that Tyson wasn't going to be matched with anybody,
not for a while.

King, who had once spent a week protesting Tyson's defeat
when his fighter had been quite visibly knocked out by Buster
Douglas, was not so brazen this time. He retired behind the
scenes, where he can operate comfortably as well, and hired
a former political image maker to craft a damage-control
game plan, a task beyond even King's powers of spin.

Sig Rogich had once served on the NSAC and had later
done public relations work for President Reagan and had
served as George Bush's assistant for media relations. He was
popular in Nevada and had much clout. A source said that
King paid Rogich $1 million for that clout, and also to write
an apology for Tyson to read.

Rogich earned his money if all he did was insist upon some
show of common sense in Tyson's first public appearance
after the fight. Left to their own devices, Team Tyson might
well have shown up in press-conference mode with Crocodile
preceding them, shouting "Mystique is a powerful force!"
Why not? They had shown no capacity for judgment so far.
But on Monday, Tyson showed up alone at the MGM to read
a prepared statement and put "I snapped" into the vocabulary of popular culture.

Dressed in a white leisure suit, with a thin bandage over
his right eye, Tyson strode into the room through a side
door and, in just four minutes and 16 seconds, managed to
apologize for, rationalize, and distance himself from as much
of that night as he could. "Saturday night was the worst
night of my professional career," he said. "I am here today to
apologize, to ask the people who expected more from Mike
Tyson to forgive me for snapping in that ring and doing
something that I have never done before and will never do
again." He apologized to Holyfield in particular and said he

258

"will not stand for any more of the nasty and insulting comments made" to the man whose ears he'd bitten.

Tyson explained the moment by saying, "I thought I might lose because of the severity of the cut above my eye; I just snapped." He suggested it was no worse than a baseball player spitting into the face of an umpire; it was horrible, but completely within the realm of modern-day sports behavior.

But he also managed to explain away his whole life in a pithy aside. "I can only say that I am just thirty-one years old, in the prime of my career, and I have made it this far because I had no other way. I grew up in the streets. I fought my way out and I will not go back again. I learned the hard way from the past because I didn't have the luxury of schools, or people to help me at a time when I needed it most."

He said he expected punishment and would "pay the price like a man." And he promised immediate rehabilitation. "I have reached out since Saturday to the medical professionals for help," he said, "to tell me why I did what I did, and I will have that help. Now I will continue to train, not just my body, but my mind, too."

He played all the right chords, but music was not what the commission was of a mind to hear. Besides, it was getting an earful from other sides. In addition to the 600-plus phone calls it received Monday before the hearing, the commissioners were picking up on all kinds of negative reaction, whether from a London newspaper that bannered its story "The Beast Must Be Banned Forever," or from President Clinton, who allowed, "As a fan, I was horrified."

Tyson begging for his job back was not what was called for. Nor would it be effective; contrition may be a powerful force, but there were now economic arguments weighing against Tyson. The ugliness of the fight, and the postfight hysteria that closed down portions of the MGM casino for several hours, was a black eye for Las Vegas tourism and a hit to the bottom line. The Hilton, which had been preparing for a junior bantamweight title fight between Johnny Tapia and Danny Romeo, canceled the fight, citing a dispute over insurance. The real message was plain: The Hilton and its casino brethren did not want to be associated with this type of entertainment.

The Wednesday hearing, to be held at the Las Vegas City Council office, had the makings of a Don King press conference, sans King. The commission was even offering media credentials. And sure enough, crowds of the curious and furious showed up on the sun-baked steps.

Inside the atmosphere was cooler, with the five commission members seated in high-backed plum leather chairs surrounded by teak paneling. Noticeably absent was Tyson himself, who, it was later learned, was treating himself to a $200,000 Ferrari 456 GT in a suburb north of New York City (by way of comparison, at the same moment Holyfield was in South Africa, meeting with President Nelson Mandela). Tyson's spiritual advisor, Muhammad Sideeq, was disappointed. "I'm naïve," he said. "I would have said, 'Yes, Michael, come. Speak your heart. Show your repentance.'" Tyson's choice to put the Ferrari through its paces could hardly have charmed the commission, but at least it simplified things from a crowd-control standpoint.

As it turned out, Tyson might have been better at winning sympathy from the commission than his lead attorney, Oscar Goodman, proved to be. Goodman, in a shocking misreading of the situation, tried to supply the commission with context, noting that "baseball players have spat in the faces of umpires, basketball players have kicked innocent people by the side of the floor, football players hit with such viciousness. . . . Mike Tyson, for thirteen years, has lived an exemplary life in the ring."

The commission had all the context it wanted, just not

enough Tyson. "I wanted to ask what you normally ask somebody," said member Luther Mack. "'Explain to me what happened.' I really wanted an honest answer."

With a minimum of back and forth from the attorneys, the commission quickly and unanimously voted to ban Tyson for at least one year and to withhold the maximum amount allowed by Nevada law, 10 percent of his purse, or $3 million. Under the rules of their decision, Tyson would not automatically be allowed to fight in July 1998, but would have to apply for a license anew. The commission admitted later that it would have preferred a longer suspension but was concerned about legal challenges. This way, though, it could rebuff Tyson at every application if it felt like it.

"From a legal standpoint," said commission member Lorenzo Fertitta, "he can come back and apply for a license in one year. But it could be a three-year or a five-year revocation. It certainly could."

This was not a slap on the wrist. Tyson's lawyer tried to put a good face on it, as if this was the best result that could have been expected. "They had to do something to appease the world," Goodman said after the hearing. "The lynch-mob atmosphere, the bloodthirstiness on the part of the public. When everything's cooled down and the world is thinking about other things and other sports and other problems I'll be able to go back there. If I have the same commission, I feel very, very confident that you'll see Mike Tyson fighting in a year."

There was instant speculation that King might try to circumvent the ruling. Most other states, it was understood, would honor Nevada's decision, but fights had been held overseas before—indeed, King had been the one promoting them. All Tyson would need would be permission to travel while on probation. But the speculation was far-fetched, and would go so far against the grain of public opinion that surely

not even King would consider such a move. Except that the
next week, King called John Davimos, the manager of IBF
champion Michael Moorer, to ask if Moorer'd be willing to
fight outside the country. Just asking.

King reconsidered that approach and never made mention
of it again. He didn't make mention of much, actually. His
empire was in some disrepair with Tyson out of action. He
had an option on Holyfield, but no promotional control beyond that. His Moorer-Holyfield bout scheduled for November 1997 was not going to be the basis of another empire,
either; Davimos and Moorer were free of King because a
clause in their contract said that Tyson had to fight Moorer
in Las Vegas within a year, and he obviously couldn't. King's
other heavyweight, Henry Akinwande, failed miserably in a
WBC title bout with Lennox Lewis, actually getting disqualified for repeated hugging. Akinwande's terrified performance,
for all his high ranking, was one more piece of evidence
against King-maneuvered fighters.

As for Tyson, he too disappeared into the shambles he had
created. He was photographed in New York, dining with
Monica or riding on the back of a motorcycle, but was otherwise lying low. He must have correctly gauged that biting a
man's ears was even more reprehensible in the public mind
than rape had been. Who would have guessed? There was no
point in contesting it, though. The people hated him. Perhaps
the man who'd placed flowers on Sonny Liston's grave the
morning of his biggest fight was happily relaxing in his mar-
tyrdom. *They didn't like me anyway. They never liked me.*

There was, predictably, some revisionist history being applied to his talents now as well. Maybe he'd just been Henry
Akinwande, with a threshold of failure that was simply dialed
in much higher. He had lost to all of the men who'd ever
stood up to him, or so the wisdom had it. He was revealed as
a fraud.

That view, however, was ridiculous. The power, the fast hands, the personality to destroy another big man's will—these were not illusory. His early and concussive string of victories was not counterfeit. His punches truly did buzz brains. And until his support system crumbled under the weight of death, until his celebrity interfered with his interest in boxing, until his wealth complicated his personal life beyond his capabilities—as it would those of any 20-something kid from Brownsville—he was as electrifying a performer as ever climbed through ropes.

He was not a great fighter, though. He did not surmount any difficulty beyond his own upbringing—and it's important to remember that the upbringing was perhaps not all that bad, anyway. From the age of 13 on, he lived in a Victorian mansion on 10 acres of land in Catskill, New York; because of his possibilities as an athlete, he was afforded enormous privilege. In the ring, he was afforded a lot of privilege as well, as concerned parties took care of the matchmaking, the publicity machine, and the political maneuvering. All Tyson had to do was destroy a few aging and melancholy King fighters to get his crowns.

But when difficulty arose, he could not come up with anything heroic. He could not summon the character to defeat a George Foreman, as Muhammad Ali had done in his dark time. In fact, presented with the shame of repeated failure, Tyson reacted with a perverse cowardice, defining himself in animal behavior when a loftier kind was required. In the end, he did not get the job done.

If any revisionism was necessary, it was in the matter of his character. He had none. His character was neither bad nor good. There just wasn't any. Even Showtime's Jay Larkin, who wanted badly to like Tyson, was uncertain what was there. "He's a chameleon," Larkin said. "He takes on different personalities as he needs to. Coming out of jail, he assumed a certain set of characteristics. I don't believe he intentionally sat down and plotted it out, but he did assume a certain flavor or coloration. And you could see it change. You could be sitting with him at dinner and it would be all 'yes, sir' and 'no, sir.' An hour later, with a different crowd, it was 'motherfuck' this."

Like some other Tyson watchers, Larkin noticed that all the great quotes had come from other sources. "How dare they challenge me with their primitive skills?" was the memorably arch line he delivered after being insulted by Bruno's effort in their first fight. It came from a karate movie. And, when he was affronted by Razor Ruddock and wondered, "Why do you say things like that when you know I'll kill you for it?"—well, that was taken out of the mouth of Lex Luthor in *Superman.*

"He's boxing's Zelig," Larkin said—passing through history without any identity of his own.

For that matter, there wasn't one original in his bunch. He was buttressed by fellow film watchers whose every antic was cribbed from the true eccentrics. Anyone with a sense of history, or perhaps anyone who had just seen the Ali-Foreman documentary, *When We Were Kings,* recognized the source, on the night of the second Holyfield fight, when Crocodile looked at Holyfield and drew a finger across his throat: Bundini Brown, Ali's helplessly devoted yeller, did it first. (For that matter, whatever Crocodile was, Bundini was first.)

Tyson, even more than the others, copped personalities effortlessly, inventing histories for the wide-eyed scribblers. Teddy Atlas certainly believed that Tyson was part of the con and not just King's empty vessel. He remembered a story in *Sports Illustrated* in which Tyson took the author on a tour of his old neighborhood. The running commentary, how he'd come back a champion and still participated in recreational mugging, was tossed off with psychotic brio; here, the message was, walks a truly dangerous man. Reading it, you shivered. "Those things," Atlas said, "I don't believe they ever happened. He lied."

Atlas always believed Tyson was empty, a willing conduit for other men's, and women's, desires. From the day he came to Cus D'Amato, he was never more than a seized opportunity. "The old man and the kid, people ran with that story," Atlas said. "But it wasn't really like that. The old man had an agenda—everybody did—but his was to leave this world with another champ. It was all compromised because of the shortness of time. So instead of making this guy face certain issues, enforce conduct as far as establishing better character habits, it was more of a race against time for Cus."

Of course, Atlas ended up estranged from both of them the first time he challenged Tyson's behavior. Maybe he's revised his own history. Then again, there's a story he likes to tell of dinnertime in the old mansion when Tyson, having eaten his spaghetti, reached for another kid's food. Camille, D'Amato's companion, told Tyson to leave it alone. Cus told him, "Go ahead, take it. You're gonna be the next champion of the world." It sounds like it could have happened.

His life was similarly greased after first D'Amato, then Jimmy Jacobs, left his world, well before their imprint could be made complete. He had money, and the ability to generate millions more, so he would never be without a mentor, some strong father figure who could confer identity upon him, or at least help script his fictions. Tyson didn't mind being used, didn't ever once make a plan for independence. He was happy to be controlled.

He'd never been able to judge his own worth as a person. He didn't seem interested in that kind of reckoning. In the only down time of his life, lying in his jailhouse cot with his boxes of books, he entertained visions of one model after another, heroes all of them. He embroidered his arms with alternate icons—Chairman Mao and Arthur Ashe. And then, out of jail, they all flew from his head; only the tattoos remained, though what they reminded him of in the mirror is anybody's guess. Other people would float through his life, leaving impressions: Wayne Newton, Sonny Liston. Zulu warriors. He was transfixed with the idea of superheroes, but he lacked the judgment to decide who in his life was like one.

He was the perfect man for King's purposes, though, smart enough to be actively complicit in the con, but emotionally disorganized enough to defer to King in its execution. Tyson had long since given up on the idea of establishing his own place in history. The money was what it was about, getting over on the people who didn't like him, who never had liked him. The money was all that satisfied his bitterness. He knew the McNeeleys, the Busters, and the Brunos were just props in a caper, and though there was a residual sorrow over his wasted promise, he played along with the proper gusto. He was sullen, he was fierce, he was as dignified as he could be —the artifice of his greatness was constructed and maintained with care. Until that shot fighter with the scripture on his shorts came along, and all was revealed.

With King's operational know-how and his rapacious attitude toward the game, it wasn't much of a trick at all to pirate all that money. Tyson earned $135 million in less than two years, without delivering one genuine or memorable athletic moment. At the end, it was a tough trade, because he would be forever notorious. But that's a lot of money, no matter how you're known.

King, meanwhile, had the greatest run of his life, a stretch so rewarding that at 1997's tax time he faxed every boxing writer in the country with news of his April 15 payout—$30 million. It is easy and painless to rip King for the cynical promotion, but he did work hard, surmounting difficulties with an élan that would be celebrated if it were anyone else's. His tenacity should be held out as an example to any would-be mogul. And it should be pointed out that he took pretty good care of himself, too.

But it was all over now. Tyson's second act had degenerated into a money grab, and he appeared to have no substantial regrets. King was enriched, though his inadvertent elevation of Holyfield to boxing sainthood would cost him in the long run. Still, they had done well. Standing in the Indiana cornfield two years earlier, they may have thought they would do better, but they couldn't complain. The comeback had worked.

Elsewhere, there were pieces to pick up. The MGM, according to sources, was pleased "overall" with their five fights, but was upset enough over the postfight melee to bow out of the boxing business for a while. But one insider insisted that the MGM had actually lost more than $3 million on each of the five fights it produced for its guests. Perhaps that is why it made no attempt to secure the Holyfield-Moorer fight. It promised to get back into the business, but meanwhile it seemed content to watch somebody else gamble on that bout.

In fact, the MGM—and all of Las Vegas—suffered horribly from the Tyson-Holyfield fallout. Dean Harrold, president of the Las Vegas Hilton, told the *Las Vegas Review-Journal,* "I think the fight was such a bust it took a lot of steam out of a lot of people. They didn't feel like doing anything. They wanted out of town, and they felt they were misled, like suckers." According to one report, the 100 or so private airplanes that had been parked at McCarran International Airport the night before the fight were almost all gone the following morning. Just 10 remained. The high-end players had bolted town.

The MGM in particular was hard hit. Casinos dream of

big-fight nights; there is New Year's Eve, there is Super Bowl weekend, and then there is a big-fight night. A-tier properties like Caesars Palace or the Mirage can expect—but not guarantee—a $5 million to $10 million pickup from their whales. Sometimes the casinos lose—"don't play well" is their euphemism—and entire bottom lines can be wrecked. (ITT, a giant conglomerate, once had to explain a bad quarter for the corporation—the corporation!—because Caesars took a hit at baccarat one night. At the Moorer-Holyfield fight, it's been said, two bettors walked away with $10 million.) The volatility is so excruciating that the Hilton was said to be restructuring high-end play to try to flatten the hills and valleys; they wanted to ratchet the play down from the players with $1 million lines of credit to those with just $300,000. Over the long run, of course, the casinos win. Otherwise the volcano wouldn't erupt, the pirate ships wouldn't duel, and less electricity might be used to light the strip. Certainly the MGM expected to win on June 28.

But that now-familiar cloud of failure wafted up from the arena again, poisoning the play. What was it about these Tyson fights that roused suspicion and dread, caused so much tension, when they had been engineered to produce a harmless recklessness? All those guys in the pinkie rings, they were meant to appropriate this staged virility, and to act like men at the tables. Instead, they and their bimbos were running down the halls in terror and then jetting right out of town. Just what had happened that night? Was it the growing anxiety produced by Tyson's increasingly urban crowd, whose style no doubt frightened the gold-nugget bunch? Or was it Tyson biting two ears, the shame of his failure being incorporated by the people who had come to celebrate his tools of terror?

There was, after the fight, a seething frustration, a feeling of incompletion that couldn't be satisfied. Nothing good had happened, or even been settled. Whatever feelings these fights provoked were still rampant. And, in a town and in a hotel where feelings were the muscle that pulled the slot machine handle, this was even going to affect bottom lines. Or worse.

When a champagne bottle popped somewhere in the casino, it was as if only then could that tension be released. With the history of these events, well, it wasn't a stretch to imagine you heard gunshots. So on what was supposed to be the casino's grandest night, even if it hadn't turned out to be Tyson's, people were hitting the decks, cops running for cover, people stampeding the valet-parking lot, knocking over the metal stanchions and creating more sounds like gunplay. The gamblers and guests panicked everywhere—"He's got a gun!"—some of them running from the casino back toward the arena, screaming. It was a magnificent hysteria. There were fights, there were elderly women in dead faints near the elevators, there were Metro police officers wrestling a man to the ground as guests watched in horror.

Some 40 people were transported to area hospitals that night with fight-related injuries, suffered in a confusion that lasted two hours. The casino was even forced to close its tables for several hours—lost opportunity on the biggest night of the year, when all it wants is opportunity. Weeks later, when the MGM Grand filed its quarterly earnings report, it boasted record income, yet had to admit the increase was actually from its sister property, New York New York, across the street. The night had been a fiscal failure on top of everything else, with reimbursement for its marketing costs of nearly $6 million for the fight probably left in the dealers' trays that night. The MGM tried to put a good face on it, but couldn't. "God only knows," said Alex Yemendidjian, the MGM Grand president, "what the additional revenue and profits would have been if things had gone more normally."

Three months later the MGM Grand would announce it

was out of the Tyson business and would not be holding the fighter to the sixth event in their contract. At the same time, it had to announce the sale of MGM stock to satisfy the clause that gave King his $15 million profit on his options. It was over. It was not a triumphant announcement.

But the MGM had seen and understood, that night in June, exactly what it had gotten itself into. People screaming and tables shut down—it was an unqualified disaster. Let's picture that night, examine the end product of this comeback, replay videotape taken as the night's disturbance reached a terminal confusion beyond which even casinos could no longer do business. Let's look at some footage from the surveillance cameras that scrutinize every hand of cards, every roll of dice, every dealer's payout.

There: At a $100 minimum blackjack table in pit 21, where a couple of NBA players and a friend are playing, you can see them jolt at the first sounds of disturbance. Yet they do not panic. Instead, the video shows a man's hand reaching into the dealer's chip tray and, with its thumb and forefinger spread, pinching off about $60,000 in $5,000 chips. Seconds later the table is tipped backward and the dealer's tray is scattered to the floor, where other disembodied hands can be seen reaching for the chips. You can see a security guard on his knees trying to recover the loot, and next to him, cheek to cheek, a man is stuffing chips into his own pocket. The man's activity is unnoticed and you can see the security guard help him to his feet and send him on his way, along with some of the $134,000 lost from the tray.

It's a fascinating sight, greed so simply enacted. The men who took the chips were probably not, by their calling anyway, thieves. Like Tyson, King, casino operators, bookmakers—they were here to make a killing within the rules of fair play. Some would have advantages of psychology, power, intelligence, or, in the case of the hosts, the advantage of statistical probability. They were all alike in ambition, the confluence of their desires having brought them together to a well-lit place in the desert, where opportunity was the chief commercial product.

Maybe it was inevitable—so much opportunity!—that some would tweak those rules, find loopholes, depart from their normal standards of behavior. Can you blame them if they did? Who doesn't want something for nothing? Who is so fussy about fair play that they wouldn't take something for nothing? The chips are right there. *Go ahead, take it. You're gonna be champion.* In the surveillance video, which was passed on to the Nevada Gaming Control Board's Enforcement Division, faces float in and out of the picture. Sure enough, frame by frame, the hands connect up with those faces; identifications and even arrests were made. Maybe this was just one of those nights when everybody got what they deserved.